D0805478

MEDICINE AND LITERATURE

MEDICINE

AND

LITERATURE

Edited by Enid Rhodes Peschel
Introduction by Edmund D. Pellegrino

NEALE WATSON ACADEMIC PUBLICATIONS, INC.
NEW YORK, 1980

First published in the United States of America
by Neale Watson Academic Publication, Inc.
156 Fifth Avenue, New York, N.Y. 10010

© Neale Watson Academic Publications, Inc. 1980

Library of Congress Cataloging in Publication Data

Main entry under title:

Medicine and literature.

1. Literature and medicine—Addresses, essays,
lectures.   I. Peschel, Enid Rhodes.   [DNLM: 1. Medicine
in literature. WZ330 P473m]
PN56.M38M4   809'.933'1   79-25912
ISBN 0-88202-189-3

Manufactured in the U.S. A.

We are grateful to the Schering Corporation, Kenilworth, New Jersey, for helping to make the publication of MEDICINE AND LITERATURE possible.

Contents

Part One:
Doctor-Writers

Part Two:
Doctors Portrayed in Literature

lists

Part Three:
Disease as an Altered—or Heightened—
State of Consciousness

Acknowledgments

I am deeply grateful to the many people who advised, encouraged, supported and assisted me throughout the preparation of this book: Raymond La Charité, Virginia La Charité, Paul E. Molumphy, M.D., Gloria Parloff, Edmund D. Pellegrino, M.D., Raphael H. Rhodes, Irma G. Rhodes, Albert Rothenberg, M.D., Richard Selzer, M.D., Joanne Trautmann, and Virginia Wilkinson.

It is also a pleasure to thank Bill Morse, Vicky Morse, Andrew Slaby, M.D., Ph.D., and Neale Watson, who helped make the vision of this book into a reality.

And special thanks to my husband, Richard E. Peschel, M.D., Ph.D., for his enthusiasm, understanding, and advice.

Enid Rhodes Peschel

Editor's Note

What does medicine have to offer literature? And what does literature have to offer medicine? New worlds of thought, insight, emotion and experience, as these essays will show. The purpose of this book is to establish a dialogue between these two seemingly disparate disciplines. A dialogue implies an interchange, a discussion of ideas leading toward a mutual understanding: a sharing. Here we do not have one group lecturing another, but rather two groups teaching each other, expanding their knowledge and their understanding.

This collection, which explores the interface between medicine and literature, is intended for both medical and literary readers: doctors, medical students, and nurses; literary scholars, college and graduate students, all people who love literature. The essays will also speak meaningfully to anyone who has been ill or who has had experience with illness. The goals of this book, the first substantial collection of its kind, are to raise questions and to heighten sensitivities, on all levels: medical and literary, ethical and social, intellectual and emotional, physical and spiritual.

In these essays, several of the finest contemporary literary scholars explore the problems—and the richnesses—of the world of medicine. By considering literature from a medical angle, these authors have learned as much as will the medical and literary people reading the essays. In addition, two outstanding psychiatrists examine literature from a medical point of view: they see literature as prophetic, to some degree, of the directions psychiatry takes several years, often decades, later. The insights of literature can help counter the thrust towards dehumanization in our health-care systems; the experiences of medicine can help bring the often overly intellectualized humanist back to reality, and to his body.

Each essay reflects a scholar's individual style, his personal way of exploring the resonances between medicine and literature. One of the greatest advantages of a collection of essays is that it is able to offer a variety of approaches and styles. Diversity, and not uniformity, is the rule —and the delight.

The book is divided into three sections: (1) Doctor-Writers, (2) Doctors Portrayed in Literature, and (3) Disease as an Altered—or Heightened—State of Consciousness. These sections are like three filaments braided together. Individually, each filament is fascinating in itself; but the whole is richer, more interesting, and more powerful because of the common bond.

Part One, "Doctor-Writers," raises questions. Why does a physician write? Does he seek to heal through his writing? And if so, whom? Himself, perhaps? The essays on Chekhov, Rabelais, and Richard Selzer, particularly, probe these questions. Other issues are raised. How is the physician's medical art related to his literary art? Do the two complement —or contradict—each other? The studies of William Carlos Williams, Schnitzler, Samuel Garth, and Céline explore these possibilities.

When the doctor is examined as the subject, what insights do we gain about medicine, about the type of person who becomes a doctor, about the types of doctors we would like to have? The essays in Part Two, "Doctors Portrayed in Literature," discuss doctors as ineffectual creatures, satiric figures, and as heroes. Shakespeare's finest healers are not doctors at all. What do these insights tell us about physicians, about ourselves, and about the nature of healing?

In Part Three, "Disease as an Altered—or Heightened—State of Consciousness," disease appears now as a torture, now as a privileged state of consciousness; now as an impediment to, now as a motivating force for, artistic creation. Syphilis, as discussed in the essay on Thomas Mann's *Doctor Faustus,* provides the protagonist with a heightened state of consciousness. An illness or an impairment, as Weintraub illustrates in "Medicine and the Biographer's Art," may be the source of an artist's greatness, his uniqueness of vision.

The relationships between psychiatry and literature are probed. Although literature sometimes precedes psychiatry in certain discoveries about the human mind and spirit (see Slaby and Tancredi, "Literary Insights and Theories of Person"), at other times medicine may precede literature, as discussed in the essay about the surrealist André Breton.

Disease is considered not only as a physical and mental process, but also, especially in the essays by Biasin and Hartman, as a language. How are the signs and symbols of literature like the signs or symptoms of disease? Hartman's "Words and Wounds" explores the relationships between the hurting and the healing powers of language. After all, language, the stuff of literature, is also the means of communication between the patient and his physician. Both medicine and literature share the imperious need to communicate, and to be understood.

The book closes with Trachtenberg's study of Whitman's "This Compost": a symbol of the body decomposed, and recomposed as Life. For as Thomas Mann writes in *The Magic Mountain,* "all interest in disease and death is only another expression of interest in life."[1]

What do medicine and literature have to offer each other? The intertwining filaments explored in this book offer glimpses of the dialogue that can go on and on. Medicine and literature share profoundly, intimately an abiding concern for language and for those who wish to—who need to—communicate. The dialogue between medicine and literature is, essentially, a continuing interchange between the flesh and the word: between man's body and his spirit. Both medicine and literature probe, although from radically different perspectives, the same subject: the truths that are revealed—and concealed—in man.

Enid Rhodes Peschel

NOTE

1. Thomas Mann, The *Magic Mountain,* trans., H. T. Lowe-Porter (New York: Alfred A. Knopf, 1946), p. 495.

Introduction

To Look Feelingly—The Affinities of Medicine and Literature

George Santayana, the most literary of modern philosophers, says that
only literature "can describe experience for the excellent reason that
the terms of experience are moral and literary."[1] Owsei Temkin, one
of the more philosophical of medical historians, says that medicine is
"not only science and art but also a mode of looking with compas-
sionate objectivity. Why turn elsewhere to contemplate man's moral
nature?"[2]

In their emphasis on ways of looking at morality, Santayana and
Temkin provide us with two conceptions which merge in medicine and
literature and which ground their natural affinity for each other. For both
are ways of looking at man and both are, at heart, moral enterprises. Both
must start by seeing life bare, without averting their gaze. Yet, neither can
rest in mere looking. To be authentic they must look with compassion.
Medicine without compassion is mere technology, curing without healing; literature without feeling is mere reporting, experience without
meaning.

Medicine and literature are united in an unremitting paradox: the
need simultaneously to stand back from, and yet to share in, the
struggle of human life. They must see clearly but they must also be
involved in the outcome of the struggle. Thus both of them are moral
experiences. For medicine, Paul Valéry put it this way: "you doctors
are the champions, the strategists in the struggle of the individual
against the law of life."[3] Literature, in Santayana's words, "has its
piety, its conscience; it cannot long forget without forfeiting all dignity that it serves a burdened and perplexed creature, a human animal struggling to persuade the universal Sphinx to propose a more
intelligible riddle."[4] To look compassionately is the summit of artistry
for both medicine and literature; to take part in the struggle is the
morality they share.

Medicine and literature are linked, too, because they both tell the
story of what they see. The patient's history that a physician writes is
really a tale, the narrative of the patient's odyssey in the dismal realms
of disease. The writer, too, must contemplate the same perplexities of

being afflicted, which are part of being human. Illness is inextricably woven into the tapestry of every human life. No serious writer can avoid it entirely.

The writer's tale transcends the clinician's history because his or her language is charged with meanings. The writer of literature can evoke a vicarious experience of illness and suffering, whereas the writer of the clinical record evokes only diagnostic or prognostic possibilities. The writer's charged language forces all of us to look at human experience without averting our gaze because we are made to look with feeling for the subject of those experiences.

Clinical language itself can be a thing of beauty in those rare instances in which the artist is also a practicing physician, as in the case of William Carlos Williams, Thomas Browne, Oliver Wendell Holmes or Richard Selzer. In their hands even the lugubrious details of anatomy and pathology become instruments of poetry or evocations of the joy and peril of man's embodiment.

Often, physicians who become serious writers abandon the clinic wholly or visit it only intermittently. But they retain the clinician's way of looking. Their writing carries that special imprint peculiar to those who have felt, smelled and cured among fevers, madness, blood and abscesses. We think of Rabelais, Crabbe, Smollett, Chekhov, Maugham, Keats, Céline or Walker Percy, who completed their medical training, or Michaux or Breton who interrupted theirs. We think of Walt Whitman who worked in a doctor's office and as a volunteer nurse, and whose panegyrics of the body in all its afflictions and exaltations are unexcelled for vividness.

In the last decade these affinities between medicine and literature have come to be exploited in medical pedagogy.[5] In a dozen medical schools courses in literature are serving several goals in unique ways: teaching empathy with the ill person, giving insight into the peculiarities of the medical life and the doctor's place in society and culture, underscoring the dilemmas of medical morals, and improving the use of narrative forms in history taking. These medical uses of literature offer some hope for buffering the encroachments of technology to which today's scientifically trained clinician seems so especially susceptible.

Much effort has been expended in recent years by psychiatrists, behavioral scientists and older clinicians to teach empathy to young physicians. The results have not been particularly satisfactory. The example of respected clinicians remains the most useful method for teaching how the physician may project himself into the existential state of the patient and thus treat him more sensitively and humanely. Literature offers an alternative because it has such power to evoke vicarious experiences. Through the eyes of the sensitive creative writer, the student physician can experience something of what it is to be ill, in pain, in anguish, or dying. The imaginative teacher will use passages from the worlds of poetry and prose and, by careful explication of the text, will help students to learn to see with compassion.[6] The writer's eye is not beclouded; his vision can open the eye of the neophyte physician in the personal, profound and penetrating ways peculiar to true literature.

No medical lecturer could evoke the experience of illness with the intensity achieved, for example, in Homer's depictions of the lacerating and flesh-tearing assault of spear and arrow, or the confusion of madness and genius in the sick brain of Mann's Adrian Leverkühn, or the agonies of Montaigne's kidney stone, or the pleasurable malaise of a mild illness in Virginia Woolf's *On Being Ill,* or the indignities suffered by Tolstoy's dying barrister at the hands of his paternalistic doctors.

Is there a better way to help the student feel something of the joys, the difficulties, the foibles and failings of the medical life than through the literary depictions of the species *homo medicus?* Few portraits of humans are as mordant as the portraits of physicians in Martial's *Epigrams,* Petrarch's letters, Bernard Shaw's *Doctor's Dilemma* or Joyce Carol Oates's *Wonderland.* On the other hand few humans are as sympathetically portrayed as George Eliot's Lydgate, Balzac's Dr. Bénassis, or Miguel de Unamuno's Dr. Monegro. Writers have inquired into the doctor's life because they could not be indifferent to it. The physician is too intimately bound to hopes and fears of the ill in their struggle against disease and death. The physician who cares as well as cures fulfills one of the noblest ideals of human services. The affinities between medicine and literature have not prevented dissonances as well as admiration.

It is easy to forget that the physician's major diagnostic tool, despite the burgeoning of electrical, chemical and radiological techniques, remains the clinical history. That history is itself a story, a complex, personal variegated story in the life of a human being. Each story is unique. Yet, history taking is the physician's most neglected skill simply because it is so taken for granted. Like any skill it needs cultivation; it needs to be formed on the best models of the narrative form. Premedical courses in literature are surely necessary but not sufficient. They do not carry over into professional life in most cases. Narrative skills, and expository prose need reenforcement in the course of medical education.

Literature also teaches the physician something of the significance of symbol and language as the media linking human minds and personalities. Language is the instrument of diagnosis and therapy, the vehicle through which the patient's needs are expressed and the doctor's advice conveyed. Understanding the nuances of language, its cultural and ethnic variations and its symbolic content are as essential as any skills the clinician may possess.

As noted in the opening quotations from Santayana and Temkin, literature and medicine are moral enterprises. Literature lays open for view the moral dilemmas, conflicts, triumphs and failings of human beings. Aspiring physicians need to be sensitized to the complexities of the moral contexts within which their advice is given or their judgments of their patient's behavior are rendered. Literature, through its power to evoke vicarious experience and develop empathy, places the physician in a concrete human situation. As it enhances his perceptions of the moral choices people face, so does it sharpen his awareness of even the simplest of human decisions.

Finally, these utilitarian ends must not obscure more subtle but really the most important service literature performs for all humans— enhancement of the experience of life itself. For the busy physician later in life, confident of his craft and perhaps a little bored with it, literature has special virtues. It takes him from the grinding reality of the clinic into realms of imagination, lyricism and drama; it provides those moments of delectation without which the soul shrivels. Literature refreshes the physician's view of the men and women he sees as "patients" and restores them to their real roles in the human drama. Literature gives meaning to what the physician sees and it makes him see it feelingly. Whatever enriches the doctor's sensibilities must perforce make him a better physician.

In this book, Enid Peschel offers us the reflections of belletrists and critics of the affinities of medicine and literature. In these original essays, literary insights are offered on a wide range of the conjunctions of the writer's and the clinician's art. They examine the special vision of physicians who are simultaneously writers, such as William Carlos Williams and Richard Selzer, and the creative writer's depictions of illness in Thomas Mann, or Proust, the image of the physician in Camus, Céline, Roger Martin du Gard and Flaubert, the healing and wounding powers of language in the essays by Hartman and Biasin.

The resulting tapestry richly presents the subtle encounters between persons and matters medical and persons and matters literary; it shows medical uses of literature and the literary uses of medicine. Linked by a common need to see life bare, to look and see, and to see feelingly, medicine and literature enhance each other. In doing so, they enhance man's capacity to heal himself in spirit and body. Should we expect less? After all, Aesculapius of Greek myth was the son of Apollo. The genetics of the spirit may be even more powerful than the genetics of DNA.

Edmund D. Pellegrino

NOTES

1. George Santayana, *Atoms of Thought: An Anthology of Thoughts from George Santayana,* ed., Ira D. Cardiff (New York: Philosophical Library, 1950), p. 261.

2. Owsei Temkin, *The Double Face of Janus* (Baltimore: The Johns Hopkins University Press, 1977), p. 37.

3. Paul Valéry, *Idée Fixe,* trans., David Paul (New York: Pantheon, 1965), p. 51.

4. George Santayana, *The Life of Reason or the Phases of Human Progress,* reviewed by

the author in collaboration with Daniel Cory (New York: Charles Scribners, 1954), p. 333.

5. See, for example, *Human Values Teaching Programs for Health Professionals,* Report No. 7, Institute on Human Values in Medicine, published by the Society for Health and Human Values; and Anthony R. Moore, *The Missing Medical Text* (Melbourne, Australia: Melbourne University Press, 1978), p. 249.

6. See the annotated bibliography complied by Joanne Trautmann and Carol Pollard, *Literature and Medicine: Topics, Titles and Notes* (Philadelphia: Society for Health and Human Values, 1975), 209 pp. Of interest, also, is the *Newsletter of the American Physicians Poetry Association,* Richard A. Lippin, M.D., ed. (3901 Conshohocken Avenue, Philadelphia, Penn. 19131), which publishes poems by contemporary physicians.

Part One:
Doctor-Writers

Someone asked me why a surgeon would write. . . . It is to search for some meaning in the ritual of surgery, which is at once murderous, painful, healing, and full of love.

Richard Selzer, *Mortal Lessons*

Physician, heal thyself.

Luke 4:23

A Physician Healing Himself: Chekhov's Treatment of Doctors in the Major Plays

Stephen Grecco

> Now, for example, a simple person looks at the moon and is moved as before something terribly mysterious and unattainable. But an astronomer looks at it with entirely different eyes. . . . With me, a physician, there are, also, few illusions. Of course, I'm sorry for this . . . it somehow desiccates life.[1]

In addition to being a playwright and a writer of short fiction, Anton Pavlovich Chekhov was also a doctor. "I look upon medicine as my lawful wife and literature as my mistress," he tells friends in conversation and in letters, without, however, indicating which he actually preferred to be with. On one occasion we learn that his mistress is "dearer to me than a wife," but on another she is not to be mentioned, "for those living in sin will perish sinfully."[2] Thus in a lighthearted but telling way Chekhov implies that his particular *ménage à trois* provided many of the same pleasures and perversities one normally associates with more traditional triangular arrangements.

That he used a metaphor connoting personal intimacy to express ambivalent feelings about his divided professional loyalties would be unremarkable were it not for the fact that this doctor-writer throughout much of his adult life had neither wife nor mistress, a situation biographers generally attribute to a demanding work schedule and persistent ill health; yet, important as these factors might have been, they are surely only partial explanations for his reluctance to become closely involved with eligible women or, for that matter, more than casually attached to various male and female friends.

To say that he feared passionate involvement with the opposite sex or was somehow socially retarded is to deny the love he expressed for the actress Olga Knipper, whom he married two years before his death of tuberculosis at age forty-four, or the devotion he felt for several friends and family members, particularly his brother Alexander and his sister

Mariya. But to many who knew him he projected a palpable aloofness, an "absent air" that conveyed the impression he was first and foremost an observer of life, not a full participant in it, "an observer distant and as it were senior . . . like an adult playing with children and pretending to be interested when he really wasn't."[3]

If we accept the assumption that Chekhov was fundamentally a sad and alienated man, and there is ample evidence in his life to assume that he probably was, he fits well into the company of scores of other great writers whose art reflects a joy so patently missing from their own lives. It may be, of course, that significant literary achievements can come only from alienated souls, that some combination of personal and metaphysical unhappiness is a *sine qua non* of true creativity. Although Chekhov himself says relatively little about the possibility, his imaginative works, notably his mature dramas, testify that he thought extensively about the reasons behind his inability to relate more meaningfully to other people. Undoubtedly, it was a painful subject for him to explore, which is why I believe that much of this reflection occurred on a subconscious level, perhaps the only place where one so immediately affected could have given it serious consideration both as a fact of life and as a possible source of creative inspiration.

Throughout his career as a writer, Chekhov dutifully paid homage to his medical training as a powerful influence on his writing. In a biographical sketch attached to a letter to a neuropathologist who had been his classmate in the Moscow University medical school, Chekhov wrote:

> I don't doubt that the study of the medical sciences seriously affected my literary work; they significantly enlarged the field of my observations, enriched me with knowledge, the true value of which for me as a writer can be understood only by one who is himself a physician.

He goes on to praise his acquaintance with the natural sciences and the scientific method, adding that he did not belong to those writers who have a "negative attitude toward science, nor am I one of those artists who think that they can arrive at everything by the intellect alone."[4]

It is interesting to note that Chekhov felt obliged to qualify his allegiance to scientific principles; his study of medicine antedates by several impressionable years his interest in writing, and one wonders if perchance during this formative period young Anton came to accept more deeply than he wished to remember the prescripts of his "lawful wife." The time during which he prepared to become a doctor was coincidentally the heydey of scientism, and it is highly conceivable that his studies exaggerated in him certain constitutional tendencies that led him to regard as unreliable his all too natural feelings and emotions. One might even say that Chekhov's initial attraction to literature as a coprofession was an inevitable reaction to the conditioning he underwent as a medical student and later as a doctor.

Chekhov the medical practitioner routinely saw men and women in moments of crisis and pain, people whose psychic and physical distress might have overwhelmed him had he not developed the necessary emotional defenses. In this respect he was similar philosophically and temperamentally to many of his fellow physicians—although noticeably dissimilar to other notable Russian men of letters of the period (Tolstoy and Gorki, for instance), who tended to be much less suspicious of the subjective response that Chekhov scrupulously guarded himself against. "A play must be written in which people can come, go, dine, talk about the weather, and play cards," he lectures pragmatically, "not because that's the way the author wants it, but because that's the way it happens in real life."

As an artist, Chekhov continually strove for objectivity in his work, a feat that he accomplished with surprising regularity in his major dramas, principally in the depiction of character: it is an axiom that there are no real heroes or villains in his later plays, only complex individuals who exhibit both positive and negative qualities. Nonetheless, if one examines closely the physicians in these plays, one can see that the much-heralded Chekhovian impartiality has been exercised with considerable restraint. The three men in question, Dorn in *The Seagull*, Astrov in *Uncle Vanya*, and Chebutykin in *The Three Sisters*, are delineated in ways that are curiously uncomplimentary. Amiable and gregarious on the surface, they are revealed as cynical and loveless types, enigmatic in their conversation and behavior, disdainful of the medical profession because it no longer provides much satisfaction while it continues to fill them with a crippling, oftentimes irrational, sense of guilt.

Yevgeny Sergeevich Dorn is a fifty-five-year-old bachelor obstetrician whose main function as a doctor in The *Seagull* is to deliver not babies, but valerian drops, the tranquilizer of turn-of-the-century Russia. Once considered a romantic idol, he is now little more than a walk-on in a real-life drama that permits him precious few occasions for center-stage action. Polina Andreevna, a married woman who has loved him for many years without receiving very much love in return, mothers and flatters him, listens patiently as he complains about the weather and approaching old age. Periodically he breaks out into song when the conversation becomes too threatening or tosses out non sequiturs to fill up uncomfortable pauses. At one point she loses all patience and beseeches him: "Yevgeny, my dear lovely man, take me into your own home. . . . Our time is passing by, we are young no longer, and if at the end of our lives we could only stop hiding, stop telling these lies. . . ."[5] He's too old to change the way he lives, he says, then hurries off to administer his favorite anodyne.

He likewise fails Masha, Polina's daughter, who comes to him ostensibly seeking advice concerning her unrequited love affair: "I don't love my own father . . . but I like you a lot. Deep in my heart and soul, I feel somehow you are close to me. . . . Help me or I'll do something stupid" (Act 1, p. 18). Unfortunately, the fatherly affection—and daughterly recognition—she craves is not forthcoming from the doctor, who is in all likelihood (as he was in an early draft of the play) her biological father.

A year later he is back at the Sorin estate, where he finds himself being teased about his finances by Medvedenko, a witless schoolteacher, whom Masha has married in desperation. Dorn replies: "Money? I've been in practice for thirty years, a practice which gave me no peace, my friend, when neither day nor night belonged to myself, and what did I manage to save in all that time?" (Act 4, p. 40). Only two thousand rubles, we are told, most of which he spent on a trip to Genoa, his favorite non-Russian city because its packed streets make it an ideal place in which to lose oneself in a crowd.

Dorn's skill in detaching himself emotionally from potentially charged situations is further illustrated at the end of the play, when Konstantin, the young man his putative daughter really loves, commits suicide off-stage by shooting himself. Hearing the gunshot and suspecting the worst, the doctor excuses himself from a card game and goes out to determine what the noise actually was. He returns a half minute later and informs the gathering that a bottle of ether had burst. He then breaks into song ("Once again I stand before you, enchanted. . . ."), takes a fellow cardplayer by the waist and leads him to the footlights, calmly instructing him to take the boy's mother away, for "the fact is, Konstantin Gavrilovich has shot himself. . . ." The curtain comes down before we have a chance to see how anyone else in the play reacts to the bad news.

Although he is his junior by at least fifteen years, Dr. Mikhail Lvovich Astrov is presented as a more eccentric and embittered version of Dorn. *Uncle Vanya* opens with Astrov's complaining to Marina, an old nurse, about how his practice has aged him: "From morning till night always on the go, I get no peace, and at night I lie under the bedcovers, scared they may drag me out to a patient." The complaint was triggered by the death of a railman who was recently brought to him for treatment: "I put him on the table to operate, and he went and died on me under the chloroform. Just when I didn't need it, my feelings came back again, and I was tortured so much by my conscience I felt I'd deliberately killed him. . . ." He reluctantly accepts a glass of tea from Marina, but refuses her offer of something to eat. What he truly wants is a glass of vodka, which is his form of valerian drops, for the good doctor delights in getting drunk. "When I'm in this condition, I become shamelessly arrogant, even insolent. Oh, there's nothing I feel I can't do then! I tackle the most difficult operations and do them superbly." But it is doubtful if anyone fully believes him. Serebryakov, the ill-tempered and gout-stricken professor of literature, says what kinder souls sense but are disinclined to verbalize: "He knows as much about medicine as I—about astronomy."

The people on the estate are remarkably tolerant of Astrov's drinking, even when he occasionally turns nasty and tells them they come across as "tiny insects . . . microbes." No one seems offended, possibly because they confuse his drunken confessions with theatrics and refuse to take him seriously. He tries again: "I've started putting on years, I've worked too long and too hard, I've become petty and vulgar, as sordid as one can be. My feelings are gone, dead to the world, and I really don't think I could ever grow close to another person. There's no one I love, and . . . no one I ever shall love." The only thing that still fascinates him is beauty, but as he freely admits, "that isn't love, you see, or devotion. . . ."

Haunted by his personal and professional failures, he takes to painting and turns out cartograms of the district to show how it has changed over the past fifty years. In an earlier version of the play Astrov had been known as the Wood Demon and, as in *Uncle Vanya*, was given long speeches in which he speaks about nature and about the possibility of someday finding true happiness. But these soliloquies, like Dorn's snatches of popular songs, simply furnish a cover for his growing despair. Our suspicions are confirmed when he is presented with an opportunity for change. Yelena, the professor's young and attractive second wife, speaks for her stepdaughter, who is in love with him. "Do you like her?" she asks. "Yes, I respect her." "Do you like her as a woman?" Astrov pauses: "No. . . . My time has already gone by. . . . Besides, I've not time for . . . When could I have the time?" (Act 3, pp. 80–81). Unable to reciprocate Sonya's love, Astrov agrees to leave the estate and never to return, albeit not before he recovers a bottle of morphine that Vanya took from his medical bag. "Listen, if you've made up your mind once and for all to finish yourself off, then go to the forest and shoot yourself there. But give me back the morphine, or there will be all sorts of talk and guesswork and people will think that I gave it to you. . . ." Clearly, Dr. Astrov is prepared neither for a wife nor for a second dead man preying on his conscience.

In act 1 of *The Three Sisters* Dr. Chebutykin declares that nature has created us for love alone. In true Chekhovian fashion, he roars immediately afterwards with laughter, and it is only in retrospect that we realize what this laughter meant. Now sixty years old, alcoholic, and admittedly grossly incompetent as an army doctor, Chebutykin passes his time by reading fillers from newspapers and flirting with Irina, the youngest of the three sisters. Irina, in her early twenties, dreams of a young prince charming, while Chebutykin, who treats her as a daughter, fantasizes about her as a wife. "Balzac was married in Berdichev," he says, quoting from a newspaper. This apparently senseless remark is repeated twice, once by the doctor and once by Irina, both seemingly taking for granted that matrimonial bliss may yet be possible in their own little corner of the world if Balzac was able to find a mate in a backwater such as Berdichev. Chebutykin explains his bachelor state to Andrey, the girl's brother. "I didn't have time to get married because life flashed by like lightning. Yes, and because I was madly in love with your mother, who was already married. . . ." Rationalization and fantasy are about all the doctor has left to sustain him, even though his skills as a physician (slight as they are) are badly needed by the townspeople. During a terrible fire that is engulfing part of the town, Chebutykin is called upon to help. Instead, he purposely becomes drunk:

> To hell with them all . . . to hell. . . . They think I am a doctor, I am able to cure every kind of illness, but I know absolutely nothing at all, I've forgotten everything I know, I remember nothing, absolutely nothing at all. . . . Last Wednesday I treated a woman in Zasyp—she died, and it's my fault she died. Yes . . . I knew something or other twenty-five years ago, but now I remember nothing at all. (Act 3, p. 136)

He begins to cry and wonder if he is truly human after all.

> Perhaps I am not really a person, but only pretend that I have hands, and feet, and a head. Perhaps I don't even exist at all, but it only seems to me that I walk, eat, sleep. . . . Oh, if only I no longer existed! . . . And that woman, the one I killed on Wednesday, came back to my mind . . . and in my heart and soul I felt twisted, corrupt, ugly . . . I went and got drunk.

Momentarily consumed by guilt and remorse, Chebutykin pulls himself together remarkably quickly and in the final act is once again his old self. The army is leaving town and he with it, but he promises Irina that he will return. "They'll retire me in a year, I'll come back here and live out the rest of my days near you. . . . Yes, I'll come back to you here and change my ways, change them at the core . . . I'll turn into such a quiet, hon . . . honorable, proper little fellow. . . ." He stumbles over the word honorable, and well he might, for the doctor has been asked to witness a duel between the maniacal Solyony and the Baron, lately Irina's fiancé and Chebutykin's rival for her attentions.

Chekhov describes the doctor as being in a "complacent mood which does not abandon him" in the course of the whole act. This look of complacency is merely a subterfuge, however, an extension and perversion of his professional mask. He knows full well that the Baron is no match for Solyony, yet he allows the duel to take place anyway, going so far as to hide the facts from Irina, who presumably could have taken some action to stop the absurdity. When Masha, her sister, expresses concern that Solyony might wound the Baron or even kill him, Chebutykin blandly responds: "The Baron is a fine person, but one Baron more, one Baron less—what does it matter, anyway! Let them! It doesn't matter." But, of course, it does matter, and it should matter a great deal to someone who has taken the Hippocratic oath.

Why Chekhov chose to describe these men as he did is surely open to debate, but it is my contention that he was in large measure unconsciously attempting to objectify and thereby exorcise through his dramatic art that part of himself—the impersonal rationalist embodied in the guise of a doctor—which he intuitively felt inhibited him from functioning freely on an instinctual level. Such a method of externalization, inherently available to him as a complex and sophisticated artist, put him in the vatic position of being able to discover (if ever so subliminally) the source of a debilitating behavioral pattern and its probable path of development. In this respect these three dramatic portraits can be viewed as psychological representations of Chekhov by Chekhov, deliberately selective and stylized so as to isolate what was most in need of healing.

Dorn in *The Seagull* is most like the real doctor. Here we see Chekhov becoming increasingly aware of the dysfunctional nature of his empathetic response, the implications of which are manifestly beginning to concern him. A doctor is a human being as well as a scientist, he seems to be saying to himself, and as such has an unstated obligation to minister to both spirit and flesh, is not by virtue of his training relieved of the necessity of attending to the very real needs of the soul. The injunction is a heady one to someone whose obvious quest for emotional privacy very likely was instrumental in his choosing a scientific career.

Dr. Astrov is the man Chekhov feared he was rapidly becoming. Whereas Dorn is still capable of making positive choices but refuses to do so because of inertia and indifference, Astrov is projected as an individual who has delimited himself into a state of near immobility. What existential freedom he heretofore possessed is now moribund. He knows the faith he claims to have in people is turning inexorably into mistrust, and for the first time he sees the spector of misanthropy hovering around the corner. Astrov's real responsibility for the death of the railman can only be guessed at, but his morbid obsession with the incident is indicative of the guilt he bears for having brought about the spiritual demise of others in relationships that might have survived had he been more skillful in his handling of the affairs of the heart. Sonya may one day love and marry someone else, but until she does, Dr. Astrov will continue to count her among his unsuccessful operations.

The murderous Chebutykin is a *reductio ad absurdum* of what Chekhov knew he was in part and what he was destined to become entirely if he permitted his intellectual self to continue dominating his emotional self. His marriage to Olga Knipper is proof that he did not allow this to happen, marking as it did an important turning point in Chekhov's life and work. The passions that were too long held in reserve were finally given free rein ("I have just received your letter, read it twice—and I kiss you a thousand times. . . ."). Significantly, there is no physician in his last work for the stage, *The Cherry Orchard,* which he wrote during the years of his short-lived marriage. The most positive of his four major dramatic works, the play in one respect represents the peace Chekhov made with the world of science. In a letter to Olga not long before he died, the doctor-writer had a favor to ask of his wife:

> I have already told you, I am a physician and a friend of the Women's Medical School. When *The Cherry Orchard* was announced, the students requested me, as a doctor, to arrange for a performance of the play for the benefit of their auxiliary; they are terribly poor, many of them are expelled for failure to pay tuition. . . . I said I would take up the matter with the directors, did so, and obtained their promise. . . . Some of the students may call on you in Petersburg; receive them, talk to them, be as gracious as you can. . . .[6]

NOTES

1. Anton Chekhov, in Ernest J. Simmons, *Chekhov* (Boston: Little, Brown and Company, 1962), p. 480.

2. In Avrahm Yarmolinsky, *Letters of Anton Chekhov* (New York: The Viking Press, 1973), p. 230 and p. 44.

3. Ronald Hingley, *A New Life of Anton Chekhov* (New York: Alfred A. Knopf, 1976), p. 183.

4. Yarmolinsky, *Letters,* p. 352.

5. All quotations from the dramatic works are taken from *Anton Chekhov's Plays,* trans. and ed. Eugene K. Bristow (New York: W. W. Norton & Company, 1977). Act and page references are included in my text.

6. Yarmolinsky, *Letters,* pp. 465–66.

Rabelais:
The Book as Therapy
Raymond C. La Charité

Unbridled energy, creative frenzy, teasing playfulness, bristling intellect, Democritean moralism, power, and humanity characterize Rabelais's art and imbue his fictional worlds with that especial blend of Apollonian wisdom and Dionysian merriment which his readers the world over appreciate and whose mysterious unicity they seek to penetrate. His verbal structures, teeming with life, generate a polysemous and kaleidoscopic world. Visions of unequaled clarity and transparency alternate with troubled images of refracted luminosity. Whenever and wherever the reader chooses to enter the world of Rabelais's books, he is struck by an overriding aura of celebration and pensiveness. In every sense, Dr. Rabelais's literary masterpieces constitute an absorbing study of man: what he is, what he is capable of, where he has been, where he is, and where he is going. And it is axiomatic of his profoundly comic vision that whatever befalls man, good or bad, and whatever he does, sublime or foolish, he is a reproductive physical organism whose component elements—body and mind—are subject to sickness and disease and, more often than not, in need of change and diversion, renewal and cheer.

François Rabelais (ca. 1494–1553), like his fictional characters, led a full and eventful life. A man of prodigious intellect, extraordinary erudition, and unabashed interest in just about everything, he devoted himself especially to philology, theology, law, and medicine. He became a monk and an ordained priest, a practicing and eminent physician, a father of three, a friend of powerful churchmen and diplomats whom he accompanied and served on missions to Rome, and the author of the comic saga *Gargantua and Pantagruel,* whose four unique books *(Pantagruel, Gargantua, Third Book, Fourth Book)* rank him among the giants in arts and letters. Michelangelo, da Vinci, Shakespeare, Montaigne—these are his peers.

Rabelais's interest in medicine dates from about 1521. He was awarded the degrees of bachelor of medicine in 1530 and doctor of medicine in 1537, both from the Faculty of Medicine of the University of Montpellier, where he also taught for a brief time. In general, Renais-

sance medicine was a branch of humanism and its students were principally involved in the interpretation and clarification of the ancients, in
particular Plato, Aristotle, Hippocrates, and Galen. Hence, we have no
treatise on medicine by Rabelais himself; what we do have are his comments on and editions of Hippocrates's *Aphorisms,* Galen's *Small Art of
Medicine,* and Manardi's Latin letters on medicine. But Rabelais's knowledge of medicine and the world of sickness and disease is far from merely
bookish: he served for a time on the medical staff of the Hôtel-Dieu
Hospital in Lyon and also did dissections, which was a rather daring and
innovative initiative, since the Church was opposed to the practice.

As one might expect, his comic novels are not to be divorced from
his knowledge of medicine. In fact, in Rabelais's art, the interpenetration
of literature and medicine is so pervasive that one would have to say that,
for him, literature is indeed medicine, and medicine the stuff of literature.
There are very few pages in Rabelais that do not exude in one way or
another some sense of medical lore. However, his fiction is a burlesque
"fearsome," "terrible," "horrible," "heroic" saga of giants, and therefore the reader is confronted not by a medical tract, but by an earthy,
carnavalesque poetry of medicine.

With the possible exception of surgical instruments per se (one
character, Friar John, does use a cross as a scalpel in order to dissect and
dismember a horde of attackers), I think it safe to say that Rabelais's
novels incorporate the whole of Renaissance medicine. Two principal
characters, Pantagruel and Panurge, consider the study of medicine and
/or practice it, and a third, Rondibilis, a minor character in the *Third Book,*
is a doctor and is called upon to give his opinion as to whether Panurge
will be cuckolded in the event he marries. The depiction of Rondibilis as
physician is straightforward; in many other cases, however, the state of
the art and its practitioners are mocked, as when Pantagruel decides to
avoid the study of medicine for the reason that "the profession was far
too wearying, besides being melancholy, and that physicians smelt of the
suppository, like old devils."[1]

More significant, however, are the presence and range of medical
discussions involving birth, pregnancy, child rearing, sexual organs,
and so on. Throughout the *Third Book,* for instance, Pantagruel and
Panurge argue about the production of semen: Pantagruel posits the
brain as the seat of production, while the ever ithyphallic Panurge
opts for the testicles, for "when a man loses his head, only the individual perishes; but if the balls were lost, the whole human race
would die out." In this case, testicles and the head provide the basic
imagery for the generational and cognitive patterns of the book. Similarly, Panurge, poeticizing the virtues of the heart and the bloodstream, develops an outlandish and endearing physiological-economic
system wherein "everyone lends and everyone owes, where all are
debtors and all are lenders." In *Pantagruel* as in *Gargantua,* on the
other hand, there are not only hilarious episodes involving obstetrics

and gynecology, but also extensive seriocomic presentations of various principles of hygiene and diet to be adhered to in the upbringing of the young giants.

Anything and everything medical is grist for Rabelais's mill: every conceivable part of the human anatomy, with a special predilection for genitalia; the function of various glands, aging, potency, sexual development, abscesses, infections, skin diseases, stench, the digestive tract, excrement, urine, various excretions and secretions, wounds, fractures, bandages, salves, drugs, laxatives, and much, much more. And he especially delights in pathological imprecations ("May St Anthony's fire burn you, the epilepsy throw you, the thunder-stroke and leg-ulcers rack you, dysentery seize you, and may the erysipelas, with its tiny cowhair rash, and quicksilver's pain on top, through your arse-hole enter up, and like Sodom and Gomorrah may you dissolve into sulphur, fire, and the bottomless pit, in case you do not firmly believe everything that I tell you in this present Chronicle!") and in anatomical assaults ("He beat out the brains of some, broke the arms and legs of others, disjointed the neck-bones, demolished the kidneys, slit the noses, blackened the eyes, smashed the jaws, knocked the teeth down the throats, shattered the shoulder-blades, crushed the shins, dislocated the thigh-bones, and cracked the fore-arms of yet others"). Hence, our appreciation of his comedic operations also involves our recognition of their grimness.

But it is his uncanny use of the human body as a pulsating, throbbing metaphor for the whole of life that best illustrates his sensual and luxuriant imagination and his manipulation of physiology and medicine for esthetic and teleological ends. In Rabelais, everything is mirrored through the prism of the body, and especially through its alimentary-excretory-copulative needs and propensities. The lusty skits which ensue inevitably lead to paroxysms of uproarious—and beneficient—laughter, cleansing and purifying, as it were, and titillating too, the body and spirit of the reader. Hence, the doctor-novelist ministers to our needs, and the book becomes a prescription for our renewal.

Sexual and alimentary effusions are to be found on nearly every page; discourse and intercourse, orality and anality conjoin in a boisterous and rollicking exploration and demystification of physical-spiritual consonances. If an episode is called upon, for example, to lampoon the legal system as nothing but hot air, the litigants are appropriately named Kissass and Sniffshit. Unerringly, language and the mouth—supposedly the organ of verbal and intelligible discourse—are graphically replaced by the anus; the world is thus shown to be upside-down, the buttocks replacing the head, the entire system satirized as verbal offal, speaking through its anus, in a copious defecation of words. Hence, when the intellectual conduits are constipated, the doctor points to health by calling upon the intestinal tract.

Throughout *Gargantua and Pantagruel,* an endless vocabulary of elimination, urethral imagery, terms of swallowing and regurgitation, colorful embellishments on copulation, phallic and orificial thematics, and so on —in a word, Rabelais's joyful bawdy body—combine with all other elements to create a structure of healing. Life is good health, and the role of the book-medication is to bring it about through the sustaining and curative power of laughter. Indeed, for Rabelais, the physiology of laughter and the creation and maintenance of good health are synonymous, the one feeding off the other.

In the following brief discussion of Rabelais's first novel, *Pantagruel*, I should like to show the interplay of sickness and health as a structuring principle that reveals the restorative properties of the book.

For all its emphasis on the positive aspects of man's gustatory, excremental, and sexual shenanigans, the novel pays a great deal of attention to man's physical as well as his intellectual diseases and disabilities. Health and wholeness are obviously the standard, and the plurivalent comic sallies of the work illustrate the many modifications to which human beings and concepts are subject. This interaction of health and sickness, of the whole versus the damaged, is perhaps the most persistent of the novel's many patterns.

Although the conceptual aberrations or sicknesses that *Pantagruel* exposes in matters of education, religion, and law constitute a substantial part of the pattern under consideration, it is the physical dimension of the health-sickness motif that is of immediate significance here. It first appears in the prologue, in the guise of toothaches and more especially in the evocation of syphilitics, to whom Rabelais will be partial throughout his works:

> There are those in the world—these are no fairy-tales—who, when greatly afflicted with toothache, after expending all their substance on doctors without any result, have found no readier remedy than to put the said Chronicles [a popular book to which the narrator compares his tale] between two fine linen sheets, well warmed, and apply them to the seat of the pain, dusting them first with a little dry-dung powder. But what shall I say of the poor victims of pox and gout? Oh, how often we have seen them at a moment when they were well anointed and thoroughly greased, with their faces shining like a larder lock-plate, and their teeth rattling like the keys on the manual of an organ or a spinet when it is being played, and their gullets foaming like a wild boar which the hounds have driven into the toils. And what were they doing then? Their one consolation was to have some pages of this book read to them. And some of them we have seen who would have given themselves to a hundred barrels-full of old devils if they had not felt a perceptible alleviation of their pain from the reading of the said book, while they were being kept in the sweat-room.

In fact, Rabelais placed his book under the aegis of syphilitics, gouty people, and tipplers. This fun-loving, reveling internal audience needs help, to be sure, but their exuberant and earthy attitude toward life— infection, inflammation, and worse being their calling cards—is the corrective the book seeks to bring about. Hence, disease generates art. More important, the narrator bills himself as an "abstractor of quintessence," thereby linking his enterprise with that of medieval alchemists who not only sought to extract gold from base metals but also to discover a universal cure for diseases as well as a means to prolong life indefinitely. As a result, the book he prescribes for the sick—and for the healthy—is a potent and fertile agent of transformation and creation, an elixir to be kept close at hand and absorbed like the tippler's wine. The word is soothing, comforting, revivifying, a resuscitative salve, the essential and inexhaustible therapy.

Those in need of medical attention are plentiful in *Pantagruel.* Gargantua, Pantagruel's father, is concerned about his health and worries that his sadness over the death of his wife in childbirth might bring on a fever. On the other hand, Pantagruel suffers a gigantic stomachache, for which his physicians prescribe a laxative combining "four hundredweight of scammony from Colophon, a hundred and thirty-eight cart-loads of cassia, and eleven thousand nine hundred pounds of rhubarb, not to count other messes." He also swallows seventeen copper pills, each containing a man with pick and shovel, their goal being the location and dislodging of mounds of ordure; after they stack it in baskets and reenter their pills, Pantagruel forces himself to vomit, throws everything and everyone up, "and in this way Pantagruel was cured, and restored to his former good health."

Conversely, as in the case of Kissass and Sniffshit, excrement is often used in order to effect or indicate a cure. When a cocky, mouthy student refuses to speak intelligible French, Pantagruel grabs him by the throat and so scares him that his lexical bravura dissolves and comes to rest at the bottom of his pants, his fecal speech now being labeled "natural." When another character is decapitated in the course of battle, Panurge, the ever-resourceful rascal and healer, breathes new life into the man by first placing the head on his codpiece in order to keep it warm, then bathing it in wine and dusting it with powdered excrement; there follow ointment, vein-to-vein surgery, stitches, and finally breathing, eye movement, yawning, sneezing, and ultimately farting; only at the last does Panurge pronounce himself satisfied that the man is alive and beyond danger.

Miraculous medical virtues are also ascribed to urine. When Panurge is neither extolling nor using the extraordinary properties of his suggestive codpiece, he displays all the knowledge of an apothecary as he concocts a diuretic brew for Pantagruel, causing him to release a urinal deluge of such magnitude that an entire enemy camp is drowned. On another occasion, Pantagruel releases urine of such temperature that it creates clinical hot baths. And when Panurge wishes to humiliate a haughty Parisian woman, whose favors he had sought in vain, he smears her clothes with an estrous concoction that attracts six thousand male dogs, whose sexual antics and urinary prowess reduce her to a laughing-stock and her house to a floating ark. It is as though the Rabelaisian text is out to demonstrate the viability of one of the admonitions of the popular *Regimen sanitatis salernitanum* (A Regimen of Health from the School of Salerno), a medieval medical poem: "Do not retain your urine nor tightly compress your anus. / Follow these rules and you shall live a long time."

Still, of all the physical manifestations of health and sickness that permeate *Pantagruel,* it is the recurrence of a wound and its cure that holds center stage. Normally, this is demonstrated through the inordinate size of the female genital area, as in the case of Pantagruel's mother, whose dimensions are "a good three acres and two roods in size." But the best example is a veritable scatological *tour de force* in which Rabelais has Panurge spin a tale about a lion and a fox who come upon a hag who has just fallen on her back, displaying to both an unusual perforation. Inasmuch as the lion has but recently had his leg cut by one man, then cured by another, he is full of compassion and quick to succor the injured. Because he suspects that the hag's "what-d'ye-call-it" is, naturally, the result of a hatchet-blow, he asks the fox to administer first aid with his tail while he runs around gathering up moss with which to stop the wound. It would be difficult to find in all literature a more poetic, bawdy, ribcage-shattering anecdote; even Aristophanes's tale of a bird who ate sand and excreted bricks and thus helped to build the pyramids cannot compare. At all events, in the Rabelaisian context, the *wound* serves a dual purpose: it is both the object of titillating impudence and the symbol of restorative considerations. The lion and the fox are concerned with reme-dial means, with healing, and so they seek to recreate what they perceive as an original whole. Just as the world of *Pantagruel* is sickly and in need of medical attention, the hag's "physical deformation" depicts imbalance and disharmony.

In a dedicatory preface to the *Fourth Book,* Dr. Rabelais places himself squarely in a long line of illustrious personages—Hippocrates, Plato, Galen, and others—who extolled the virtues of cheerful medicine: "Ev-erything that is said must aim at one effect, must be directed to one end: to cheer the patient up." For Rabelais, surely the greatest wordsmith the French language has ever known, the laughing book, with its irrepressible exuberance and sheer joy, is the best antidote for sickness and unhappi-ness, and a recommended substitute for the physician.

NOTE

1. References are from *The Histories of Gargantua and Pantagruel,* trans., J. M. Cohen (Baltimore: Penguin Books, 1955). Helpful studies in English are Mikhail Bakhtin, *Rabelais and His World,* trans., Hélène Iswolsky (Cambridge: The M.I.T. Press, 1968); Dorothy Coleman, *Rabelais: A Critical Study in Prose Fiction* (Cambridge: Cambridge University Press, 1971); Donald M. Frame, *François Rabelais: A Study* (New York: Harcourt Brace Jovanovich, 1977); and Thomas M. Greene, *Rabelais: A Study in Comic Courage* (Englewood Cliffs, N.J.: Prentice-Hall, 1970).

From Hero to Horror:
Louis-Ferdinand Céline, M.D.
Bettina L. Knapp

Céline (1894–1961) was what one might call the mythomanic type. In *Death on the Installment Plan,* for example, he describes his childhood as having been horrendous, ignominious; it was spent in utter filth, poverty, and degradation. His father is depicted as cruel, vulgar, coarse, and brutish, and his mother is represented as pathetic, vicious, crippled, and a mender of old, ragged lace. Certainly there is nothing unethical in creating a fictional world; and the novel can be an ideal medium in which to do so. When the fiction is passed off as fact, however, when myth is fed to journalists and the reading public, the validity of the story related becomes questionable. Céline chose to fantasize about the wounds he had received in World War I. For years his reading public and acquaintances alike thought he had been trepanned: that he had suffered severe head wounds. So Céline wanted everyone to believe! What was the actual story? He had suffered a fracture of the shoulder bone, the result of shell fire. It was a serious enough wound and he had to spend several months in a military hospital because of it. But the wound was no trepanation.

When writing his doctoral dissertation (a requirement in France for the medical degree) on Ignaz Philipp Semmelweis (1818–1865), Céline did not fantasize. On the contrary, he showed sincerity, admiration, and idealism in this youthful work. Céline pointed out that Semmelweis discovered the contagious nature of puerperal fever fifty years before Louis Pasteur proved the existence of bacteria. Semmelweis—the precursor of antiseptic medicine, the man who had devoted all his life and sanity to scientific investigation with the purpose of reducing suffering and death in the hospitals of his day—became Céline's hero.

With admiration Céline related Semmelweis's story: after completing his studies at the medical school in Vienna, Semmelweis spent many long days observing the great doctors at work, such as Doctor Skoda, whose diagnostic techniques were notable for their finesse, whose dissecting procedures were remarkable for their precision. As Semmelweis's knowledge of medicine deepened, Céline inferred derisively, he came to have less and less faith in the abilities of the so-called great doctors and surgeons. Why? Céline questioned. It was because the mortality rate in the hospitals, and in the obstetric wards in particular, was very high. An unexplored area opened up for this creative physician. Dr. Skoda recognized the young man's talent, as well as his rebellious spirit, and he feared it. He realized only too well that the most brilliant students are the ones most likely to destroy or overthrow their masters. Skoda evidently was not prepared to accept the innovative and to suffer dethronement from his powerful position in the hospital. Rather than hire Semmelweis as an assistant upon his graduation (1844), as he had promised to do, Skoda chose another doctor, justifying his bad faith on the grounds of the other man's seniority. Despite this setback, Semmelweis continued his work in surgery and, later, in obstetrics. He questioned and probed: was puerperal fever contagious? how was it contracted? how did it spread?

As Semmelweis's martyrdom grew, so Céline's anger and resentment also increased and were focused on all those who persecuted his hero. Despite the disbelief, mockery, and jealousies Semmelweis encountered during the course of his investigations, Céline stated with fervor, he pursued his work. He was not emotionally strong enough, however, to overcome the barage of insults and ridicule leveled at him. "Never had a human conscience," Céline wrote, "been so covered with shame [as Semmelweis's] . . . during the months of 1849." Too many misunderstandings had arisen; too much ill will had been activated because of Semmelweis's hygienic directives. Semmelweis was ordered by the Viennese hospital authorities to leave the hospital and the city. In Hungary now he started to work on his study of the *Etiology of Puerperal Fever.* He preached cleanliness once again in the hospitals, and again was vilified; unable to withstand the attacks and unflagging hatred, his mind gave way. He suffered attacks of paranoia. He became dangerous. Convinced he was being pursued by enemies, Semmelweis ranted and raved, screamed, and fought. One day he rushed into an anatomy class in the Medical School in Budapest, grabbed a scalpel and made an incision in the cadaver, touching some putrefied tumorous area with his knife. Inadvertently, he cut himself slightly with the scalpel. His wound bled. He was disarmed. It was too late. Infection had already set in. When Doctor Skoda heard of the incident he went to Budapest and took Semmelweis back to Vienna with him. He was placed in a mental institution and died two months later at the age of forty-seven. Ironically, he had proved his own theory. He had been his own guinea pig.

The hero figure emerges in all of its power and point in Céline's dissertation. Admired not only because of his innovations, perseverance, and talent, Semmelweis was also idealized because he was fired by a messianic spirit and was working for the good of humanity. It is generally during a person's adolescence that hero figures come into being. Viewed psychologically as helping figures, they are usually idealized. They are an expression of dissatisfaction with one's own lot, and with that of humanity as well. A bearer of new cultural elements, the hero is an initiator of untried ways. He represents standards of perfection: he becomes capable of extricating individuals from a joyless world and from pressing problems. The hero-worshiper, whether an individual or a collective, projects or identifies with the legendary or historical figure and in this way gives the undeveloped ego the strength it lacks. Once the ego has been strengthened, as is frequently the case during the more mature years, the need for the hero figure diminishes or disappears.[1]

Clearly, Semmelweis was Céline's hero during this period. He possessed the qualities of imagination that Céline admired in that Semmelweis allowed his thoughts to wander freely and to penetrate uncharted territories—reaching a kind of no man's land. It was from this region that he brought back his message, his discovery. Semmelweis was also a fighter who defied conventions: an intellectual revolutionary who attempted to impose a new scientific canon upon an ungrateful and even hostile group of physicians. The hero's real test hinges on how successful he is in forging his ways and ideas upon the world. Semmelweis failed this test because he gained only animosity from his contemporaries and was unable to cope with the forces that sought to destroy him. His mind gave way. No one understood his motives, and that destroyed him. Céline's rage and hatred found fertile field in Semmelweis's detractors.

The idealism exhibited by Céline in his dissertation on Semmelweis indicated a desire on his part to dedicate himself to the betterment of man's lot on earth, and perhaps to follow in his hero's footsteps insofar as his interest in science was concerned. One might be led, therefore, to believe that the Semmelweis-type, the doctor as healer and as medical phenomenon, would be reborn in Céline. When idealism, however, is extreme, disappointment soon sets in, followed by resentment and rage at those who are unable to understand the lot of the innovator. Whether Céline was distressed over his own lack of abilities as a physician or with scientific investigation in general, is not known. After he received his medical degree, he practiced medicine off and on, in a desultory manner. What has come to light is Céline's extreme sense of solitude, his bitterness, and his inability to relate to his fellow men. Alienation ensued and with it, rancor and hatred made deep inroads in Céline's psyche.

Céline's protagonist Bardamu in his first novel, *Journey to the End of the Night* (1932), is the antithesis of Semmelweis. Although a doctor, Bardamu has no goal in life. He wafts along on currents, whatever these may be. He has no hope for the future and is paralyzed by fear (of death in particular), so much so that he is unable to cope with life. He becomes a psychological paralytic, incapable of sizing up situations or being able to act to his advantage. Such an attitude results in feelings of contempt for everything and everyone around him, increasing still further his loneliness and despair. Bardamu became anti-French, antirich, antipoor, antihealthy, antisick. His tirades and hatreds spilled over to encompass all of humanity. On shipboard, for example, when returning from Africa, he looks at the passengers with mounting rage. He sees them as a collective entity—a microcosm of the world—diabolical, gruesome, hepatic, toothless, syphilitic, flea-infested, eczema-covered, pimply, fat, slovenly, attracting clusters of flies and bugs of all sorts. He was revolted by them, and he feared them. As for the Black Africans, they are described as follows:

> These niggers are all dead and stinking; you'll soon find that out. They squat there all day; and you wouldn't believe them capable of even getting up to go and piss against a tree, and then as soon as it's night, my God! . . . They all go hysterical, all nerves, all bloody-minded. Part of the night itself is gone crazy—that's what the niggers are. I'm telling you. The set of dirty beggars! Degenerate scum.[2]

Some primitive instinct within Céline had been stirred and rumbled in his depths. He could not accept passivity, laziness, lack of direction and focus in others, perhaps projecting onto the collective certain of his own unconscious characteristics.

Ambivalence is also involved in the medical cases delineated in *Journey to the End of the Night*. Céline goes into great detail when describing an example of sadism: a couple beating their ten-year-old daughter in order to become sexually aroused. He reveals a modicum of humanity, however, when castigating a mother who prefers to risk her daughter's life (the girl was hemorrhaging from a self-induced abortion) rather than to have her hospitalized because that would allow the neighbors to discover the cause. Bardamu's reactions are notably bizarre when calling upon a family with an illegitimate infant. He maltreats the child; the parents are aghast and finally ask him to leave. Bardamu cannot account for his unpleasant manner nor does he really try. Most frequently Céline underscores the vile, vicious and venomous side of mankind when depicting Bardamu's patients. He seems to take pleasure in fluoroscopic descriptions: skin abrasions, sores, infectious diseases, and in most cases, he exhibits a lack of feeling. As a physician he seems untouched by those he examines, as though he did not care whether his patients lived or died, provided that his fees were paid. He rarely if ever gives of himself to his patients and only on occasion does he participate in their turmoil or develop any kind of understanding for the destitute or the dying. Céline's doctor-protagonist makes no attempt at heroism, no attempt to right a wrong. One wonders why he ever bothered to study medicine. Certainly it was not out of any devotion to mankind.

The protagonist in *Death on the Installment Plan* (1936), Ferdinand, is also a doctor, and even further removed from Céline's ideal figure: the Semmelweis-type physician. A satire in part, *Death on the Installment Plan* is a grotesque novel marked with bitterness, coldness, and cruelty—echoing the grin of tragic laughter. The hero's emotional condition (rage, passion) takes on physical dimension (nausea, vomiting, excrement) in this work and is an expression of Céline's hostility through projection toward himself as well as toward society in general.

Regurgitation scenes in *Death on the Installment Plan* are unique in literature and unforgettable. Ferdinand's most violent vomiting spell occurs when he confronts his father and strikes him. Prior to this incident, his father has been described as sadistic and given to uncontrollable bouts of rage. Ferdinand's vomiting is so acute, so spasmodic, so complete—the ejection of evils, poisons, and decayed, infected, parasitic entities—that it seems it will never stop. Up to now Ferdinand has accepted his father's insults and condemnations which slowly eroded his own personality. His giant effort at rebellion, described viscerally by Céline, indicates that something positive within Ferdinand's psyche is taking root, being born out of the chaos. Other forces come into play at this time: the realization, perhaps, that his father has acted as he has all these years because his son and his wife have been willing to put up with his behavior. Had they been active and forceful individuals, the father might not have gotten away, so to speak, with these destructive outbursts. Henceforth, Ferdinand's relationship with his father changes of necessity: he is no longer to be dominated or stifled by him. The change which took place in the parent-child confrontation was so sudden, so extreme that it disturbed Ferdinand's entire orientation. His father is no longer the paragon of strength to be feared; his image has been reduced to that of a weak, screaming mass, a helpless, degraded entity. He is nothing. Ferdinand's reaction is traumatic. He breaks out in sweat; he shivers; he is crippled with vertigo, anguish, and vomits in a way he has never experienced before.

> I began to vomit. . . . I even pushed to make it come up. . . . That made me feel a lot better. I vomited everything. . . . The shivers started in again. . . . They shook me so hard I didn't know who I was anymore. . . . I was surprised at myself. . . . I threw up the macaroni. . . . I started in again. . . . It did me a whole lot of good. Like I was getting rid of everything. . . . I threw up everything I could all over the floor. . . . I pushed and strained. . . . I bent double to make myself puke still more and then came slime and then froth. . . . It splattered, it spread under the door. . . . I vomited up everything I'd eaten for at least a week and then diarrhea too. . . .[3]

This purgation had some positive consequences for Ferdinand. It led to a total break with his father. Since he was thrown out of the house, he was forced to develop and shift for himself.

With the passing of years the Semmelweis hero figure dimmed still further in Céline's mind. In its place, hate increased. Céline concentrated his venom—with particular viciousness—on the Jew, the Black, and the Oriental, although other groups were not slighted. Céline's sentiments were articulated in three polemical tracts: *Bagatelles for a Massacre* (1937), *School for Cadavers* (1938), and *Some State of Affairs* (1941). These found fertile field in France prior to and during World War II. In ancient times the evils of a community supposedly disappeared along with the animal. When Céline cursed the Jew, for example, in his polemical writings, he sought to destroy an entire population and thus exhibited his brand of scapegoat mentality. Never was there any discussion of morality or sober assessment of political, economic, or social situations in these works. Céline was in effect ridding himself, but not really, of all the unacceptable sentiments lodged within his own unconscious and projecting these onto a minority group.

During the Occupation of France, Céline advocated rapprochement with Germany. He also shared Nazi racial feelings concerning the superiority of the white race and stated his thoughts in such pro-Nazi newspapers as *La Gerbe, Au Pilogri, L'Emancipation Nationale, L'Union Française*. In his publications, pro-Nazi meetings and lectures, and in his polemical tracts, Céline expressed sentiments such as: "Urns for the Jews. . . . Luxate the Jew to a post. . . . I didn't wait for the High Command to bedeck the Crillon with flags to become a collaborator. . . . I have been anti-Jewish from the very beginning. . . . I want an alliance to be made with Germany, and right away; not a small, precarious alliance. A real alliance, solid, colossal."[4]

In 1942 Céline went to Berlin for a brief visit, ostensibly to see some German hospitals. He had good friends in the medical corps, such as Doctor Karl Epting, Doctor Haubolt, and others he had known in Paris before and during World War II. After his return, he pursued his existence as a verbal collaborator with the enemy. A month after French and English troops landed in Normandy, and fearing allied reprisals, Céline and his wife, Lucette Almanzor, left Paris for Germany en route to Copenhagen, where some years before he had converted his royalties into gold bullion. He received a *Passierschein* through Germany and sojourned for a while at the Park Hotel in Baden-Baden, then Kränzlin (Brandenburg), at Sigmaringe, where many collaborators and members of the Vichy government (including Pétain and Laval) had been given asylum by the Germans. In Copenhagen Céline and his wife were given shelter and hospitality by an old friend, Karen Jensen. In time (1946) he was denounced to Danish authorities as a French collaborator and remained in prison for fourteen months and his wife for two. After that date he promised the Danish authorities not to leave Denmark until given official permission. He was allowed to live at Konprinssessegade, then at Körsor, a small port town on the Baltic Sea. In February 1950, Céline was condemned by default in France "to one year of imprisonment and fifty thousand francs fine." He was declared "to be a national disgrace." Able to take advantage of the amnesty law of August 1947, he and his wife returned to France in 1951.

Céline emerged from the holocaust a broken man: he was cornered and did not know where to turn. His works at this time were a *massa confusa* in which he revealed himself as a shattered being, fragmented, splintered as crushed glass in: *Guignol's Band* I (1944) and II (1964); and *Fairy-Play for Another Time* I (1952) and II (1954). Not a single instant of repose is reflected in these works, only feelings of entrapment, enslavement, and hurt.

Céline had come a long way from those early days when he looked upon Semmelweis as his hero; when integrity, perseverance, and scientific investigation were paragons of greatness. Now a man against the world and cosmic order, Céline's personality in many ways resembled the symbolic meaning of the swastika. Originally, the swastika stood for natural harmony, since it symbolized the "sun" and in Sanskrit *su* means "well" and *asti* is defined as "being." The Nazis, however, reversed the image, indicating their desire to turn *against* cosmic and natural well being, showing their need to annihilate.[5]

Céline's turbulent and chaotic inner world took on collective stature in his trilogy *From Castle to Castle* (1959), *North* (1960), and *Rigodon* (1969), novels which take readers to Germany after his flight from France in 1944. In these volumes the eidetic images are excoriating—unforgettable —and reflect the mental erosion of a man whose inner world is peopled with ghouls, grotesquely deformed foul beings—horror heroes. The action in *From Castle to Castle* focuses on Sigmaringen, a sinister castle. The creatures inhabiting this darkened realm are mutilated beings: Generals (Pétain, von Raumitz, Abetz), government officials (Laval), a female devourer who stands with her hounds outside of her room waiting for her victims to enter, never to reemerge; bands of nymphomaniacs, an insane vicar, lice- and flea-infested people, syphilitics and mentally deranged people. Ignominious and thanatoid forces are at work in this miasmic world where depravity, decay, and degeneration cohabit.

This Walpurgisnacht atmosphere comprises a description of a cancer ward which is unparalleled in literature. The narrator in his capacity as doctor is supposed to care for advanced cancer cases. The descriptions given are so vivid, so detailed that each word carries affective power: the images revolt the reader not only by their gory and sordid nature, but also by the author's own propensity for the macabre and unfeeling. Tumors of all sizes and shapes are described with clinical accuracy: bulbous, bloody, parasitic excrescences, putrescences. The narrator suggests that some women can even be strung up and swung by their tumors. Hysterectomies are always in order because women, he states, are in need of being emptied like "rotted rabbits."

Other medical prodigies besides the narrator live at Sigmaringen. There is a surgeon who enjoys operating without anesthesia, the better to watch his patients wail and moan. His method: first, sever an ear, then gouge out the eyes, and finally cut the entire globular mass away from the torso. The surgeon is always pictured with scalpel in hand, very nearly panting with pleasure as he watches more and more future patients come his way. Indeed, it is he who single-handedly creates the headless group of children that run about frantically at Sigmaringen. Children are usually equated with joy and hope, but these headless children are hideously grotesque, gesticulate madly, grunt, and screech; their features are contorted, distorted, inflated—a rictus engraved on their "headless countenances."

The last section of *North* centers on the relationship between wife and husband; a sad commentary on marriage. The wife is a modern version of a Bacchante or Maenad, a woman struck by the "rage" ("mania"), a phallus-bearer who burns for men; who is only interested in the male as a fecundating agent. This kind of woman belongs to no man but rather to all men; she is anonymous, a transpersonal being, an incarnation of the Great Mother. Céline's Maenad, Inge von Leiden, is a covert prostitute-type. She is married to a paraplegic, owner of an immense estate, and it was through her husband that she obtained both title and fortune. Hard, ruthless, and even brutal, she is fed up with her defective husband. He represents everything that is atrophied in life: a waste product.

How will Céline destroy Inge's husband whom Céline considers a useless, nonfunctioning entity? One day as the handyman carries the paraplegic to the courtyard, he drops him, either by mistake or on purpose, into a cesspool which has not been emptied in three years and is filled to the brim with the excrement of four-hundred cows. When the husband is fished out of the cesspool, dead, he is in a fetal position, "folded over on himself, a large trunk with atrophied legs, covered over with yellow and black liquid manure."[6] The fact that he has not died in a beatific manner, but rather in the most ignominious manner (bathed in excrement), indicates that he truly does represent refuse; since he is no longer a source of nourishment to humanity, he is worthy only of destruction.

Rigodon, a fusion of verbal collages and associative blocks, also takes the reader into polluted and miasmic areas. One of the most abrasive and excoriating images in all of Céline's works is his description of a group of lepers whom the narrator meets in Germany. No detail is spared the reader: eyes and noses are like masses or clots of bloody, oozing pustules; the members of these beings are half eaten away with rot—and evoke feelings of nausea in the reader. As the images depicted grow more and more unbearable, a second vision is superimposed: a nun enters the picture and begins bandaging the lepers. Céline's replications go beyond the world of appearances in this instance. The bandages represent one more of those deceits society is wont to heap upon its members. Leprosy for Céline is concomitant with evil. Hidden under the bandages, the disease is allowed to fester, to grow unchecked and to become all the more virulent since its destructive path goes unobserved.

From Hero to Horror! Céline completed the circle that was to be expected since the seeds of hatred, as well as those of intense admiration, had found flower in his doctoral dissertation. With the passing of years, Céline's wrath focused on the establishment, those Doctor Skodas who lacked understanding and sensitivity. They represented for him success as doctors and as scientists; and by denigrating them, he seemed to purge himself of his own feelings of disappointment brought on by his own undistinguished medical career. That he projected onto his protagonists such characteristics as laziness, lack of perseverance, and the inability to pursue scientific investigation, might also imply an unwillingness on his part to accept his own negative characteristics which were manifested in the creatures of his fantasy. Céline's frustrations had evidently reached such a point of hatred rather than compassion, anger instead of understanding, that they emerged as flaming forces. These were focused on individuals, groups, and nations in his polemical tracts. In his novels, such rage evidenced itself frequently in his minute descriptions of sores, pustules, fungi, tumors, sexual aberrations— acting as a catharsis to relieve him temporarily of his powerful obsessions.

Céline's rancor, however, is indicative of something deeply fearsome from society's point of view. The creative individual—Céline is a case in point—enjoys a very special position in the world. He is a kind of forerunner of what is to be, the prototype of many people, a prophet, a "retort in which [the] poisons and antidotes of the collective are distilled."[7] How many times has it been said of a painter—a Cézanne or a Van Gogh, for example—"he saw into the future . . . he lived before his time . . ."? Such statements are meaningful. A writer with Céline's intuition and perception is possessed of sensitive antennae that lie deep within the fibers of being. He senses the unknown; he transmutes the impalpable into the palpable, the evanescent into the eternal. The artist Céline responds more powerfully to the deepest layers within himself—to that transpersonal realm, named by C. G. Jung as the collective unconscious. Great creative endeavors—and Céline's is to be placed in this category—must be looked upon not merely as personal expressions, but also as revelations; not simply as individual offerings extracted from the author's depths, but also as an indication of what lies hidden "behind the scenes" for the collective and of what is likely to come to pass in the world of reality. For this reason the artist's audience must be doubly aware of his message and conscious of what he has produced.

If the trajectory in Céline's novels has been from Hero to Horror— and if he represents inner forces at work in the collective psyche (his works are immensely popular in France today)—what can be said about the future?

NOTES

1. C.G. Jung, *Symbols of Transformation* (New York: Pantheon Books, 1956), p. 112.

2. Louis-Ferdinand Céline, *Journey to the End of the Night,* trans., J.P. Marks (New York: New Directions, 1961), p. 165.

3. Céline, *Death on the Installment Plan,* trans. Ralph Manheim (New York: New Directions, 1966), p. 121.

4. In Bettina L. Knapp, *Céline: Man of Hate* (University: University of Alabama Press, 1974), pp. 93–130.

5. Gerhard Adler, *The Living Symbol* (New York: Pantheon Books, 1961), p. 134.

6. *Oeuvres de Louis-Ferdinand Céline,* Vol. V (Paris: André Balland, 1969), p. 111.

7. Eric Neumann, *Depth Psychology and a New Ethic* (New York: G. P. Putnam's Sons, 1969), p. 30.

Samuel Garth and the Dispensary: The Project and the Poem

John F. Sena

The physician in the eighteenth century was often a public figure with manifold interests. Unlike many of his twentieth-century counterparts, he was not circumscribed in his activities nor estranged from his contemporaries, but was, instead, deeply involved in the political, social, and literary life of his time. John Arbuthnot, for instance, was as well known among his contemporaries as a political satirist and a Tory apologist as he was for his theories on the relationship between diet and disease; Hans Sloane, while Physician to Christ's Hospital, began his collection of artifacts, which became the basis for the British Museum; Richard Blackmore, Mark Akenside, and Tobias Smollett were acclaimed as creative artists as well as medical practitioners. The interests and achievements of these physicians—and numerous others—went beyond medicine; yet, none was more of a public figure or more of a Renaissance man than Samuel Garth.

Garth excelled in three diverse areas: medicine, politics, and poetry. He began his medical training at Peterhouse College, Cambridge, in 1676, at the age of sixteen, and received from Cambridge his B.A., M.A., and M.D. Little is known of his university career beyond the fact that his residence at Cambridge was not continuous between his master's and doctor's degree. Owing perhaps to the lack of emphasis at Cambridge on the study of anatomy, Garth, following the path of numerous English physicians, traveled to Leyden to further his medical education. He was admitted to the Royal College of Physicians in 1693, where he became deeply embroiled in the most bitter and significant medical controversy of the period: the struggle between the apothecaries and physicians over the creation of a dispensary for London's sick poor. Although he began his professional life as a spokesman for the poor and continued to aid the downtrodden and indigent until his death in 1718, his medical career ranged over the entire economic and social spectrum. He was, for instance, the personal physician to the King, George I, and to the greatest military hero of the age, the Duke of Marlborough, as well as physician-general to the army; he attended royalty—the Prince of Denmark and the Duke of Wales; and he was physician to such socially and intellectually prominent figures as Lady Mary Wortley Montagu and the great essayists Joseph Addison and Richard Steele. Although Garth was involved in medical and political controversies throughout his life, no one, not even the most acrimonious of his enemies, ever seriously impugned his medical ability or his professional ethics. Rather, he was universally praised for his consummate skill and for the generosity with which he bestowed his talent; he was, in short, as Alexander Pope epitomized him in *A Farewell to London*, "the best good Christian."

Although Garth as a physician treated both Whigs and Tories without prejudice, he was, nevertheless, highly partisan in his political activities. A staunch supporter of William III and the Hanoverians, he fought openly on behalf of Whig causes, even when they posed a threat to his safety. When, for instance, in 1710 the English grew disenchanted with their government's policies in the War of the Spanish Succession, he helped to organize anti-Tory rallies and public demonstrations at substantial personal risk. He also served the Whig cause by acting on numerous occasions as a secret courier and emissary (he carried messages, for example, from the Whig government to the Duke of Marlborough when the general was fighting in the Hague in 1711). He undertook an even more delicate task shortly after the abortive rebellion of James Edward in 1715 when he met secretly in Paris with the exiled former secretary of state, Henry St. John, Lord Bolingbroke, in the hope of persuading him to abandon the Tory party and to join forces with the Whigs.

In addition to being an accomplished physician and a political activist, Garth was, in the words of William Ayre, Pope's early biographer, "one of the best Poets of his Time."[1] He was the author of *Claremont,* a well-known topographical poem celebrating the estate of the Duke of Newcastle, as well as the general editor of the most famous translation of Ovid's *Metamorphoses* to appear in the eighteenth century, a translation which was carefully calculated to lend support to the Hanoverians. But undoubtedly his most popular and significant literary creation was a lengthy mock-epic poem entitled *The Dispensary.*

Behind Garth's poem lay a half-century paper-and-pill war between the Society of Apothecaries and the Royal College of Physicians over the free medical treatment of London's sick poor.[2] The conflict began as an economic issue, but soon raised humanitarian questions as well concerning the obligation of medical practitioners and society in general toward the indigent and the ill. The number of apothecaries in London grew rapidly in the last half of the seventeenth century, from three hundred in 1660 to more than eight hundred by 1698 to more than two thousand a few years later. The proliferation of apothecaries made it increasingly difficult for them to earn an adequate living if they restricted themselves to the selling of drugs exclusively. Thus many apothecaries supplemented their income by prescribing drugs in addition to selling them; by recommending cures in addition to keeping their shops; by, in effect, practicing medicine. This was not especially difficult for them to do, for they had bona fide prescriptions from physicians on file. They simply had to recommend the same drugs or regimen for their patients that the physicians had prescribed for theirs. Naturally, the apothecaries' treatment would be effective only if they could recognize analogous illnesses; if, that is, they could determine whether their patient's illness was the same as the illness of the physician's patient whose prescription was being copied. Although they frequently made inaccurate analogies, with suffering or death as the tragic result, the apothecaries grew in wealth and prestige throughout the latter quarter of the seventeenth century.

Most physicians were incensed at the presumption of the apothecaries. The apothecaries, they felt, lacked the necessary professional training for the practice of medicine; they were mere pretenders perpetuating a cruel fraud on the ignorant masses. Sparked, then, by humanitarian impulses and economic self-interest (since they were losing patients), the physicians attempted to counter the apothecaries by opening in 1675 and 1687 dispensaries at which London's sick poor could be examined by physicians without charge. These two attempts were failures, however, for although the poor received free medical advice, they could not afford to buy the necessary drugs. It was at this critical juncture that Garth and four other physicians devised a plan that overcame this obstacle: all physicians who wished to support the dispensary project were asked to contribute ten pounds apiece for the preparation of drugs on the dispensary premises. The poor could then receive not only free medical advice but drugs at a nominal cost as well. The average cost of a prescription at the dispensary was one penny.

The dispensary project was bitterly opposed by the apothecaries as well as by a number of influential physicians within the Royal College of Physicians, among them William Sydenham, Edward Tyson, John Radcliffe, Richard Blackmore. The reason for the opposition of these physicians was, ironically, economic. A friendly apothecary, it must be remembered, could refer a great many patients who required sophisticated treatment to a specific physician. Thus some physicians were less afraid that the apothecaries would attract poor patients away from them than they were that, by supporting the dispensary, a fertile source of referrals would dry up. With the dispensary project being attacked from outside the Royal College of Physicians by the apothecaries and from within by the group that courted the apothecaries' favor and came to be known as the "Apothecaries Physicians," the project was in dire need of a defender, a spokesman who could humiliate the apothecaries and their supporters, while setting forth the humanitarian goals of the dispensarians. Samuel Garth responded to this need by writing *The Dispensary,* becoming the chief apologist and publicist of the project as well as the creator of one of the most famous mock-epic poems in the English language.

The Dispensary met with immediate acclaim. Three editions were published between May and June of 1699, a fourth in 1700, and a fifth in 1703. In all, ten editions appeared during Garth's lifetime, two of which were pirated. The poem begins with a description of the College of Physicians, once the scene of vigorous scientific investigation, but now the lair of the God of Sloth. The God is awakened from his lethargy by the noise of workmen reconstructing the building that will house the dispensary. The God Sloth decides to foment a struggle between, on the one side, the apothecaries and their allies and, on the other side, the physicians responsible for the dispensary. He hopes that in the ensuing dissension his reign of "dull indolence" will be restored. The apothecaries meet and, after invoking the goddess Disease through a burnt offering of drugs and old prescriptions, hear various courses of action proposed to meet the threat, including advice from Mirmillo, a member of the College who has always been more interested in money than in medicine. Ultimately, they conclude that the issue must be decided by a war, which is described in mock-heroic fashion, with caustics, emetics, cathartics, syringes, and assorted medical paraphernalia used as weapons: "Each Combatant his Adversary mauls/ With batter'd Bed-pans, and stav'd Urinals."[3] The combat ends when Apollo interposes "in form of Fee," thereby diverting the attention of the apothecaries. The poem concludes with William Harvey advising all practitioners of medicine to study science more and lucre less.

The chief villains of *The Dispensary* are, as one would suspect, the apothecaries and the physicians who support them. Their opposition to the dispensary project is seen by Garth as symptomatic of the moral decline, the lack of idealism and altruism, infecting the medical profession. Charity and benevolence, compassion for mankind, and ethical behavior are being menaced by a growing materialism and selfishness; greed and avarice threaten to undermine medicine's traditional humanistic values. Garth's attacks on the antidispensarians are both direct and allusive. He excoriates his enemies directly through witty and caustic character sketches, while he employs allusions to heroic works of literature—*The Iliad, The Odyssey, The Aeneid*—to encourage his readers to view the disparity between the grandeur of the classical world and the pettiness of segments of the modern world. This latter use of heroic or epic literature for satiric purposes may be described as a mock-heroic or mock-epic technique. It is not classical literature that is being satirized; rather, heroic literature is being used as a standard to allow the reader to make moral judgments about contemporary society.

Garth's success with the satiric character sketch may be seen in his description in Canto II of Colon, a man identified by the poet as Samuel Birch, Master of the Society of Apothecaries from 1714 to 1715:

> In Morals loose, but most precise in Look.
> *Black-Fryar's* Annals lately pleas'd to call
> Him Warden of *Apothecaries-Hall.*
> And, when so dignifi'd, he'd not forbear
> That Operation which the Learn'd declare
> Gives Cholicks ease, and makes the Ladies fair.

In starch'd Urbanity his Talent lies,
And Form the want of Intellects supplies.
Hourly his Learn'd Impertinence affords
A barren Superfluity of Words.
In haste he strides along to recompence
The want of Bus'ness with its vain Pretence.

(75–86)

As Warden of the Apothecaries, Colon is an apt representative of the hypocrisy, incompetence, and deceit of apothecaries in general. Instead of being genuinely interested in relieving distress and curing disease, he is concerned merely with creating the illusion of being a healer: he effects a "precise" appearance to mask his professional incompetence and his "Morals loose." Appearance or "Form" is, in fact, his stock in trade, the basis for his medical success, for by dazzling the eyes of his patients with "starch'd Urbanity" and inundating their ears with "barren" words, he is able to divert attention away from his lack of ability. The only remedy he knows for curing the sick—other than talking them to death—is probably an enema or clyster, an "Operation" that hardly reflects a broad knowledge of drugs.

Garth's combination of the satiric character sketch and classical allusion may be seen in an episode that occurs early in Canto IV. Mirmillo, identified by Garth as Dr. William Gibbons, a member of the Royal College of Physicians who was a staunch antidispensarian and an indefatigable supporter of the apothecaries, addresses the apothecaries preparatory to their mock-heroic clash with the physicians. Then Askaris, an apothecary (identified by Garth as "Pierce"), deferentially says to Mirmillo:

. . . Each Word, Sir, you impart,
Has something killing in it, like your Art.
How much we to your boundless Friendship owe,
Our Files can speak, and your Prescriptions show.
Your Ink descends in such excessive Show'rs,
'Tis plain, you can regard no Health but ours.
Whilst poor Pretenders trifle o'er a Case,
You but appear, and give the *Coup de Grace.*
O that near *Xanthus* Banks you had but dwelt,
When *Ilium* first *Achaian* Fury felt,
The Flood had curs'd young *Peleus's* Arm[4] in vain,
For troubling his choak'd Streams with heaps of slain.
No Trophies you had left for *Greeks* to raise,
Their ten Years Toil, you'd finish'd in ten Days.

(76–89)

Mirmillo is ironically praised in this passage, not as a healer, but as a destroyer; not as a giver of life, but as a virtually heroic purveyor of death. The bond between him and the apothecaries, instead of being based on a mutual desire to relieve distress or to share medical information for the benefit of the patient, is based on self-interest and greed. Mirmillo, who said several lines earlier, " 'Tis plain, my Int'rest you've advanc'd so long," is indebted to the apothecaries for their referrals. And the apothecaries are grateful for his prescriptions, which allow them to practice medicine on the ignorant and unsuspecting masses: " 'Tis plain, you can regard no Health but ours." Instead of being honored for his skill with a scalpel, the physician is praised for his prolific pen, which he wields for the benefit of the apothecaries. What is ignored, of course, in this unholy alliance is the welfare of the patient.

This passage undermines both the antidispensarian physicians and the apothecaries in a fairly direct manner; Garth's allusive technique can be seen in the concluding lines, which are a close imitation of a poignant and well-known speech from Homer's *Iliad.* In Book 21, the river god Xanthus (also called Scamander) berates Achilles for killing so many Trojans and piling them in his river:

> 'Tis not on me thy Rage should heap the Dead.
> See! my choak'd Streams no more their Course can keep,
> Nor roll their wonted Tribute to the Deep.
> Turn then, Impetuous! from our injur'd Flood;
> Content, thy Slaughters could amaze a God.[5]
>
> (234–38)

While reading the text of *The Dispensary,* Garth's audience—one familiar with the classics—would, presumably, also be mindful of the passage being imitated from *The Iliad.* With both *The Dispensary* and *The Iliad* simultaneously in mind, the reader would have an additional basis for judging the stature and character of Mirmillo. Whereas Achilles, for instance, was of heroic bearing, a larger-than-life warrior fighting for a noble cause, Mirmillo is a petty and avaricious charlatan fighting to preserve his and the apothecaries' right to bilk the sick poor. Whereas Achilles was united to his men by bonds of idealism, love, and trust, Mirmillo and the apothecaries are held together by their mutual greed. There is one way, however, in which Mirmillo is superior to Achilles and all his men: he is capable of killing more people in less time than all the Greek armies.

Garth's allusion to the destruction of Troy—"No Trophies you had left for *Greeks* to raise, / Their ten Years Toil, you'd finish'd in ten Days" —would have had a special significance for the physician-poet's audience, for the English believed the popular myth that they were the descendants of the Trojans. It was thought that the Trojan civilization had been transplanted to Rome by Aeneas and that his descendants had founded England. London, in fact, was traditionally referred to as "Troy-novant." Garth's allusion to Troy, then, carries apocalyptic overtones: just as the destruction of ancient Troy may be traced ultimately to an immoral act —the abduction of Helen—so too many the "New Troy" fall because of the avarice and selfishness of the apothecaries and their supporters. As soldiers smuggled inside of Troy precipitated its downfall, so too is the threat to London from enemies within the city. To avoid this calamity it is necessary for medical practitioners, as Garth advises elsewhere in *The Dispensary,* to emulate the integrity, altruism, and devotion to duty of physicians such as William Harvey, Thomas Wharton, and George Bates, and for society in general to place greater emphasis on collective humanitarian and charitable projects such as the dispensary.

Although *The Dispensary* enjoyed enormous contemporary fame, its popularity has declined with the passage of time. This is undoubtedly the result of the topical nature of the work. *The Dispensary* was deeply rooted in a controversial medical debate; it reflected local and indigenous attitudes and issues. Once that controversy ended and passions cooled, much of the impact and relevance of the poem dissipated. Had Garth moved in the direction of *The Rape of the Lock* and focused on the follies of an age with an amused detachment rather than on a topical squabble in which he was highly partisan, had he created a poem more imaginative than self-consciously didactic, *The Dispensary* might have maintained more of its contemporary popularity. Even so it remains one of the most compelling examples in English history of the manner in which literature and medicine can complement one another. The dispensary debate gave birth to the poem, gave it its villains and heroes, its issues and principles, while the poem itself probably contributed more to the final success of the dispensary than any document or, for that matter, individual associated with the project.

NOTES

1. *Memoirs of the Life and Writings of Alexander Pope* (London, 1745), 1, 304.

2. For a comprehensive treatment of the debate between the apothecaries and the physicians over the establishment of a dispensary, see Albert Rosenberg, "The London Dispensary for the Sick-Poor," *Journal of the History of Medicine* 24 (1959), 41–56, and Frank Ellis, "The Background of the London Dispensary," *Journal of the History of Medicine* 20 (1965), 197–212.

3. *The Dispensary,* in *Poems on Affairs of State,* 4, ed. Frank Ellis (New Haven and London: Yale University Press, 1970). All quotations from *The Dispensary* are from this brilliantly annotated edition.

4. That is, Achilles, son of Peleus.

5. *The Iliad,* trans. Alexander Pope, ed. Maynard Mack, in *The Poems of Alexander Pope,* Twickenham Edition, 8 (London, Methuen, New Haven: Yale University Press, 1967).

The Surgeon's Mate:
Tobias Smollett and
The Adventures of Roderick Random
Harold Gene Moss

Few physician authors of eighteenth-century England have attracted as much attention to their dual vocations as has Tobias Smollett (1721–71), author of five major novels, journalist, playwright, hack writer, translator, and surgeon. At fifteen years of age Tobias Smollett was sent by his grandfather to medical studies at Glasgow University and to a medical apprenticeship with one Dr. John Gordon. At eighteen, Smollett moved to London in hopes of a literary career, but found only frustration, which he later transposed into Melopoyn's story, chapters 61–64 of *The Adventures of Roderick Random.* After this disappointment, Smollett obtained a commission as surgeon's mate in the squadron of Commodore Ogle bound for the West Indies as part of the action against Cartegena in the War of Jenkyn's Ear (details again drawn into *Roderick Random,* in chapters 16–20). In the eight years that followed, he initiated friendships within the medical community of London (some of which he maintained throughout his life) and published at age twenty-six his first and most widely read novel, *The Adventures of Roderick Random* (1748). From that point onward, his career was devoted largely to his writing, including journalistic prose, translation, and the authorship of four more novels: *The Adventures of Peregrine Pickle* (1751), *The Adventures of Ferdinand, Count Fathom* (1753), *The Adventures of Sir Lancelot Greaves* (1762), and *The Expedition of Humphry Clinker* (1771). The last differs in form from the others because it is an experiment in the epistolary novel—written entirely in letters—in which Smollett projects an extraordinary richness of imagination. The complex development of different personalities and perspectives, the interactions of these characters, and the contrasting views of shared experience have won Smollett a lasting place among novelists, for in *Humphry Clinker* he advances the study of the human mind much in the direction of later psychological writers—Henry James, James Joyce, Marcel Proust, and André Gide.

To be sure, critics have studied *Humphry Clinker* more closely in relation to health and disease than any other Smollett novel, and the most significant of these approaches demonstrates that the structure of this novel devolves from the journey of the protagonist, Matthew Bramble, from a state of congestion of humours, constipation of bowels, and defensive ill-nature to an open and healthy state of mind and body.

This theme—the revival of health from a "diseased" state—is generally present in *Roderick Random,* but it is interwoven with the romance tradition in which the novelist originally began writing. The romance as it was practiced by early British authors regularly focused upon the life of a young man who is frustrated in his efforts to establish himself within society. Some distortion in the values of the parental generation or perhaps the corruption of society in general interferes with the flourishing of the protagonist's virtues. The plot carries us from a rapid account of the character's birth, through the vicissitudes of maturation, up to the moment when conventional norms are reestablished by his marriage. With only slight variations, the design of *Roderick Random* follows this broad pattern.

Now within this structure of action Smollett introduces events and images wholly unique to such fiction and derived, I believe, from his own experience as a physician. The many autobiographical aspects of the novel deserve and have received attention; I shall pass by them to look instead for matters of deeper concern within the fiction, for some principle of organization as profoundly important to *Roderick Random* as the search for health is to *Humphry Clinker.*

Ten chapters in the middle of *Roderick Random* contain five episodes of extraordinary literary power in which Smollett's protagonist is forced to confront essential biological threats. These scenes move rapidly from commonplace descriptions into surreal images of disorder and disruption. Smollett provides us with images of the internal, psychological confusion experienced by Roderick as his maturation proceeds. The process by which the easy assumptions of childhood are lost begins with the chaos of young Rorie's first storm at sea in chapter 28.

Smollett begins the episode by developing the effects of the storm on the fleet, then focuses on Roderick's ship, and finally on the young man himself. When his friend Jack Rattlin is thrown from a yardarm to the deck, a tense controversy breaks over whether to amputate his broken leg. Random and his fellow surgeon's mate, Morgan, argue with the chief surgeon, Mackshane, and are eventually vindicated in their wish to repair the limb rather than amputate it. But the vindication leaves behind a malice that influences events in all five episodes and is instrumental in the last of them.

Roderick thus becomes the object of the hatred of those in charge (the captain, surgeon, and chief mate) and is almost immediately arrested as a spy (chapter 20) and chained as prisoner to the deck just as the *Thunder* begins a bloody all-night battle with a French man-of-war. Roderick describes his second trial as follows: "I concealed my agitation as well as I could, till the head of the officer of the marines, who stood near me, being shot off, bounced from the deck athwart my face, leaving me well-nigh blinded with brains."[1] The nightmare continues: ". . . when a drummer coming towards me . . . received a great shot in his belly, which tore out his entrails, and he fell flat on my breast. The accident entirely bereft me of all discretion." Bathed in broken limbs and blasted tissue, Roderick endures the entire night in a spectacular confrontation with destruction and the biological limits of human life.

Within fifteen pages of text, Roderick's third trial occurs at the battle of Cartegena when, once again, "honest Rattlin" is a casualty, this time his left hand torn apart by grapeshot. Rattlin's philosophical calmness in the face of his pain and loss inspires the following reverie from Roderick: "I was much pleased and edified with the maxims of this sea philosopher, who endured the amputation of his left hand without shrinking; the operation being performed, at his request, by me . . ." (chapter 32). The chief surgeon, the parson, and the purser—the obvious "professionals" in the ship's cockpit—run mad with fear. The surgeon "went to work" at his trade "and arms and legs were hewed down without mercy." The parson "stripped himself to the skin, and besmearing his body with blood, could scarce be withheld from running upon the deck in that condition." And the purser merely sat upon the floor of the cockpit, lost in tears and lamentations.

Young Roderick's fourth and fifth "trials" each involve more direct threats to his own health and well-being, first through a near-fatal fever (chapter 34) and then through a treacherous beating by the ship's evil first-mate (chapters 37–38). The passage ends with Roderick so badly disfigured that rural peasants, who find him in a barn where he has sought shelter, mistake him for the devil and find a woman rumored to be a witch who might exorcise this bloody beast.

For several reasons these five episodes carry special significance in the design of the novel. First, the episodes are literally central to Smollett's arrangement of chapters in Roderick Random; the whole is sixty-nine chapters long, and the twenty-eighth through the thirty-eighth lie exactly midway. Second, these five episodes signal the end of the protagonist's youth and the beginning of his adulthood. They begin with Roderick as an inexperienced young man, carry him through his first venture at sea, and finally into his earliest sense of professional and personal identity. The defiance of foolish and arbitrary authority leads rapidly to the young man's sense of his own capability, particularly in contrast to the petty and knavish acts of surgeon, parson, and purser.

Finally, the vents of these chapters generate a special power through their bizarre, surrealistic descent into the nightmare of biological disorder. Smollett places before us images of broken bones, smashed limbs, "atomized" tissues, brains and blood, deadly fever, and finally Roderick's own body beaten beyond human recognition. In each case, Roderick is made to sort out as a surgeon and as a man what he can—and cannot—do in the face of the limits of human condition. The lesson Roderick learns from these events embodies the larger purposes of the novel. For their imaginative power alone, these five episodes deserve special attention. Their link with the main threads of action in the sprawling narrative and their centrality to the plan of the fiction mark them as a deliberate focal point for the emotional material the fiction communicates. Just as Matthew Bramble's journey to health is the central theme of *Humphry Clinker,* so the young man's face-to-face confrontation with death and his lessons in life's values are the theme of *Roderick Random.*

We cannot prove that the five central episodes of the novel arise from the personal experiences of their author because the necessary biographical information does not exist. And yet what we know of Smollett's twenty-six years prior to writing the novel, what we know of medical practice in the eighteenth century, the details he supplies in the novel itself about the misguided efforts to care for the ill and to cure their illnesses, all we can muster as circumstantial evidence suggests that these episodes were adapted more or less directly from his medical practice and transposed as images of the greatest power into the heart of his first novel.

The design of his last novel, *Humphry Clinker,* is clearly based on an idea of health and disease; I believe that his first novel, *Roderick Random,* is marked just as strongly by his experience as a doctor. From the beginning of his literary career to its end, Tobias Smollett enriched his fiction with medical notions and images derived from his brief practice of medicine.

NOTES

1. All citation is to *Roderick Random* (New York: Dutton, 1975) by chapter enumeration.

The Doctor as Man of Letters
Henri Peyre

It has often been remarked that the links between medicine and literature are much closer in several countries of continental Europe than in Britain and especially America. Many leaders of medical education in this country have been heard to deplore this situation. Repeatedly, they have recommended for future physicians more intensive reading in the humanities, less reliance on narrow specialization, a fuller awareness of the literary and artistic heritage of the West. Such had already been, in the seventeenth century, the admonition of Thomas Sydenham, viewed by many as the founder of modern clinical medicine, who reportedly preferred future doctors to steep themselves in Lucretius and Montaigne instead of concentrating prematurely on anatomy and physiology. Such was, two hundred years later, Pasteur's advice to the young. In our own age, when every profession is concerned with its "image" in the press and public opinion, doctors have had reason to deplore the relative absence in modern American fiction of unforgettable pictures of physicians such as appear in Balzac, Zola, Thomas Mann, Roger Martin du Gard, and a score of Spanish, Russian and German novelists.

The loss, due to the reluctance of doctors to venture into literary creation and to the scant interest apparently taken by writers in physicians as characters or types, is, in this writer's opinion, even more to be lamented by the students and lovers of literature. It is true that in English-speaking countries there were relatively few sons of doctors who eventually made a name for themselves in letters, when compared to the large number of sons of clergymen and of rabbis; and the few who did, like Ernest Hemingway, do not seem to have been prone to reliving the anguish and the ordeals of the general practitioners or the surgeons about whom they must have heard in their youth. The romance of modern microbiology or of recent surgery has not apparently thrilled many American or English imaginative writers or even biographers, since the author of *Arrowsmith* (1925). Not even the foibles and the absurdities of a profession which occasionally must assume airs of dogmatic omniscience have tempted, in the English language, those who might have portrayed them as human, hence fallible and vain, as Jules Romains, a friend of several doctors, and Flaubert and Proust, both sons of doctors, have done.

The marked specialization of medical education in America, even for psychiatrists and "soul healers," as well as the high and respected degree of professionalism required from physicians, may in part account for the relative isolation of doctors from other intellectual groups. Medical students abroad are less exclusively engrossed in their training as interns; they associate in cafés with students of philosophy, literature, law, with future poets and artists, and even with lazy "bohemians." Yet, in the century of Hawthorne, Whitman and Howells, and even in the early decades of Viennese psychoanalysis, many American medical students went abroad for their education and mixed with future novelists and politicians in Edinburgh, Munich or Paris. Any of us who has associated with doctors in this country and has pierced the veil of shyness with which many modestly cover up their liking for literature, has remarked the independence of their tastes and the deeply humane attention which they bring to pursuits in which they do not claim to be experts.

Physicians in other countries have often proved to be more rash. They have not shied from offering a post mortem diagnosis on the ills that afflicted Montaigne, Pascal, Swift, Goethe or Byron. Speculations have long been rife on the special urinary or sexual ailment which Rousseau may have suffered from, according to his own testimony, or on the extent to which epilepsy may have conditioned the behaviors of Dostoevsky or Flaubert and inflected the course along which their talents developed. Medical theses on the hypothetical effects of syphilis on the sensibilities of Stendhal, Heine, Baudelaire are numerous. The impact of asthma on the life-style of Proust, on his view of life, and even on the structure of his sentences, has been tentatively assayed by a few of the several medical experts who have been drawn to the novelist, the earliest being a French M.D., Georges Rivane, and one of the latest an American, Dr. Milton L. Miller, who entitled his psychoanalytical study of Proust *Nostalgia.* In some cases, it may have been easy for professionals of literary criticism to deride the dogmatism of medical apprentices who, undaunted by the scantiness of objective documentation and reassured by the noninterference of the patient dead for a hundred years or more, boldly diagnosed the disease they believed had tormented the dead author and probed as well into the death urges of creators. Some of the early attempts by psychoanalysts to decree what had lain at the root of Baudelaire's alleged "failure" (by Dr. René Laforgue in 1931), and even later and more sophisticated ones, such as a woefully inadequate one, a posthumous analysis of Camus by Albert Costes (*Camus et la parole manquante: Étude psychanalytique,* Payot, 1973) have failed to win the approval of literary specialists. A frequent flaw of the studies on artists and writers which have proliferated since Freud is that they do not stress sufficiently how the creator came to terms with his complexes—be he Kafka, D.H. Lawrence or S. Beckett—and how he triumphed over the real or imaginary difficulties that stood in his path: precisely, through his creation.

Still, some of the most balanced and insightful biographical studies of writers to have appeared in our century are the works of doctors. The French in particular have not been chary of praise for the literary achievement of their medical men who combined an eminent professional career with literary insight, philosophical originality and talent as writers. Both Pasteur and Claude Bernard, in the latter half of the nineteenth century, thinkers and stylists of uncommon gifts both, were elected to the French Academy, as has been in our time a biologist who was a prolific author, Jean Rostand, and more lately Dr. Etienne Wolff. A famous surgeon, the late Henri Mondor, never felt that he had to choose between his activity in operating rooms and his many biographical and critical studies of Mallarmé and other French poets. Another doctor, Jean Delay, also elected among the forties of the French Academy, is the author of the most authoritative psychological study of Gide: *The Youth of André Gide* (University of Chicago Press, 1963). Students of literature have often voiced their gratitude to the Spanish physician Gregorio Marañon (1887–1960). The author of expert studies on sexuality, he was also attracted to the literary type and to the myth of Don Juan, "the man constantly loved, eternally incapable of loving," whom he diagnosed as an effeminate person and a weak braggart (*Don Juan and Don Juanism,* Buenos Ayres, 1947). He discerned in the Swiss writer Benjamin Constant a case of what he termed "intellectual Don Juanism," in a book published in Havana in 1937. Marañon then studied another Swiss, Frédéric Amiel, who was a complete contrast to Constant. Amiel, an awkward professor, poor, lacking in charm and eloquence, fearful of sex, who made room and that, reluctantly, for only one night of love in his bachelor's existence (he died at sixty); yet who, to his own surprise, involuntarily attracted the adoration of several women. He confided daily his hesitations and cogitations to his diary of sixteen thousand pages, which has never ceased fascinating posterity. Dr. Marañon selected him as the archetype of a class of men not often analyzed by doctors or by critics: the shy ones. His volume on Amiel, published in Spanish and in French in 1938, is entitled *Estudio sobre la timidez (A Study of Timidity).* There, the Swiss professor is placed by his Spanish biographer alongside, of all men, Casanova, since both wrote lengthy memoirs, or rambling diaries, "in order to clothe with dignity the failure of their victory over themselves."[1] Amiel, indeed, appears to have intrigued posterity almost as much as the boastful and adventurous Venetian.

Medicine is traditionally considered an empirical science, practiced by prudent experts whose concern is for the individual patient and his idiosyncracies rather than for the philosophizing about illness. "Il n'y a pas de maladies; il n'y a que des malades," as a trite French saying puts it. ("There are no such things as diseases; there are only sick individuals.") In English-speaking countries, lofty philosophical speculations on the expanding universe, on the structure of matter, on the extent to which indeterminacy can be combined with determinism, have been indulged in more often by physicists than by physicians. In continental Europe, for better or for worse, the temptation to erect ambitious systems has not been so stubbornly resisted by the very same experimenters who display the most meticulous submission to facts in their clinical work. The allurements and prestige of a comprehensive hypothesis on "the human phenomenon," on the degree to which chance and necessity interweave in mankind's history have seduced some of the most respected biologists and physiologists of Germany and France. Jacques Monod and François Jacob, two Frenchmen who shared the Nobel prize for medicine in 1965, each published five years later a philosophical treatise in which they pondered, Dr. Jacob on *The Logic of Life* (Pantheon Books, 1974), Dr. Monod on *Chance and Necessity* (Knopf, 1971).

If their extrapolations from the scientific domain into the philosophical, from the biosphere into the noosphere, as the anthropologist Teilhard de Chardin termed them, entail much risk, and have aroused dissent (as those of Laplace and Huxley and Haeckel had done before them), they have also brought a much needed reminder to other contemporary philosophers, in an age which has revived metaphysics, that their structures are in danger of remaining mere verbalism if they fail to take into account the recent revolutions in genetic science.

In other fields strewn with even more pitfalls, those of art and the psychology of races and nations, some of the boldest, and occasionally most illuminating speculations of our century in the French language are those of a doctor, Elie Faure. The fame and influence of that physician who long had a dual career—he was a general practitioner as well as a writer on art and literature—have grown steadily since his death in 1937, at the age of sixty-four. His many books read like an exalted hymn to life and to beauty. They utter a passionate indictment of all negativism, pour scorn on constraints imposed by bourgeois prudence and traditional religion. Through an ironical whim of fate, that lyrical enthusiast of the poetry of materialism and of the Nietzschean will to power, whose thought had first been stimulated by Lamarck and Haeckel, came from a stern Huguenot family. He was a conscientious doctor, intent upon assisting the poorer classes after he defended his M.D. thesis in 1899 on "the treatment of lupus through the new tuberculin of Koch." He served as a military doctor in World War I; then, heeding the advice of his brother Jean-Louis Faure, a surgeon of great repute, he specialized as an anesthesist and as an embalmer. His eager curiosity embraced many a writer of the past, from Shakespeare to Michelet, and the whole realm of art, the analysis of the national character of seven or eight countries. His *History of Art* in four volumes (1909–1921), followed by a profound philosophical study on *The Spirit of Forms in Art* (1927), was soon translated into English in New York and has lately been reprinted in France in paperback. It is written with partiality, often with utter disregard for logical continuity and calm objectivity; it is in several respects the authentic precursor of André Malraux's equally passionate and boldly encyclopedic disquisitions on art.

The dismal experience of trench warfare, of crowded military hospitals, of sick and wounded soldiers dying by the thousands for lack of adequate or competent medical care powerfully impressed the young doctors who served in the French and the German armies. It induced some of them to become writers so as to leave a graphic testimony of their revulsion for the senseless slaughter and to inspire the survivors with the zeal to work for a better understanding among nations. Elie Faure died two years before World War II broke out in Europe, but in time to foresee the wreckage of his hopes to convert nations to a common fraternal goal. He had set great hopes in a doctor younger than himself, Louis-Ferdinand Céline, who crashed impetuously into the literary world in 1932 with his semiautobiographical novel, *Journey to the End of the Night.* Faure soon was sadly disappointed, not only by the gross ingratitude of Céline, who specialized in vituperation and chose to rejoice in universal decomposition, but also by his advocacy of racism and his acclaim of Nazi anti-Semitism.

Two other French medical men stood closer to Faure's views on the need for doctor-authors to help rebuild mutual understanding among nations. Both became widely read novelists and interpreters of other countries. One was André Nepveu, who adopted the pen name of Luc Durtain. The son of an eminent bacteriologist, he specialized first in comparative physiology in Dr. Richet's laboratory, then in laryngology. He wrote about his war service in an ambulance at the front, then composed poems and novels about the United States: *Quarantième Étage* (1927), *Hollywood dépassé* (1938), followed by a lively and perspicacious relation of his travels round the globe, *Le Globe sous le bras* (1936).

The other was Georges Duhamel. The son of a whimsical and erratic doctor, he became a doctor himself and served in a mobile surgical unit in World War I. The two volumes of vignettes about wounded, disabled and dying men in hospitals which he published count among the most truthful and the most poignant inspired by that war: *Vie des martyrs,* the new martyrs being the suffering soldiers, and *Civilisation,* a bitter indictment of our claims to being civilized. From then on, exchanging the physician's career for a literary one, Duhamel became a successful essayist and novelist. Unlike other doctors whose concern with the ills of the body inclines to a materialistic view of their fellow beings, Duhamel became the advocate of feeling, of a soft-hearted and often self-blinding attitude to life.

In countries other than France, even in those where a literary career brings with it less glamour, some doctors have been tempted to dramatize or relate aspects of their medical experience and have won fame thereby. One of the best sellers in the period between the two wars was *The Story of San Michele* (1929) by a Swedish doctor Axel Munthe, trained in Paris by Charcot, encouraged to write by Henry James and Maupassant. His account of the fashionable clientele of French aristocrats and wealthy American expatriates that he acquired in Paris when he diagnosed the soon to be fashionable disease of colitis is hilarious. Flushed with his success, he even dared to advocate eliminating pâté de foie gras from the diet of the overfed rich! When he grew tired of the snobs and neurotics, he transferred to Naples, where he took part in attempts to end a cholera outbreak, then settled in a house in Anacapri, which he turned into a bird sanctuary. He exchanged his endeavors to cure the Parisians of colitis for the just as preposterous task of protecting the birds of Italy from hunters and gourmets. His unpretentious anecdotal book is one of the most entertaining written by a member of the medical profession.

The Italian Carlo Levi is, like Axel Munthe, the author of one very successful book of memoirs blending humor and pathos: *Christ Stopped at Eboli,* published in Italy soon after the collapse of Fascism. It was translated at once into several languages. Subsequent volumes of political and moral essays by the author failed to win a similar fame. Carlo Levi, born in Torino in 1902 into a Jewish family, was a doctor by profession who soon exchanged medicine for painting, which he considered his favorite avocation. Mussolini's government had exiled him, in 1935–36 to a forlorn southern village of Lucania, beyond the line where, as the saying went in those parts, Christ must have stopped: there he lived under police surveillance, and was worshipped by the superstitious peasants, upon whom he took pity and from whom he later parted with regret and affection. Italy had counted a number of thinkers, novelists and dramatists who hailed from Naples, Calabria and Sicily; but none of them had ever taken much interest in the backward, almost pre-Christian southern population, living without hope and outside redemption. The average Italian had traditionally preferred to read about Lapland or China rather than about his Mezzogiorno. It took an anti-Fascist liberal and a doctor who was also a talented writer to force his countrymen to face the tragic plight of their forlorn provinces.

The German Alfred Döblin (1878–1957) and the Viennese Arthur Schnitzler (1862–1931), both of Jewish extraction, also gave up their careers as physicians in the middle of their lives to devote themselves to their literary work. Döblin, who had been close to the German Expressionists in 1910–30, scored a resounding success with his simultaneist novel, *Berlin Alexanderplatz,* in 1929; he then emigrated to Switzerland and France. His special professional field had been neurology. His books evinced scant interest in medicine. Schnitzler, whose real name had been Zimmermann, was the son and brother of doctors. Early he had specialized in the study of functional aphonia and its treatment through hypnotism, on which he wrote a monograph in 1889. He gave up his private practice when his dramas and stories made him famous. Doctors appear often in his plays; there are as many as fifteen of them in his comedy *Professor Bernhardi* (1912). They are frequently lovable, reflective people who voice the gentle, refined, mildly skeptical creed of the author, typical of the urbane literary groups of pre-1918 Vienna which then opposed the brutal naturalism of the Berlin writers.

Very different were two other German doctors who maintained their practice until late in their lives and drew upon the exceptional knowledge of human nature thus acquired to make their literature concrete, brutal at times, harsh on the foolish self-destructive urges of individuals, yet full of pity for their powerlessness and their suffering. Both were tempted by poetry. The younger of the two, Gottfried Benn (1886–1956) is among the best poets of his generation. Hans Carossa, born in 1878 in Bavaria, died also in 1956. Both were sons of doctors and had to wage a stubborn fight against their families in order to be allowed to follow their medical vocation. Carossa has narrated his childhood studies in a Catholic school, then the admonitions of his father on the grave moral responsibilities of a doctor, in two delightful volumes of memories of his childhood and youth, translated in America as *Boyhood and Youth* in 1932 (New York: Brewer, Warren and Putnam). His first outstanding novel, in 1913, was entitled *The End of Dr. Bürger* and related the despondency and suicide of a physician who had failed to save his ailing fiancée from death. His next novel, *Der Artz Zion (Dr. Gion),* appeared in 1931 and was translated here soon after. It offers one of the most truthful pictures of the disturbed and chaotic postwar years in Republican Germany. Dr. Carossa had seen the war on the French front, then in Rumania. As a physician there he had to attend to disgruntled veterans, impoverished widows, heroin addicts, syphilitic and mental patients. In his fiction there is none of the romanticized picture of disease or the presentation of sickness as a sign of election that one finds in the works of Proust or Thomas Mann. Carossa, less glamorously and more graphically, faced up to the harrowing problems of a doctor who, doing his best to cure his patients of their disorders, espouses their anguish and becomes obsessed with feelings of guilt as well as with compassion. He always insisted on remaining a physician first and a man of letters next. His close participation in the miseries and political vagaries of Germany after 1918 induced him to side with what he regarded as the forces of youth and life as against the temptation to despair and the consent to disorder. His leaning toward a vague mystical pantheism blinded him to the Hitlerian peril and he later repented having been too absorbed in his profession of curing people to discern what nihilism lurked under the Nazis' rhetoric of hatred. Important surgeons and other big medical bosses accustomed to obedience in nurses and interns, doctors who require obedience from their patients, sometimes assume a dogmatic attitude and prefer order and hierarchy to the forces of anarchy.

Such was likewise, when Hitler came to power in 1933, the choice that Gottfried Benn made for a time. He parted from his former literary friends (Heinrich Mann, then Klaus Mann, Alfred Döblin) when he rallied to Nazism for a while. Soon however he realized his mistake and asked to serve as a doctor in the army, that "aristocratic form of emigration," as he called it. He had been a medical officer in the German army in Belgium and had actually witnessed the execution of the English nurse Edith Cavell. His gruesome assignment had been to serve as a military physician in a house for sick prostitutes in Brussels. He published his early poems in 1915 under the title of *Fleisch* and several short stories based on a doctor's life. Back in civilian life, he specialized in skin and venereal diseases: few branches of medicine afford such opportunities for watching human beings unmasked and resigned to forsaking all pose and pretence.

Benn's entry into literature in 1912, at the time when Expressionism had made rebelliousness and brutality in vogue, had been a resounding one. He was just then completing his medical studies with a thesis on the incidence of a certain form of diabetes in the army when his poem, "Morgue," crudely cynical and strangely powerful, appeared. In the wake of Baudelaire, of the Rimbaud of the early poems, of Walt Whitman, and at marked remove from the elegance of the Symbolists, the youthful doctor literally opened up the corpses of drowned waifs; he dissected drunks and prostitutes, touched rotting intestines and burst bladders, sang disgusted hymns to carnality and sexuality. One line in *Fleisch* has remained famous and is characteristic: "Die Krone der Schöpfung, das Schwein, der Mensch" (the crown of creation, the pig, man).[2] Another poem in *Fleisch* entitled "Requiem" vividly conjures up nude bodies, their skulls split, on operating tables, and newborn babes in caskets. And another, "The Doctor," is even more outspoken, or degrading: "I know the smell of whores and of madonnas after they have defecated, on awakening in the morning, or when drowned in the tides of their menstruation; men come into my office their sex organs are atrophied . . . Do you think it was for such malformations that the earth grew . . . ? You talk of soul. What is your soul? The old hag soils her bed nightly; the aged man smears his decomposed thighs. . . . With pimples on their skin and their rotten teeth, they copulate, tight against each other; he sowing sperm in the furrows of her flesh and taking himself for a god along a goddess."

Gottfried Benn eventually outgrew such cynicism and composed poems that have won the admiration of many in and outside of Germany. But he always maintained that his poetry and his whole literary career would have been inconceivable without his medical orientation. From his physician's career, he learned to think coldly and objectively and to criticize himself. He repeatedly recalled that a majority of modern artists have been psychopaths, neurotics, dipsomaniacs and sickly people. "Nevertheless their effigies stand in the Pantheon and in Westminster Abbey. Above all else rises their work, immaculate and eternal, the flower and the light of life."[3] Benn, in his bitterness, was close to Zola, to the Naturalist group of novelists of 1870–90, and to one of his favorite masters, Nietzsche. He did not want poets to shy away from violence and pessimism, but he asserted that life could eventually be justified as the muddy substance on which some flower of beauty may bloom. As a clinician and as a poet, he wished to ignore neither the most repulsive ugliness nor the creation of beauty. A hundred years earlier, Henri Cazalis (1840–1909), a French doctor who was the close friend of Mallarmé and a fierce pessimist glorifying the Hindu Nirvana, wrote poetry under the name of Jean Lahor. His dual purpose as he envisaged it was, as a medical man to alleviate pain and sorrow in a world where evil is rampant, as a man of letters to cultivate beauty and perhaps help men rise, through the beautiful, to the good.

It is a commonly voiced complaint, in these last decades of the twentieth century, that what once was imaginative literature has become the almost exclusive preserve of professors whose favorite and monotonous subject is the relating of their wrestling with language and their fight —usually all too victorious—with the temptation of silence. A number of them, in France in particular, seem to exult in the assertion that a writer is by definition a person who has nothing to say and that his stories need have no relation whatever to reality. Some of us have protested angrily against such sadistic starving of literature and devoutly wished that it might again be given a content and deal with people in the flesh and with a spirit. Physicians who enjoy the privilege of observing men when they are off their guard, women with no makeup, their hair undyed, their breasts flagging, also have the insight to pierce through to the rock bottom of human personalities. They need not fear the charge of clinging to an anthropomorphic view of their fellow beings which some European novelists consider as the unforgivable sin committed by their predecessors. Better than men of most other professions they may, when they turn to writing, bring to life whole, real persons, endow them with vicarious existence and, as it were, experiment *in vivo*.

Physicians who experience the urge to write and muster up the courage to do so would gain much from discarding the barbaric, overtechnical, often needlessly obscure language in which they indulge in their learned papers. The recent success in this country of volumes like Dr. Lewis Thomas's *The Lives of a Cell* or of Dr. Richard Selzer's *Rituals of Surgery* and *Mortal Lessons* bears evidence to the eagerness with which the public would welcome imaginative writing by medical men or works of higher, and artistic, popularization by them. Even in terms of crass publicity and so as to restore the standing with the press and the public of their often maligned profession, it is to be wished that more doctors would summon up the courage to be writers as well as expert clinicians, to be again men living among men and not just specialists addressing themselves to other specialists. The medical profession, in the last decades of the century which has witnessed its preeminence, might well welcome more, and better, literature arising from its very midst.

NOTES

1. Grégorio Marañon, *Amiel, un estudio sobre la timidez* (Madrid: Espasa-Calpo, 1962, 9th ed.), p. 3.

2. See the second stanza of "Der Artz," the introductory poem of *Fleisch,* published in 1917.

3. In Pierre Garnier, *Gottfried Benn* (Paris: André Silvaire, 1959), p. 31.

Poets and Physicians in Arthur Schnitzler's "The Bachelor's Death" and "An Author's Last Letter"

Richard H. Lawson

It is all too easy to interpret Arthur Schnitzler's turn to literature and eventual abandonment of medicine—a process commented on by, above all, Schnitzler himself in the autobiography of his youth[1]—as an instance of a young man's rejecting his father's world and indulging the dreams and preoccupations of his own childhood. And it is equally too easy to cast a stereotype in which the physician lives happily on in the mind of the poet. Too easy because, while the stereotypes may be superficially and perhaps partially applicable, the facts are not that simple. Nor are the literary works of Schnitzler that dwell on the relationship between poet and physician. Two such short works, not at all simple by virtue of their shortness, will be the objects of our examination.

Schnitzler was born in 1862 into the Jewish upper middle class that comprised the backbone of professional, intellectual, and artistic Vienna before and at the turn of the century. His father, Johann Schnitzler, migrating to Vienna from Hungary, had by dint of much effort become a highly successful physician, successful in research and editing, in administration, and not least in the practice of his specialty, laryngology.

As perhaps the most distinguished laryngologist in Vienna, Johann Schnitzler—who as a student in Budapest had attracted attention by writing dramas both in Hungarian and German—counted among his patients an array of prominent actors and singers, who were also his friends. Arthur, who from an early age accompanied his father to the theater and on visits to theater people, was thus exposed under the paternal aegis to the world of art, which fostered an empathy with that world. Not less through his father's influence—it was simply the atmosphere of their house, as Arthur Schnitzler remembered it—was he exposed to the world of medicine and led to empathy with *that* world. From early boyhood Arthur assumed, as his father assumed, that he would pursue a medical career, although it later occurred to him that he had no special scientific bent and preferred such fields as history, psychology and, in a vague and romantic way, literature.

He began his medical studies at the University of Vienna at the then customary age of seventeen. If not an excessively diligent medical student —perhaps because by his nineteenth birthday he had written twenty-three complete (though unpublished) dramas and begun thirteen others, this in addition to an active social life—nevertheless he persevered and earned his M.D. degree just after his twenty-third birthday. He had developed a primary interest in nervous and mental diseases, an interest that was rooted, as he put it, less in the medical than in the poetic dimension. By the time he had published his first poem and his first belletristic essay, he noted that studying medicine was a stupid thing for him to have done.

Still, we find him pursuing both a medical and a literary career side by side: on the medical side, residency, clinic, scientific publishing,[2] and private practice (his specialty was laryngology); on the literary side, the publishing of poems, dramas, and novellas. From about 1890 his literary publication increased strikingly; we may infer that a definitive decision for literature was made, if not yet acted upon, at about that time or slightly later. It is likely that he had already made the decision before he entered private practice in 1893 at the death of his father. He remained active as a physician, however—though on a decreased scale—into the late nineties.

Although Schnitzler eventually ceased to be a practicing physician himself, he peopled his plays and his fiction with a significant number of physicians. About one-half of his plays, over one-third of his combined fiction and drama, present physicians in roles of primary or secondary importance.[3] Often a given work includes both a physician and an artist —in effect a sharing of the components of his own person. Much less often, to be sure, are the physician and the artist placed in the forefront of a work in such a way that they interact significantly upon each other: one may speculate that that was an especially ticklish creative task. Two such instances, the first from midcareer (from the literary point of view), the other published posthumously, are the novellas "The Bachelor's Death" (1908)[4] and "An Author's Last Letter" (1932).[5]

The action in "The Bachelor's Death" is precipitated by a late-night summons of a physician to the home of his old friend, the fifty-five-year-old bachelor. The servant reports that the bachelor, having suffered a sudden attack of illness, expressed a desire to see his three old friends: not only the physician, but also the author and the merchant. The physician is too late by a quarter of an hour to be able to exercise his healing arts. Soon after his futile arrival, he is joined by the merchant, and then the author—or rather the poet, as he prefers to call himself. The three friends, not particularly close to each other, are only moderately affected by grief. They are ill at ease in one another's presence and at what their now dead friend may have had in mind in summoning them.

The physician, whose capacity for observing physical detail is manifestly superior to that of his friends, notes an opened desk drawer and in it an envelope bearing the words "To My Friends"; in it a letter, to be read aloud. The merchant, with the physician's concurrence, asks the poet to do so. The bachelor's last letter, actually written nine years earlier, dwells upon the even then ambiguous nature of his relationship with his friends (then five, of whom now three are present). Towards the end of the letter, he declares; "I have had all your wives. Every single one." And describes his sexual relationship with each woman in such a way that each husband (or widower) now present recognizes his own wife and the state of his own marriage at a certain time in the past.

It is the physician who first moves to leave the death-scene; servants will take care of what needs to be done further. The merchant elects to return home in the spring dawn on foot, but the poet accepts the physician's offer of a ride. During the ride the poet chatters away; the physician tunes him out. At the physician's gate the carriage is dismissed and they bid each other goodnight. The poet walks off, clutching his breastpocket. In it he has the bachelor's letter, which he intends to put among his own effects—so that when at his death his widow finds it, and realizes that he has never reproached her for her adultery, she will whisper in gratitude at his grave, "You noble man . . . you great man."

Even from the above plot summary the chief personal characteristics of the physician and the poet emerge. The former is observant, mature, considerate (not least, of himself), urbane, and ironic. The latter is pompous, egotistic, inconsiderate, insecure, and not less ironic. But what is most revealing are the instances of personal interaction between the two.

The physician, smiling painfully as he recognizes the purely professional reason for his own presence—and that too late to be of avail—in the house of the bachelor, recognizes that the merchant might have a comparable legitimation. "And you," he turns to the latter, "were probably his financial adviser." He does not turn similarly to the poet, and the omission and its implication are conspicuous. In fact, there is a continuing pattern of such implicit scorn. While the poet is descanting on his recent—just three days before—walk and conversation with the bachelor, a monologue in which grief is well-seasoned with self-importance, the physician goes to an adjoining room. Not solely, it becomes clear, in order to smoke. For as he speculates about the bachelor's not having a profession, his train of thought goes somewhat as follows: oh, well, if the bachelor hadn't had the advantage of being wealthy, he could always have taken up pen-pushing for a living. His having this unkind thought about the dead bachelor ironically brings the physician back to his perhaps greater antipathy for the living poet. For he recalls that the bachelor, with his intellectual bent, had voiced many a maliciously perceptive observation on the literary works of their mutual friend the poet.

The physician's antipathy toward the poet is due at least in part to the latter's theatrical oversensitivity, reflected in his fixed contemplation of the dead bachelor, in his pained expression upon encountering the physician, in his scornfully raised eyebrows upon learning that the bachelor had mistresses, and even in his reaction to the stuffiness of the room in which the body of the bachelor lies.

A second reason for the physician's antipathy is doubtless the poet's often petty interpositions as the physician plays his professionally conditioned role of taking charge of the situation. The poet insists on an equal —and more than equal—view of the bachelor's final letter, which it is his office to read aloud. In the course of the poet's reading, the physician reasserts himself with frequent interruptions, ostensibly, and perhaps actually, to obtain greater clarity of expression from the reader. In this little battle for dominance, ironically fought with a weapon provided by a dead man, the letter, the physician is probably more on edge than his demeanor reveals. Why else should he at one point fail to recognize the timbre of his own voice? The poet, ever sensitive, responds to the change of voice with a quick malicious glance, then chokes up when the physician in turn commands him ("befahl der Arzt") to read the end of the letter. When the merchant takes over the reading, the exquisiteness of the subliminal battle for supremacy is signaled by the poet's now commanding—the same verb ("befahl der Dichter")—the merchant to read on. The chief matter of the letter—that they have all been cuckolded by their late friend, the bachelor—is, consummate irony, accepted by all three auditors with more equanimity than the two prime contenders can bring to bear on their personal interaction.

It is the physician, ultimately dominant, who can then afford to be magnanimous and offer a ride to his friends when their peculiar assemblage is declared at an end—by himself, naturally. We are perhaps not surprised that the merchant declines the offer, that the finale will include only the two contenders in the battle for dominance, the physician and the poet. But if the poet has perhaps been dominated by the physician in a situation made to order for that dominance, the poet will not forever remain dominated in his own eyes. For, as we know, he will magnify himself post mortem in the eyes of the innocent—but not so innocent— person whom he can still dominate: his wife.

In "The Bachelor's Death," the letter left by the bachelor is catalytic to the revelation of the relationship between physician and poet. In "An Author's Last Letter," the letter itself comprises the central revelation of the relationship between physician and poet. It is the poet's last letter, as the title of the story tells us, but its content is such as to provoke the physician to whom it is directed to a final appended response—a completion as it were, by Anton Vollbringer, M.D., whose surname means "the completer," and implies as well, in contrast with the poet, "the achiever."

The poet has left the letter, part polemic, part narrative, addressed to the physician who attended—the last of many physicians—the poet's mistress in her fatal illness. This last physician by chance turns out to be an old schoolmate, rival more than friend, of the poet. The poet, his sensitivity heightened by the impending death of his mistress, feels moved to unburden himself on paper as his mistress lies dying in the next room, and just before he puts a bullet into his own temple.

The style of the poet's last letter is as convolutedly and painfully ironic as the contents. There is a quarrelsome introduction, directed at the physician for whose eyes it is intended; then the story of the poet's love affair with Maria, whose fatal illness, a cardiac affliction, and inevitable and imminent death he at first believes will unlock untapped reserves of poetic talent in him. Even as he describes their love nonpareil, he wishes for her death, so that his talent may be truly realized. On subsequently perceiving the depth of his vanity, if not the mediocrity of his talent, the poet assures his physician-reader that he was prepared to commit suicide by jumping off a cliff. He restrained himself, he continues, not out of cowardice, but out of consideration for Maria, who was then in a weakened but still conscious condition. As she lies now unconscious at death's door, he does shoot himself—not, however, before permitting himself the notion that the blonde nurse in attendance was indicating to him a willingness to be seduced.

We see that it is not an altogether laudable figure of a poet that Schnitzler here presents—rather a fleshing-out of the possibilities inherent in the poet in our first story. But again, what we are really concerned with is not poet per se, but poet vis-à-vis—or more accurately in this instance, page-à-vis—physician. Why precisely—the German word *gerade* ("precisely") recurs with emphatic frequency—*this* physician, whom he had known in school and for whom he feels an inexplicable antipathy? He supplies his own answer, in the process explaining the inexplicable: he can conceive of this relationship as a facet of his expiating for his wish for Maria's death. And, we can infer, and less complexly, he feels reciprocal disdain from the physician.

The real sequence of their mutual hatreds is neither evident nor relevant. What is evident is that the hatred, just as in "The Bachelor's Death," is rooted in rivalry, in contest for dominance. The poet outlines what he regards as the philistine success-story of the physician: "You have made your way . . . from the impoverished circumstances of your youth . . . your profession satisfies and fulfills you. . . ." The poet tauntingly assumes that by now the physician has even become self-assured enough to enjoy feminine affection without having to pay cash for it. There is no reason for you, the physician, to be envious of me, the poet, because, says the latter, you never regarded a poet's fame—professional as well as, by implication, amorous—as anything worth striving for. So again, why do you hate me, I who am neither better nor worse than you, only different? Anyway, the morphine that you gave Maria—quite possibly an overdose —is doing its work, and she is deep in sleep.

It is soon clear that the poet's aversion to this physician is typical of his low regard for physicians in general. When Maria faints—the frequent overt symptom of her heart condition—at the ballroom soon after the poet has met her and swept her into his eager arms, the call goes out for a doctor in the house. At last one appears, but only after Maria has regained consciousness. The poet interrupts his narration gratuitously to remind his reader, Maria's final physician, that he, the poet, had in fact boldly and correctly diagnosed Maria's illness as a cardiac defect before any physician had done so. Whatever the professional diagnoses, the worst for the poet is that physicians have already forbidden Maria exertions of the degree that characterizes not only dancing, but also marriage. After the poet asks Maria's mother for her daughter's hand, the mother is favorably impressed; nonetheless she withholds consent until a consultation with her family physician can be arranged. The latter tells the poet plainly that Maria's heart cannot stand the excitements of marriage, particularly of a love match. The poet, no doubt reacting almost as much to doctoral prohibition as to sexual passion, persuades the scarcely reluctant Maria to flee with him without the sanction of marriage.

Maria and the poet are extremely happy together, but Maria's health —perhaps it would have done so in any case—deteriorates further: marked fatigue and fainting spells of increasing severity. The physician who has to be summoned confirms that Maria is doomed, whether within a few days or a matter of months. In any case a further change of locale (the lovers have been touring Italy) cannot but be beneficial. A need for a higher elevation is indicated. Here occurs the crisis in the poet's perception of Maria's impending death as it affects his talent. He ceases to wish her death for the benefit of his subsequent artistic intensity, coming to the insight that he has indulged in a flight of vanity and fantasy. Among the bases for his new insight and his new hope that Maria may live is the comforting truism that physicians sometimes make mistakes—comforting, it is clear, to his contentious psyche as well as to his hopefulness for Maria.

For a time, indeed, it appears that the poet's change of heart, his hopefulness, not to speak of relative abstinence, are reflected in the stability of Maria's health. But now her sensitivity to the poet's greater concern for her health leads her to wonder whether her condition may not in fact be more serious than she has been told. A new locale, a new physician; an internationally known specialist, he seems almost by fate to be vacationing at the very resort at which Maria and the poet are now staying. He quickly recognizes Maria's hopeless condition, but he consoles the poet with the observation that in this particular sort of affliction one can never be absolutely sure and that—what hardly accords with the nature of his profession—from year to year he has come to believe more and more in miracles. In any case, one must move to a lower elevation, and practice absolute abstinence.

And indeed, Maria's condition appears to stabilize even further. Not however, for very long after the move—the final move—to the lowlands, effected three weeks before the writing of the letter. There is no more of the familiar symptomatic attacks, but rather a gradual weakening and wasting away. The poet comes to the ultimate realization that she is doomed—and that after her death he will again most likely write comedies, cool, slick, and daring, just as before. But for the moment, to relieve the patient's suffering, still further medical intervention is required. And so still another physician is summoned, who, as we know, is the poet's former schoolmate and the person for whom the poet's last letter is intended. The poet considers the supposition—and, in the light of what we have been considering, it is probably true—that "precisely" (we are clued by the reappearance of the word "gerade"), precisely this physician's person is responsible for, at any rate connected with, the poet's final resolve to take his own life.

Here the letter breaks off. The physician to whom it was addressed and among whose final effects it was found, Dr. Anton Vollbringer, added a few comments with the evident intention of having the manuscript published. Those comments reveal by no means an idealized physician whom we can facilely contrast with the poet. Rather there is revealed a small-minded, overdefensive, all too morally correct physician. He believes that the poet committed suicide so as to be relieved of the necessity of creating the promised miracle-work of literature. "For without true morality," the physician sententiously explains, "there is no genius." And the poet's every line bespeaks an absence of genius.

The physician defends himself against the charge of being a philistine—if the poet didn't actually call him that, he says, the implication is nonetheless clear. An antipathy for the poet he can't deny, but whoever reads the poet's letter could hardly call the physician's antipathy unjustified. The medical fee that the poet left him in a sealed envelope he has given to charity. The blonde nurse, to whom the poet presumed to impute sexual availability, was in fact from a good family, was even at that time the physician's fiancée and is now (some ten years later) his wife and the mother of his three children.

On their honeymoon the physician and the blonde nurse visited Vienna and had the opportunity to attend a performance of one of the poet's plays. The play was so bad that it was a long time before the physician, and especially his wife, could recover from the painful impression it made on them. In fact, he asserts, none of the poet's plays proved to have any staying power. One's imagined immortality often turns out to be of distressingly short duration. (As short, one might add, as that of a forgotten physician.) And finally, of the poet: "May he rest in peace."

But we may doubt that he will, if there are physicians in the hereafter with whom to interact. As we have seen, and as the popular critical view declares, "the physician Schnitzler lived on in the poet Schnitzler"[6]—but hardly, to judge from the sometimes wrenching psychological detail of our two stories, in the amicable fashion suggested by the popular critical view. Above all, these two stories do not support the sentimental extension of the critical view that may be subsumed in the equally characteristic assertion that poetic and medical elements in Schnitzler "went hand in hand."[7] They went anything but hand in hand, unless we wish to envision a kind of intellectual and psychological arm-wrestling.

NOTES

1. Arthur Schnitzler, *Jugend in Wien, eine Autobiographie,* ed., Therese Nickl and Heinrich Schnitzler (Vienna: Verlag Fritz Molden, 1968), pp. 93–192. Available in English as *My Youth in Vienna,* trans. Catherine Hutter (New York: Holt, Rinehart and Winston, 1970).

2. Arthur Schnitzler, "Über funktionelle Aphonie und deren Behandlung durch Hypnose und Suggestion" (Functional Aphonia and Its Treatment by Hypnosis and Suggestion), *Internationale Klinische Rundschau* 3 (1889), columns 405–08, 457–61, 494–99, 583–86. Reprint (Vienna: Wilhelm Braumüller, 1889).

3. Maria P. Alter, *The Concept of the Physician in the Writings of Hans Carossa and Arthur Schnitzler* (Bern: Herbert Lang, 1971), pp. 19–20.

4. Arthur Schnitzler, "Der Tod des Junggesellen" in *Gesammelte Werke: Die erzählenden Schriften* (Frankfurt am Main: S. Fischer Verlag, 1961), 1, pp. 962–72. Available in English as "The Death of a Bachelor" in *Little Novels,* trans. Eric Sutton (New York: AMS Press, 1974), pp. 259–79. All translations in the text are my own.

5. Arthur Schnitzler, "Der letzte Brief eines Literaten" (An Author's Last Letter) in *Gesammelte Werke: Die erzählenden Schriften* (Frankfurt am Main: S. Fischer Verlag, 1961), 2, 206–30.

6. Heinz Rieder, *Arthur Schnitzler: Das dramatische Werk* (Arthur Schnitzler: The Dramatic Oeuvre) (Vienna: Bergland Verlag, 1973), p. 15.

7. Ibid. It is fair to note that Rieder is chiefly concerned with Schnitzler's dramas. He does not make the interliterary distinction in this case, however, speaking rather of "dichterische [und] ärtzliche Elemente" ("poetic [and] medical elements").

William Carlos Williams: The Diagnostic Eye

Marie Borroff

William Carlos Williams began his medical career early in life. He went directly from high school to the University of Pennsylvania Medical School, where he was the second youngest student in a class of 120. He entered in 1902, and received his M.D., at the age of twenty-two, in 1906. After interning in New York City and studying pediatrics for some months in Leipzig, he returned in 1910 to practice medicine in Rutherford, New Jersey, his home town, retiring after suffering a stroke in 1951. A number of his short stories—"A Face of Stone," "The Use of Force," "The Girl with a Pimply Face," "A Night in June"—give us vivid glimpses of a small-town practice having as its clientele largely the uneducated and poor.

> She looked dirty. So did he. Her hands were definitely grimy, with black nails. And she smelled, that usual smell of sweat and dirt you find among any people who habitually do not wash or bathe.
> The infant was alseep when they came into the office, a child of about five months perhaps, not more.[1] ("A Face of Stone")

Williams's poems tell us less about his day-to-day experiences as a practicing physician than his stories do. In the nine hundred pages of the three volumes of his collected short poems, we find only a dozen or so poems devoted to encounters between doctor and patient. Others allude obliquely to the setting of Williams's professional life—"Between Walls," for instance, with its description of the broken pieces of a green bottle lying between "the back wings / of the // hospital." One of his best-known and most frequently anthologized lyrics, the title poem of the series *Spring and All,* begins with such an allusion. It will provide us an entryway into the working of the poet-doctor's imagination, the consciousness we find dramatized in the words on the page before us. I quote it in its entirety.

By the road to the contagious hospital
under the surge of the blue
mottled clouds driven from the
northeast—a cold wind. Beyond, the
waste of broad, muddy fields
brown with dried weeds, standing and fallen

patches of standing water
the scattering of tall trees

All along the road the reddish
purplish, forked, upstanding, twiggy
stuff of bushes and small trees
with dead, brown leaves under them
leafless vines—

Lifeless in appearance, sluggish
dazed spring approaches—

They enter the new world naked,
cold, uncertain of all
save that they enter. All about them
the cold, familiar wind—

Now the grass, tomorrow
the stiff curl of wildcarrot leaf
One by one objects are defined—
It quickens: clarity, outline of leaf

But now the stark dignity of
entrance—Still, the profound change
has come upon them: rooted, they
grip down and begin to awaken

One thing to be noticed immediately is the absence from the poem of the *I* familiar to us in nature poetry. (Compare Wordsworth's "I Wandered Lonely as a Cloud," or Yeats's "I shall arise and go now, and go to Innisfree," or even Joyce Kilmer's "I think that I shall never see / A poem lovely as a tree.") The opening line, "By the road to the contagious hospital," implies someone who is passing along that road, but that someone never reveals himself explicitly; the poem gives us only the perceived landscape. This being so, it is legitimate to ask why the road to the contagious hospital should be mentioned at all, why it should be there at the beginning of the poem. The question has a biographical answer, of course: the contagious hospital is there because Williams was a doctor. But for the literary critic, the question has another meaning, and calls for another kind of answer. What difference would it make to the poem, what lessening of power, if any, would result, if the line were omitted, or if it were changed to "By the road to the city," or "the road to school," or "the road home"?

Since the speaker is nowhere to be found, we must study the landscape itself as he presents it to us, to see what it consists of and what is emphasized in it. In so doing, we find our attention directed, as in a landscape painting, to one object in the scene, with the rest of the description serving as background. This center of interest, revealed in the third stanza, is

> the reddish
> purplish, forked, upstanding, twiggy
> stuff of bushes and small trees
> with dead, brown leaves under them
> leafless vines—

It is this "twiggy stuff," not the fields, patches of water, and trees, that is "by the road," and it is this also, in its multiple aspect, that is referred to later in the poem and in its concluding lines as "they":

> They enter the new world naked,
> cold, uncertain of all
> save that they enter. . . .
>
> Still, the profound change
> has come upon them: rooted, they
> grip down and begin to awaken

With the plural pronoun comes personification, implied also by the adjectives *naked* (which of course applies also to leafless twigs), *cold,* and *uncertain,* as well as by the actions of gripping down and beginning to awaken.

"Spring and All" is something like a landscape painting, but it differs in that it presents a protagonist engaged, by definition, in an *agon,* a dramatized struggle. The "stuff" of red-purple twigs is alive, in contrast to the "dried weeds," "dead, brown leaves," and "leafless vines" also mentioned in the poem. In its attempt to grip down, to awaken, and to put forth leaves, it must contend against the lingering cold of winter and against the wind that brings that cold to bear. At this moment, the forces of renewal and the constraints of winter are in almost equal balance; there are "patches of standing water" in the fields, and the fields are "muddy," but the earth has not yet thawed completely. Spring "approaches," but has not arrived. The new season must prevail in due course ("tomorrow / the stiff curl of wildcarrot leaf"), but the shift in its favor is barely beginning.

The personification of the roadside bushes and small trees is carried out in highly specific and allusive terms. The lines "They enter the new world naked, / cold, uncertain of all / save that they enter" can be fitted without difficulty into a description of the reawakening vegetation of early spring, but they speak even more eloquently of human birth. And they carry suggestions of the memorable statement in The Book of Job:

"Naked came I out of my mother's womb, and naked shall I return thither" (1;21). The newly born child, as it emerges naked into the world, is also separated from the warmth and peace of the mother's womb. The word *familiar,* in the phrase "all about them / the cold, familiar wind," thus implies unwelcome or officious "familiarity": the intimate and un-gentle handling to which the newborn is routinely subjected, and to which it responds with a squall of indignation. Looked at retrospectively, certain words in the earlier description of "the reddish/purplish, forked, upstanding, twiggy / stuff of bushes and small trees" abet the emergence of the pattern. *Reddish* and *purplish* suggest the infant's crimson face, and *forked,* like *naked,* has allusive power, bringing to mind another of the great descriptions in our literature of the condition of man. In *King Lear,* act 3, scene 4, the banished king, seeing the disguised Edgar clothed only in a blanket amid the raging of the storm, exclaims,

> Why, thou wert better in thy grave than to answer with thy un-
> cover'd body the extremity of the skies. Is man no more than this?
> . . . Thou art the thing itself; unaccommodated man is no more but
> such a poor, bare, forked animal as thou art.

(Notice *bare* as well as *forked;* Lear has earlier invoked all "poor, naked wretches . . . that bide the pelting of this pitiless storm.") One can in all seriousness say of this poem that it has an obstetrical theme.

The drama of emergent spring, of the vegetative life-force pitted against lingering winter cold, is contained within a larger and, for the reader of Williams, a more important drama. The struggle is not simply "there," as if on a real stage; it has been seen for us—or rather, since it is not visible in the sense in which objects, colors, and shapes are visible, it has been imagined for us. We could not have seen for ourselves, in the spectacle of reddening roadside scrub, the ordeal of birth, the stark dignity of entrance. Though the speaker of the poem has not entered it explicitly as the traditional "I" of nature poetry, he has been there all along as the personal consciousness to which the landscape has presented itself and by which it has been interpreted. The encompassing drama of "Spring and All" is, in Wallace Stevens's words, "the poem of the act of the mind." From that act, dramatized by the words on the page, it is possible to sense the qualities of that mind and, if we are on the right track, to find those same qualities displayed in other poems. Let us see.

Nothing is more important in forming our conception of the sort of man who is speaking the poem than our sense that his account of the scene is authentic. By that I mean not only that it is factual—that every-thing in it can be found in the New Jersey landscape exactly as described —but that the selection of details and the words in which they are ex-pressed carry conviction, have an epitomizing, on-target force. We—at least, we who live in Williams's American Northeast—recognize that kind of early spring day, those clouds with their mottled shapes and blue color moving overhead, that cold wind, those preternaturally vivid roadside bushes with their peculiar coloration. And without thinking about it, we take the speaker to be a native of the described locale. The poem tells us this, if we need to be told, in its predictive statement:

> Now the grass, tomorrow
> the stiff curl of wildcarrot leaf.

(*Wildcarrot* is a colloquial telescoped form of the two-word vernacular name for *Daucus carota,* also, more sentimentally, called Queen Anne's lace. The capsule description of the plant's preferred terrain in Peterson's *Field Guide to Wildflowers of Northeastern and North-central North America* is oddly apt: "Roadsides, fields, dry waste ground.") The man we meet in this poem is one who knows the wild flowers that grow in his locality. He is also one who has lived through cold spring days in his region, and seen summer emerge from them. He knows the landscape in process, what it is and what it will become. This is his home ground.

The landscape in "Spring and All" is seen in passing, from "the road," by one who is native to the place and who is traveling through it on unspecified business of his own. Even so, he brings to the experience no distractions or preoccupations; indeed, no self-consciousness. (Thomas Whitaker has spoken, with reference to another poem by Williams, of a "transit unblurred by concern for before or after.") He is in that sense at liberty, his attention free to turn to anything that may happen to catch his eye. But I have already indicated that he does more than "see." What he divines below the surface of the visible, what most deeply interests and moves him, is a vital presence engaged in a process of self-definition. In an imaginative act of self-projection, he identifies himself with that presence and that process; the poem is an implicit tribute to both. The point of view of the description shifts from the road to the roadside twigs and small branches themselves, upstanding in the midst of the cold, familiar wind. The landscape as we finally see it is portrayed from the inside out. The effect is rather like that of a painting in which light seems to come from within.

Having said this, I must once again insist that "Spring and All" is not a pictorial poem: it renders the landscape as a theater in which opposing forces contend. Once we understand this, we can recognize the extent to which its descriptive content is rich in suggestions of energy and activity. The clouds are described in static visual terms as "blue" and "mottled," but they are also a "surge." The wind drives them (the speaker knows its direction), and this same wind, as it plays about the roadside scrub, is an antagonist in the contest between winter and spring. The bare twigs, though not in motion, are described as "upstanding," in contrast to the merely "standing" weeds and patches of water. The former word implies self-assertion, and has significant overtones of moral approval. Spring itself is personified and is shown "approaching," though sluggishly. In predicting the "curl of wildcarrot leaf," the speaker seems to have in mind the process of curling as much as the achieved shape. "Objects are defined" by growing, changing, pushing outward from center. And the opening line, whose significance I questioned earlier, fits into this pattern of action and interaction, of motion and underlying motive. A "road" is a line of direction, implying both passage and destination. Even the specification of the "contagious hospital" works to imply a physical world in which living beings affect and are affected by one another.

To complete this account of the dramatized "act of the mind," we ought to note, at least briefly, the freedom of the poem—and thus the freedom of the implied speaker of the poem—not merely from self-consciousness but from sentimentality. Nothing in the account is idealized or prettified; words like *mottled, muddy, reddish, purplish, stuff,* and *sluggish* are as unflattering as they are vivid. (Compare *reddish* and *purplish,* for example, with *red, purple, carmine,* or *crimson*). The awakening roadside growth is described, as I have shown, with empathy and respect, but there is something dispassionate, even clinical, about the description as well.

What essentially shapes the unfolding drama of "Spring and All" is the position of the speaker in the landscape in every sense of the word *position;* the relationship between the perceiving eye and the thing seen. This same relationship appears also in a number of poems by William Carlos Williams in which the speaker figures as a witness to the actions of living creatures, human and nonhuman. Like the roadside bushes of "Spring and All," these actions are seen in passing; it is rather as if a hand-held movie camera were trained upon them for a moment. Often the locus of sight is a road (the road, in fact, is a kind of signature marking Williams's poetry); often, too, the witnessed actions themselves define a trajectory, a line of march or motion with its own implied destination.

> A gull flies low
> upstream, his beak tilted
> sharply, his eye
> alert to the providing water.

A flock of sparrows "skimming / bare trees / above a snow glaze," though "buffeted / by a dark wind," manages to land on a clump of "harsh weedstalks" where it can rest and feed. A drayhorse temperamentally rolls his eyes and flattens his ears,

> Yet
> he pulls when
> he must and
> pulls well, blowing
> fog from
>
> his nostrils
> like fumes from
> the twin
> exhausts of a car.

Each creature, as seen by the poet-in-transit, goes its own gait, sometimes literally so, as when a dog passing in the rain "idiosyncratically" throws

out the left fore-
foot beyond
the right, intent, in
his stride,

on some obscure
insistence—from bridge-
ward going
into new territory.

It is this "obscure insistence," the hidden motive animating the witnessed action, on which Williams himself insists, that again and again he calls to our attention as something worthy of record. Kenneth Burke has called Williams "the master of the glimpse," and this is a valuable insight. But the record of what is glimpsed would be comparatively uninteresting if it did not demonstrate the acuteness and diagnostic power of the observer's perceptive faculties.

Human beings are seen in Williams's poems as birds and animals are seen, in terms of physical action and its immediately underlying motive. There is no added dimension of moralizing, philosophizing, or social commentary. In "A Poor Old Woman," the woman of the title is "munching a plum on / the street a paper bag / of them in her hand":

They taste good to her
They taste good
to her. They taste
good to her

You can see it by
the way she gives herself
to the one half
sucked out in her hand

In this passage, the intensity of the witnessed experience is dramatized by reiteration, and the reiterated words give us an insight into Williams's characteristic language: the words used are the words that the woman herself would use (compare "She savors their sweetness"). The verbal shape of the poem derives from the poet's imaginative identification with the figure in the scene.

"Proletarian Portrait," a poem whose title might lead one to expect a sociological theme, shows us "a big young bareheaded woman" holding one of her shoes in her hand.

Looking
intently into it

She pulls out the paper insole
to find the nail

That has been hurting her.

"The Right of Way," another poem in the *Spring and All* sequence, again presents the poet as passing motorist, this time explicitly so. Driving along with "nothing in the world" on his mind but "the right of way," he sees a man, a woman, and a child. The man's face is "half averted," the woman is "laughing" and looking up at him, the boy is looking "at the middle of // the man's belly / at a watchchain."

> The supreme importance
> of this nameless spectacle
>
> sped me by them
> without a word—
>
> Why bother where I went?
> for I went spinning on the
>
> four wheels of my car
> along the wet road until
>
> I saw a girl with one leg
> over the rail of a balcony

The poem concludes thus, in suspension. Why not? The "nameless spectacle" of "supreme importance" is nothing more or less than the conscious identity of other human beings, revealed in the instant's look, gesture, or pose as by a flash of lightning. It is the privilege of witnessing this spectacle, above all else, that our right of way as denizens of the world confers on us. Or, as Williams puts it in "Approach to a City,"

> Getting through with the world—
> I never tire of the mystery
> of these streets:

Occasionally, we are allowed to see one of Dr. Williams's patients through these same tirelessly perceptive eyes. In "To an Old Jaundiced Woman," the unlovely physical signs of disease are unsparingly described: the sore on the lower lip, the matted hair, the slobber on the handkerchief, and, finally, the despairing words:

> I can't die
>
> —moaned the old
> jaundiced woman
> rolling her
> saffron eyeballs

I can't die
I can't die

Reiteration works here as it does in the poem about the woman eating plums, except that the words are quoted directly. What moves us is the insistent energy of the death-struggle, an energy that is an ironic assertion of vital power.

Elsewhere, as in this poem, it is the vigorously self-assertive, even the ornery or obstreperous patient that the poet (and I suspect also the doctor) likes best.

Shut up! laughs the big she-Wop.
Wait till you have six like a me.
Every year one. Come on! Push! Sure,
you said it!

"Portrait of a Woman in Bed," a poem consisting in its entirety of the woman's spoken words, ends in a burst of anger giving way to weariness:

The country physician
is a damned fool
and you
can go to hell!

You could have closed the door
when you came in;
do it when you go out.
I'm tired.

In this era of preoccupation with dying and death, concern is often expressed for the patient's existence in full dignity as an individual up to and through his final moments (Cf. Dr. Elisabath Kübler-Ross's recent book *To Live until We Say Good-bye*). So far as respect for the dying patient is concerned, Dr. Williams would seem to have been ahead of his time. In "The Last Words of My English Grandmother," the grandmother of the title dominates the poem and everyone else in it, resisting almost to the end her doctor grandson's efforts to get her to go to the hospital, putting him and the ambulance attendants in their place after she has finally been forced to submit.

O you think you're smart
you young people,

she said, but I'll tell you
you don't know anything.
Then we started.
On the way

we passed a long row
of elms. She looked at them

awhile out of
the ambulance window and said,

What are all those
fuzzy-looking things out there?
Trees? Well, I'm tired
of them and rolled her head away.

Death is shown here as the act of a free agent. The old woman, who has
been described early in the poem as "nearly blind," manages to convert
the indistinctness of the trees into a derogatory remark that is the equivalent, under the circumstances, of "Sour grapes!" Her petulance has
something of bravado, something stagey about it—as when, during the
last moments of a parting that threatens to swamp us emotionally, we lash
out in an irritation at the other person that is half real, half pretense or
defense. The final act is hers—Williams takes care to let us know that her
head did not fall passively aside, that she herself turned it away—and
once that act has been accomplished, the poem is over. Elegiac comment
would be superfluous.

William Carlos Williams grew up in the age of the expatriate: Ezra
Pound, T. S. Eliot, Ernest Hemingway, Gertrude Stein. He too went to
Europe, but returned home and settled in, binding himself to those he
called his "townspeople" by treating their ailments, learning about their
lives, participating in the processes of birth and death. Though his patients seldom appear in the poems, they belong, by literal right of native
citizenship, to the domain this most indigenous of American poets
marked out as his own. Like the wildflowers whose shapes and colors he
recorded, they were part and parcel of the harsh terrain that nurtured his
imagination—the mystery on which, passing through the world each day,
he faithfully trained his diagnostic eye.

NOTES

1. William Carlos Williams, *Make Light of It: Collected Stories* (New York: Random
House, 1950), p. 167. The other three books by Williams I use are *The Collected Earlier Poems*
(1951), *Pictures from Brueghel and Other Poems* (1962), and *The Collected Later Poems* (1963), all
published by New Directions. "Spring and All," quoted in entirety, is from *The Collected
Earlier Poems*, pp. 241–42.

Richard Selzer
and the Sacraments of Surgery
Enid Rhodes Peschel

Richard Selzer is a surgeon-poet. He is the author of two books that have received wide critical acclaim: *Rituals of Surgery* (short stories, 1974), and *Mortal Lessons: Notes on the Art of Surgery* (essays, 1976). The son of Julius Louis Selzer, a general practitioner, Richard was born on June 24, 1928, in Troy, New York. Since 1960 he has practiced general surgery in New Haven, Connecticut, where he is also on the faculty of the Yale University School of Medicine. Selzer's religious rearing was Jewish, that type of Conservative Judaism that is very close to Orthodox, but early in his predominantly Catholic home town he witnessed and was drawn to the rituals and the beliefs of the Roman Catholic religion. Many were the times when young Selzer would slip into a church in Troy to observe and to absorb the rites and the mystery. Selzer is not a Catholic convert: he is deeply drawn to the mystical elements in both Roman Catholicism and Judaism. Interweaving, mingling with his Jewish background, his attraction to Roman Catholicism gives his writings substance, shape, and power; and a sense of sacredness at once pain-filled and uplifting.

When Selzer was fourteen, his father died. His father's life, and more than that, his father's death, are the major influences in Selzer's own life. For Julius Selzer was not only a physician: he also tried his hand at writing. During the depths of the depression, from 1934 to 1937, Julius "went furtive—through his empty waiting room, to his desk—and took up his pen to write fiction," writes Selzer in his humorous and revealing essay "Down from Troy."[1] Selzer was never able to read his father's manuscript; his mother thought it too scandalous and destroyed it after Julius died. But Selzer has been told that his father's novel was about a doctor who falls in love with a prostitute and during that time becomes an atheist; ultimately he loses the girl and regains his faith. A doctor, the longing for love, a condemned love, and a spiritual search—the themes of his father's novel will become the major themes of Richard Selzer's own writings as well.

Selzer says he wishes he could have read his father's manuscript, wishes he could hold it now. "It is one of my lifelong regrets that the manuscript has not been preserved. Now that I too have been reduced to the anguish of writing, it should be my holy scripture, my beacon, and my emblem. . . . Ah, if only I could weep over *his* metaphors, fondle the pages where his alphabet was spilled." Selzer longs to follow his father's mind and imagination (*"his* metaphors"). He craves to recapture an essence that is bodily as well: he would "fondle"—touch lovingly, tenderly, caressingly—the pages whereon his father wrote. Through his father's lost novel, which for the son becomes a sacred scroll, the symbol, too, of his own moral truth (it would be his "emblem"), Selzer imagines—believes—he would rejoin his father's spirit, and flesh.

Because of his quest at once spiritual and physical for his father, Selzer searches for answers in the human body itself. It is there that he seeks for truth. A "heart, a lobe of the liver, a single convolution of the brain . . . would tell all the frailty and strength, the despair and nobility of man," he writes (p. 15). This truth, which he believes "lies hidden in the body," he seeks to explore and to reveal with his scalpel, and with his words.

In the first three and lyrically intense chapters of *Mortal Lessons* ("The Exact Location of the Soul," "The Surgeon as Priest," "Lessons from the Art"), Selzer dwells at length upon several wounds—wounds that hurt and heal both the patient and the surgeon. Let us examine two of them.

"I invited a young diabetic woman to the operating room to amputate her leg," he announces (p. 16). The word "invited" is ironic: the surgeon mocks his own authority, his seeming graciousness. The word intimates too that he allured or enticed this young woman indecently, seductively almost, into the room where he would stand over, and penetrate, her body. He describes the festering limb clinically and metaphorically:

> She could not see the great shaggy black ulcer upon her foot and ankle that threatened to encroach upon the rest of her body, for she was blind as well. There upon her foot was a Mississippi Delta brimming with corruption, sending its raw tributaries down between her toes. Gone were all the little web spaces that when fresh and whole are such a delight to loving men. She could not see her wound, but she could feel it. There is no pain like that of the bloodless limb turned rotten and festering. There is neither unguent nor anodyne to kill such a pain yet leave intact the body (p. 16).

The wound first appears like an animal: large, coarse, unkempt ("the great shaggy black ulcer"). Then it is a river mouth brimming with "corruption": the word suggests the physical, and the moral. This mouth would befoul—or engulf—both the woman and the surgeon. The delta-wound's "raw tributaries" evoke the river, the ulcer, pus, and pain. The spaces between the woman's toes are gone, overrun with putrefaction:

there is no place here for love. Or so it would seem.

Why does the surgeon dwell at such length upon this festering flesh? Is he repelled, revolted by the rotted limb? To some extent, yes. But he also suffers physically, emotionally, and morally with the woman, whose pain is so terrible that nothing can overcome it that would not also harm or destroy the rest of her.

Priestlike, the surgeon "anoints" the limb:

> For over a year I trimmed away the putrid flesh, cleansed, anointed, and dressed the foot, staving off, delaying. Three times each week, in her darkness, she sat upon my table, rocking back and forth, holding her extended leg by the thigh, gripping it as though it were a rocket that must be steadied lest it explode and scatter her toes about the room. (pp. 16–17)

The accursed limb is now sanctified, for the surgeon's anointing of it is both medicinal and spiritual—a healing act, a holy act. Still the woman is not cured; and therefore neither is the surgeon who suffers for her, and with her. "Who can gaze on so much misery and feel no hurt?" asked Selzer earlier in the book. There must be an operation. "There must be an amputation in order that she might live—and I as well. It was to heal us both that I must take up knife and saw, and cut the leg off. And when I could feel it drop from her body to the table, and see the blessed *space* appear between her and that leg, I too would be well." His own life, his own health, are bound to hers, and to that festering limb.

When the woman is put to sleep in the operating room, undergoing thereby a symbolic death, her leg is uncovered. Now the surgeon is startled, overcome with gratitude, and with love. "There, upon her knee-cap, she has drawn, blindly, upside down for me to see, a face; just a circle with two ears, two eyes, a nose, and a smiling upturned mouth. Under it she has printed SMILE, DOCTOR." No, the surgeon is not the hero, nor really the healer, here; but the patient is—heroine and healer, in her deathlike and transcendent state. Whereas the surgeon-priest merely cleansed and anointed her limb, the patient has done more: cleansed, anointed, sanctified—and therefore healed—with her humor and compassion, his spirit. The wound has bound them together and joined them in an act of love. In the body, seen through the wound of surgery, lies the truth: the frailty—and the strength—of man.

On a symbolic level, this amputation scene may be read as the surgeon's (or at least as Selzer the surgeon's) castration anxieties. The limb he must sever in order to heal himself appears to him festering, foul, putrid; or "a rocket that must be steadied lest it explode and scatter" its contents. But after the amputation-castration he will feel relieved, gladdened, even consecrated: the *"space"* that will appear between the body and that limb he calls "blessed."

"So, I have learned that man is not ugly, but that he is Beauty itself," writes Selzer immediately after this amputation scene. Both men and

women are for him "exuberant bloody growths." The word "bloody"
implies sloppiness, ugliness, a wound. But blood also evokes beauty, and
blessedness: the lifeblood, or the Blood of Christ. "Growths" suggest
tumors and disease, but also life that matures and develops—exuberantly, luxuriantly.

The wound, according to Selzer, and the suffering it begets make
both the patient and the surgeon receptive to grace. "I would use the
defects and deformities of . . . [people] for my sacred purpose of writing,
for I know that it is the marred and scarred and faulty that are subject to
grace" (p. 19). These words reveal Selzer's compassion for, his suffering
with, the maimed, the outcast. Their pain, he believes, opens them to
grace. All people, both virtuous and miscreant, are subject to grace according to the doctrines of the Church; but it is the faulty—the physically,
emotionally, morally, and spiritually wounded—who particularly interest
Selzer. And so this surgeon who perceives beauty in the diseased, who
loves these people and identifies with their defects, who sympathizes so
thoroughly with their pain that he feels it as his own pain, becomes, like
them, "subject to grace." Grace is granted by God. Grace is God's unmer-
ited love and favor toward human beings, enabling them to reach toward
God, enabling them to become pure and morally strong. Grace implies
beauty, holiness, and love: Grace is man's assurance of God's love. One
receives grace as a gift from God, and through the sacraments of the
Church, which for Selzer become the sacraments of surgery.

Why does Selzer envision surgery in terms of the Roman Catholic
sacraments? The sacraments, he has said, guarantee what he craves—
God's love and forgiveness.[2] His surgery, therefore—symbolized by the
sacraments of surgery that he performs and in which he participates—is
actually his search for God and for love; and for his father who, like the
God who grants grace, will love him and forgive him.

Immediately following his words about grace, Selzer writes, "I would
seek the soul in the facts of animal economy and profligacy." Purporting
to describe the scientific and natural—economy and waste in nature—
these words imply as well the moral ("the soul"), and the immoral
("profligacy"). By linking the immoral and the moral, they reinforce
Selzer's ideas about the marred and scarred and faulty who are subject
to grace. "Yes, it is the exact location of the soul that I am after," Selzer
continues with a combination of arrogance, humor, and longing. "I have
caught glimpses of it in the body diseased. . . . It is as elusive as the
whippoorwill that one hears calling incessantly from out the night window, but which, nesting as it does low in the brush, no one sees. No one
but the poet, for he sees what no one else can. He was born with the eye
for it." And that is why Selzer dwells at such length upon the festering
limb, the ugliness of the wound. This surgeon-poet seeks, by means of
his aesthetics of ugliness—his perceiving beauty in what is traditionally
regarded as repulsive—nothing less than a holy communion. Only the
poet, he believes, (and the blind diabetic woman is certainly such a poet)
can truly see and transmit that "grace": the beauty, love, and divinity

embedded in the living, festering, wounded—and exuberantly bloody—human body.

A second wound, also repulsive, also in a way blessed in the truths it reveals to him, opens further vistas into Selzer's psyche: his mind, his heart, and his soul. Once, he says mockingly, but pridefully as well, he thought he had found "the exact location of the soul." It lay in a suppurating wound. Selzer's words dramatize, re-create the ambiance. It is late at night. The doctor has been called to treat a young man recently returned from excavating Mayan ruins in Guatamala. In the man's left upper arm, a wound: "a clean punched-out hole the size of a dime." The surgeon studies it. "The tissues about the opening are swollen and tense. A thin brownish fluid lips the edge, and now and then a lazy drop of the overflow slips down the arm." At first, the hole seemed clean; then indications of pain are noted. Finally the opening appears repulsive as the surgeon remarks the "brownish fluid" suggesting pus, or blood, or excrement. Symbolically now the wound is vaginal, or anal.

With confidence, and some complacence, the surgeon makes a speedy diagnosis: "An abscess, inadequately drained." Easily, he can handle this.

Suddenly, revulsion, like a wave of nausea, sweeps over him. "What happens next is enough to lay Francis Drake avomit in his cabin," writes our surgeon-explorer. For now the wound becomes a "crater" from which looms all the Evil of the universe. His words capture and transmit his horror, his feelings of frenzy: "No explorer ever started in wilder surmise than I into that crater from which there now emerges a narrow gray head whose sole distinguishing feature is a pair of black pincers. The head sits atop a longish flexible neck arching now this way, now that, testing the air. Alternately it folds back upon itself, then advances in new boldness. And all the while, with dreadful rhythmicity, the unspeakable pincers open and close" (p. 20). The "dreadful rhythmicity" of the creature's pincers reflects visually the horror gripping the surgeon, the dreadful rhythms of his throbbing pulse.

Darting forth, now retreating, the creature seems a "beast"; the wound is its lair. Taut and terrified, the surgeon is a "high priest" determined to vanquish this evil—all Evil. He will wait, and he will conquer:

> Here is the lair of a beast at whose malignant purpose I could but guess. A Mayan devil, I think, that would soon burst free to fly about the room, with horrid blanket-wings and iridescent scales, raking, pinching, injecting God knows what acid juice. And even now the irony does not escape me, the irony of my patient as excavator excavated.
>
> With all the ritual deliberation of a high priest I advance a surgical clamp toward the hole. The surgeon's heart is become a bat hanging upside down from his rib cage. The rim achieved—now thrust—and the ratchets of the clamp close upon empty air. The devil has retracted. Evil mocking laughter bangs back and forth in the brain. More stealth. Lying in wait. One must skulk.

> ... Acrouch, strung, the surgeon is one with his instrument; there
> is no longer any boundary between its metal and his flesh. They
> are joined in a single perfect tool of extirpation. It is just for this
> that he was born. Now—thrust—and clamp—and *yes.* Got him!
> (pp. 20–21)

The beast with its "malignant purpose" that suggests physical and moral evil appears horrifying, yet strangely alluring, to this surgeon-priest. Momentarily it even seems beautiful as he imagines its "iridescent scales." Then it becomes loathsome again, a snakelike creature, or a phallus "injecting God knows what acid juice." Despite his nausea and fear, the surgeon smiles inwardly as he grasps the irony of the situation and coins a clever phrase: his patient is the "excavator excavated." But the irony in this tale turns—symbolically, strikingly—against the surgeon.

With its pincers opening and closing continuously, the phallic creature that hides, waits, then shoots forth is an image—hideous—of the surgeon joined to his surgical instrument: the pincerlike ratchets of his clamp opening and closing ceaselessly as he waits, skulks, and thrusts and thrusts again. More, the surgeon becomes, like the "devil"-beast, an image of ugliness and of evil. But in him these characteristics are internalized: his heart "is become a bat hanging upside down from his rib cage"; and "evil mocking laughter bangs back and forth in the brain." The poet's pounding plosive *b* sounds echo, amplify the surgeon's pounding heart. The irony is fierce: the high priest–surgeon who would combat, conquer Evil is imaged by the evil, foul, phallic creature that he angrily seeks to cut down and destroy in order to heal both his patient and himself.

When the surgeon finally grasps the creature in the jaws of his hemostat, he feels exultant, exalted. The beast appears to him "the whole of the evil of the world," and he will "kill it. For mankind." Here the surgeon is not merely priest: "Here is the surgeon as Savior indeed," announces Selzer with arrogance and deliciously self-deflating humor.

Extracted from the wound, the demon drowns in the specimen jar and is carried by the victorious, somewhat vainglorious, surgeon to the medical school. There the pathologist tells him that the creature is the larva of a botfly. It was about to burrow its way out of the wound and would have died anyway. His surgery was really unnecessary.

"No, it is not the surgeon who is God's darling. He is the victim of vanity," says Selzer in summation. "It is the poet who heals with his words, stanches the flow of blood, stills the rattling breath, applies poultice to the scalded flesh." For the surgeon–would-be-healer here was actually imaged by the Evil he sought to overcome. And at best he was someone who speeded along, slightly, the course of nature. True healing for Selzer comes from love and from the poet: from words, which to his mind are like the Holy Spirit. The surgeon-healer must be for him the surgeon-poet.

What emerges from Selzer's lengthy descriptions of these two

wounds—the diabetic's festering leg and the excavator's excavated arm
—is that because of his experiences of them, the surgeon is transformed.
In the case of the diabetic woman, the physician is uplifted and healed
not by his own acts, but by his patient's: her courage, and humor, and
compassion. In the botfly case the surgeon's own courage and humor
help him face his task. Too, they bring home to him his own importance,
and his own unimportance. He learns that as a surgeon, even as the
surgeon-"priest," he has only limited powers to heal. For a priest is but
one who performs a sacred ritual or who ministers; not godlike, he is
merely a servant of God. What he can do he does by cutting. The rest is
left to the body, and to the poet. The wounds reveal to him the sacredness
not of the surgeon but of the flesh and of life. The surgeon's place in
Selzer's universe is, paradoxically, very small.

A third wound grants Selzer the vision—tragic and transcendent in
this case—of one of the sacraments. A man of letters is lying in the
intensive care unit of a hospital. He was struck suddenly with "the look
of the Wound," writes Selzer. He seemed to *see* something for the first
time, to understand "something that had eluded him all his life" (p. 44).
Lying there, dying there, the man is tended—dutifully, lovingly—by a
nurse. In Selzer's eyes, she appears a wife joined to this man through the
obligations, the rights, and the love-filled devotion of the sacrament of
matrimony:

> In the room a woman moves. She is dressed in white. Lovingly she
> measures his hourly flow of urine. . . . The man of letters did not
> know this woman before. . . . But this nurse is his wife in his new
> life of dying. They are close, these two, intimate, depending one
> upon the other, loving. It is a marriage, for although they own no
> shared past, they possess this awful, intense present, this matrimo-
> nial now, that binds them as strongly as any promise. (p. 45)

The metaphorical marriage joins the patient and the one who tends him
in the love—intense, sorrowful, and exalting—of the nursing relationship. It is a pain-filled but privileged state, one that permits a person to
transcend himself through a wound and through love, to give himself. For
Selzer, love is always inseparable from suffering; by extension, then, so
is the sacrament of matrimony. But according to Selzer it is pain precisely,
and not joy, that enables a human being to surpass himself, and in so
doing to come to know redemption and grace.

Surgery, therefore, is Selzer's search for grace. It is not an easy quest,
and one does not practice surgery easily. There is a taboo against enter-
ing the human body, laying it open. It is an act of violence, like a rape.
Not surprisingly, the opened body evokes strong ambivalences in Selzer:
revulsion and attraction, "horror and fascination" (p. 25). It appears an
object of holiness, or of dread and potential punishment.

A man under spinal anesthesia is looking into his own opened abdomen. "This man is violating a taboo. . . . How dare he look within the

Ark!'' exclaims Selzer, drawing upon his Jewish background by referring
to the enclosure in the synagogue, the Ark, in which the sacred scroll, the
Torah, is kept. "But it is too late; he has already *seen;* that which no man
should; he has trespassed." That man has seen only once. But the surgeon has elected to see again and again this tabooed, this terrible and
wonderful territory: the body of his patient, which is the image of his own
body, and of the truth concealed within it—all the strength and the frailty
of man. It is enough to drive one mad, or to make one blind. "The hidden
geography of the body is a Medusa's head one glimpse of which would
render blind the presumptuous eye." Mythic, monstrous: the body is the
Medusa's head that the surgeon must observe—and even grapple with—
day after day. And because of his ordeal, he believes he will be cursed,
and blessed.

Sometimes the entry into the body is portrayed by Selzer as an erotic
act: violent sometimes, like a rape; sometimes loving. "The flesh splits
with its own kind of moan. It is like the penetration of rape" (p. 104). But
he also writes, "One enters the body in surgery, as in love, as though one
were an exile returning at last to his hearth, daring uncharted darkness
in order to reach home" (p. 25). Requiring physical and spiritual courage,
the act described here is a search for love, for unity, and for communion.
The erotic for Selzer is never far from the spiritual: Eros joined to Agape.

Opened, the abdomen becomes in Selzer's eyes the site and the
substance of a divine transubstantiation, the place and the means of a
Mass. Not the traditional transubstantiation of the Roman Catholic
Church (the consecrated bread and wine transformed mystically into the
Body and Blood of Christ), but the actual body and blood of his patient
appear transubstantiated for Selzer into the Body and Blood. And they
permit him thereby to commune with divinity.

Central to the Mass, and to the sacrament of Holy Communion that
it celebrates, are the ideas of sacrifice (literally "making sacred," from the
Latin *sacer,* "sacred," and *facere,* "to make"; one gives up something of
value for the sake of something with a greater claim), and salvation: God
the Son gave His Body and Blood to God the Father, in order to save
man. "Sacrifice," "sacrament" and "sacred" all derive from *sacer.* By
describing surgery in terms of a Mass, the ceremony that reenacts Christ's
crucifixion and is actually called the "sacrifice of the Mass," Selzer blends
images of the Roman Catholic religion with figures from his Jewish heritage. The Old Testament priest sacrificing an animal-victim to God may
be seen, after all, as a kind of surgeon-priest. And so for Selzer's surgeon-
priest, the patient evokes at once an Old Testament animal sacrifice as
well as a Christ figure who saves the surgeon spiritually through the
symbolical sacrifice of his body and blood on the operating table: his body
and blood that become the Body and the Blood.

Selzer's depiction of surgery as a metaphorical Mass also combines
images of the sacrament of Holy Communion with words suggesting the
sacrament of baptism. The opened abdomen, he writes, "is the stillest
place that ever was. . . . This is no silence of the vacant stratosphere, but

the awful quiet of ruins, of rainbows, full of expectation and holy dread. Soon you shall know surgery as a Mass served with Body and Blood, wherein disease is assailed as though it were sin" (p. 26). This silence teems with life, with beauty, and with terror: It is a sacred silence. The "holy dread" suggests Selzer's feelings for the Old Testament Jehovah: hopefulness combined with fear. The Mass is the assurance of grace. But the Mass, like the Old Testament sacrifices, reenacts a ritual death. The "awful [implying both awe and horror] quiet of ruins" evokes splendor, stillness, and solitude. The rainbows call forth beauty, hope, and holiness: the covenant between God and Noah—the flood and the chosen one's escape in the ark; the promise that there will be no more floods to destroy the earth. God's wrath, followed by God's forgiveness. In this ambiance surgery suddenly becomes an act of Holy Communion. The Mass, like the Last Supper, is "served." The surgeon is joined mystically with the patient-Christ, and surgery has become a means to salvation. Christ gave Himself to save man: the patient upon the altar of surgery saves the surgeon spiritually—the surgeon who is operating to save, literally, the patient's life. Salvation from disease is equated in Selzer's mind with salvation from sin: the operation appears to him a symbolic baptism. Just as he seeks to purge his patient's body of disease "as though it were sin," so the surgeon-priest is in a sense purified by his sprinkling with, or immersion in, his patient's sanctified blood. It is a surgical, and a spiritual, bathing.

For Selzer, therefore, the body and blood of his patient, transubstantiated into the Body and Blood, purify the surgeon-priest and exalt him; and unite him through the reenactment of sacrifice and salvation—the awful/awe-ful Mass of Surgery—with the godhead and with grace.

Sometimes the symbolic sacrifice of the patient becomes a real sacrifice: a death, and a rendering sacred. For always the surgeon is confronted with the possibility of death. Selzer describes a terrifying experience, the one he as a surgeon fears above all others: an operation during which the patient dies on the operating table. The operation described is supposed to be a routine one, but suddenly the patient begins to hemorrhage, uncontrollably. "The surgeon suctions away the blood; even as he does so, new red trickles; his eyes are full of it; he cannot see" (p. 38). The blood—like the Medusa's head of the opened body—blinds him. Then it infiltrates him, fills his own eyes. Not a baptism now, but a drowning. The surgeon has become in some ways like his patient: the blood that surges in the patient's abdomen floods his own eyes. He feels himself drowning, "his hand sunk in the body of his patient" (p. 39). Part of him too will die during this operation.

The surgeon is frightfully, fearfully, alone. The carnivore wound would suck him in, its "mouth" devour him even as he tries to suction away the blood. "No matter how many others crowd about the mouth of the wound, no matter their admiration and encouragement, it is *he* [the surgeon] that rappels this crevasse, dangles in this dreadful place, and he is *afraid . . .*" (p. 38). A mountain climber, he is totally responsible: totally dependent upon himself and upon forces outside of himself *over which he has no control.* "The surgeon cuts. And all at once there leaps a mighty blood. As when from the hidden mountain ledge a pebble is dislodged, a pebble behind whose small slippage the whole of the avalanche is pulled. Now the belly is a vast working lake in which it seems both patient and surgeon will drown" (pp. 38–39). The lake of blood is at once horrid and holy: horrid because it means that the patient will die, that the transfusions being poured and poured in are gushing out of his body even faster than new blood can replace them. But it is holy because the surgeon is overwhelmed with a feeling of awe and with the recognition of his own insignificance. And holy as well because it evokes the Blood shed for others.

The surgeon realizes that the man on the operating table has died. Selzer writes, "Now there is no more sorrowful man in the city, for this surgeon has discovered the surprise at the center of his work. It is death. The events of this abdomen have conspired to change him, for no man can travel back from such darkness and be the same as he was." The death and the guilt—the sense of sacredness and of sacrifice—will remain with him, forever.

"To *perceive* tragedy is to wring from it beauty and truth," writes Selzer (p. 46). The tragedy of illness, the tragedies of his patients' deaths, permit him to *seize,* to *receive,* to *understand* (as the Latin *percipere,* the root of "to perceive," implies) beauty and truth. Sickness, suffering and death touch his life and transform it; and grant him through knowledge, pain, and sorrow the gifts of compassion and of grace.

Surgery for Selzer is a sacred occupation. Like his writing, surgery reflects his search—physical, emotional, and spiritual—for love and for his father. His search for his father is actually his longing for a father figure who will love him: It is not unlike a quest for God. Selzer remembers that when his father died it was then that he decided he also would become a doctor. It is not so much his father's presence, but rather his father's absence, that has directed, determined—driven his life. Surgery, Selzer has said, more than other types of medicine, immerses one in the body. His surgery, therefore, reenacts symbolically his loss of, and his search for, his father: the wound inflicted by his father's death; and his own attempts, by immersing himself in the bodies of his patients, to rejoin the flesh, and so the spirit, of his father. Surgery, like his "sacred purpose of writing" (p. 19), becomes for him a means to reach out toward salvation: to commune through a wound and through suffering with his father, with divinity, and with Love.

There are three major aspects to Selzer's portrayal of surgery: the profane or artistic (the art, the skill of cutting); the sexually symbolic (the entry into the body as an act of love, or a rape; the reenactment on his patients' bodies of the surgeon's castration anxieties); and the sacred (his blending of the Jewish with the Roman Catholic). Combined with the first two aspects, Selzer's portrayal of the sacred is what makes his vision of surgery unique: haunting, powerful, uplifting. For Selzer, in fact, the surgical experience encompasses symbolically the seven sacraments of the Roman Catholic Church.

The most important sacrament for Selzer's vision of surgery is Holy Communion. The operation, which in some ways resembles the animal sacrifices described in the Old Testament, appears to him a Mass during which the body and blood of the patient are transubstantiated into the Body and Blood. The patient becomes a symbolic Christ figure who enables the surgeon standing at the altar of surgery to transcend himself mystically: to commune with divinity, and to know grace. Through the sacred bodies of his patients, Selzer also seeks to rejoin—by means of the fleshly wound of surgery and the symbolic death on the operating table —his own father. The surgical wound is reminiscent of the wound caused him when his father died, and the patient narcotized upon the surgical table recalls the sleep of death: The wound and death that will join him with Love.

Although Holy Communion is the most dramatic and most important rite of surgery as portrayed by Selzer, aspects of the six other sacraments are also present. The surgeon's being bathed in his patients' blood is for him a kind of baptism, a spiritual purification. The sacrament of matrimony is present in his depiction of the love and marriage that unite the patient and the one tending him in the nursing relationship. Extreme unction, also called anointing of the sick, is evoked as the surgeon-priest anoints the dying, festering flesh of the young diabetic woman.

Confirmation, full membership in the church (of physicians), and the taking of holy orders are represented as well. The surgeon undergoes a long apprenticeship, a real novitiate, to become a priest of his profession. Here the imagery is as much Jewish as Roman Catholic: "I must confess that the priestliness of my profession has ever been impressed on me. In the beginning there are vows, taken with all solemnity. Then there is the endless harsh novitiate of training, much fatigue, much sacrifice. At last one emerges as celebrant, standing close to the truth lying curtained in the Ark of the body" (p. 94).

Finally, Selzer's writings may be seen as his symbolic confession and penance: his admissions of guilt and of anguish; his deflating of the surgeon's ego and importance; his making amends for his past. Throughout, it is fascinating to see that Selzer the surgeon forever humbles the surgeon while also of course praising his art and his mission of healing. But the surgeon, maintains Selzer, is not the true healer. More than healer, the surgeon for Selzer is the servant of healing, and the one who may be healed. He writes; "The truly great writing about doctors has not yet been done. I think it must be done *by* a doctor, one who is through with the love affair with his technique, who recognizes that he has played Narcissus, raining kisses on a mirror, and who now, out of the impacted masses of his guilt, has expanded into self-doubt, and finally into the high state of wonderment." This doctor may come "upon the knowledge that he has done no more than meddle in the lives of his fellows, and that he has done at least as much harm as good" (p. 18). Here Selzer accuses the doctor—himself—with having loved not life or his patients, but his art and his own ego. Yet the guilt, weighty and impacted, he says, will fester and drive him to doubt himself. And in so doing it will permit him to enter a higher state of wonderment and belief: not in himself, but in something greater—more human, and more divine. Linked to his surgery, Selzer's writings are a confession and an expiation; and a reaching out for forgiveness and for grace.

Surgery is at once an art for Selzer and a religion. The surgeon's skill and technique are essential. But these, though necessary, are not enough. Surgery for him is profane and sacred, erotic and spiritual: a searching, through the blood and the body of his patient, for his father and for healing; for truth, for love, and for salvation. The surgeon in Selzer's eyes is a priest who is the servant of healing, and so of humanity. He is the would-be healer who is healed himself—joined with love and with divinity —by means of the grace accorded him through the sacraments of surgery.

NOTES

1. Richard Selzer, *Mortal Lessons: Notes on the Art of Surgery* (New York: Simon and Schuster, © 1974, 1975, 1976 by Richard Selzer), p. 187. All quotations are from this edition; page references are given in parentheses. For a study of one of the chapters of *Mortal Lessons,* see Enid Rhodes Peschel, " 'Alchemy of the Word': Language and 'The Knife'—A Commentary on Richard Selzer's Work," *The Pharos of Alpha Omega Alpha* 42, no. 1 (Winter 1979), pp. 25–32.

2. In "Why I Left the Church," a humorous and serious "sermon" he delivered at the dedication of the Hope Unitarian Church in Tulsa, Oklahoma, in October 1977, Selzer discusses why he felt the Old Testament Jehovah was too stern a God for him.

Part Two:
Doctors Portrayed in Literature

I observe the physician with the same diligence as he
the disease.

John Donne, *Devotions*

The Clinical View of Life:
Gustave Flaubert's Madame Bovary

Eugene F. Gray

In concluding his now-famous review of Gustave Flaubert's even more famous novel in 1857, Charles Sainte-Beuve remarked that Flaubert wielded a pen as others do a scalpel. The comparison, which has since become a commonplace of Flaubert criticism, refers to the author's incisive style and to his critical, analytical view of life, what in 1852 Flaubert himself termed "le coup d'oeil médical de la vie," or the clinical view of life. For Flaubert, who in his youth had been a fervent admirer of Byron, Hugo and a host of Romantic writers, and never really lost his admiration and sympathy for them, French literature at midcentury needed more than anything else that analytical vision that is a trademark of the sciences. "As time goes on," he wrote in 1852, "art will be scientific, just as science will become artistic."[1] The novel *Madame Bovary* is Flaubert's first published attempt at filling the first part of the prescription.

Sainte-Beuve's comparison is more than a figure of rhetoric and concerns more than Flaubert's style and outlook, for Gustave Flaubert grew up in a wing of Rouen hospital, in the apartment reserved for the chief surgeon, his father. As was the case with the sons of many middle-class families of the day, Gustave was destined for a career in law, until illness forced termination of his studies; his brother Achille went into medicine, later becoming associate surgeon at the hospital and, upon their father's death, chief surgeon. The windows of the Flaubert apartment, as well as those of Dr. Flaubert's dissection room, looked out over the hospital gardens, where Gustave and his brother and sister would often play. Gustave described the scene years later:

> How many times my sister and I climbed up on the trellis and, hanging there among the vines, we would look with curiosity at the cadavers stretched out on the tables. The sun shone down on them; the same flies which circled overhead and over the flowers would land on them and come buzzing back toward us! . . . I can still see my father looking up at us from his dissecting and telling

us to go away. (Letter to Louise Colet, 8 July 1853, *Oeuvres,* vol.
7, pp. 198–99)

Surrounded as he was by illness and death, it is hardly surprising that
Gustave developed at an early age a macabre and melancholy turn of
mind, or that many of the incidents that he heard discussed at home later
appeared in his novels.

Not only was Flaubert surrounded by illness, he was afflicted by
illness, a circumstance that was to have a crucial influence upon his life,
allowing him to devote his time to literature. The first manifestation of
his illness occurred at the age of twenty-two. With his brother Achille he
was riding along a country road in utter darkness when a wagon from
which swung a lantern approached them from the opposite direction.
Suddenly Gustave fell to the floor of the carriage "as if struck by apo-
plexy," he later wrote, and with the sensation of being "carried away by
a torrent of flames." Gustave's brother carried him to a nearby farmhouse
and administered first aid—bloodletting, three bleedings one after the
other until Gustave finally opened his eyes. (French doctors at the time,
including Flaubert's father and brother, followed the teachings of Dr.
François Broussais, 1772–1838, who, believing all disease to be inflam-
matory in nature, prescribed bloodletting as his main treatment.)

Flaubert suffered further attacks, milder than the first one, and most
of his life was troubled by hallucinations, which he claimed to have cured
through willpower. He was forced to abandon his law studies, which he
detested anyway, and ordered to give up smoking, wine and women, for
the time being at least. His treatment consisted of repeated bloodletting,
castor oil, numerous infusions, a drainage wick in the neck, hot baths and
avoidance of tension, all standard treatment at the time for epilepsy, but
during Flaubert's lifetime few people were willing to pronounce the name
of the dread disease (Flaubert himself referred to his illness as a nervous
ailment). It now seems quite certain that Flaubert's illness was indeed a
type of temporal lobe epilepsy difficult to diagnose in his day.[2]

Many years later Flaubert described the sensations experienced in
his attacks in a letter to Hippolyte Taine, who was researching a book on
human intelligence:

> 1. First an indeterminate anguish, a vague malaise, a feeling of
> painful expectation. . . .
> 2. Then, all of a sudden, like a thunderbolt, the invasion, or rather
> spontaneous irruption of memory, for the hallucination as such is
> nothing else, for me at least. It is an illness of memory, a letting
> go of everything it holds. You feel the images escaping like the
> flow of blood. It seems like everything in your head bursts out at
> once like a thousand pieces of a fireworks display, and you don't
> have time to look at these internal images which pass by like a
> flash. In other cases it begins with a single image which grows
> larger, expands and winds up masking objective reality, for exam-
> ple like a whirling spark which becomes a large flame. In this case

you can quite easily think of something else at the same time.
(1 December 1866, *Oeuvres,* vol. 12, pp. 158–59)

Although Flaubert's illness had no direct effect upon his literary style, as far as can be detected with certainty, he often attributed his own emotional states to his characters, and especially to Emma Bovary. John Lapp has studied this practice in detail.[3] The following passage taken from *Madame Bovary* is the most striking example, and parallels in essential details the description given to Taine:

> She was no longer conscious of herself, except through her pulsating arteries, which seemed to burst forth like deafening music filling the countryside. The ground beneath her feet was more yielding than water, and the furrows of the field seemed like huge brown breakers. Everything contained in her head, remembrances, ideas, escaped at once, in a single movement, like a thousand pieces of a fireworks display. Madness was taking hold of her, she grew frightened. . . . She felt her soul leaving her much like an injured person, who while dying feels existence flowing from his bleeding wound. . . .
> It suddenly seemed as if globules the color of fire were bursting in the air like bullets which explode as they hit, and were whirling, whirling, only to melt finally in the snow between the branches of the trees.[4]

The fear, the escape of Emma's memory or self, the multiple fulgurant images, the blotting out of reality without loss of consciousness are all characteristic of Flaubert's own experience.

"Country Customs" is the subtitle of *Madame Bovary.* Having grown up in a medical milieu, Flaubert was well equipped to chronicle the life of Charles Bovary, health officer in a village in Normandy. Lacking the financial means and the education to attend medical school in Paris, Charles Bovary has to be content with study in Rouen, the diploma of health officer, and a practice in his native region. He meets Emma, a pretty farm girl, when he goes to her farm to set her father's broken leg. Emma has received a convent education, which sets her apart from other farm girls, and has aspirations for an elegant life. The young health officer represents new horizons for her, and they are married after the death of Charles's first wife. But Emma, surrounded by mediocrity, finds life in a village oppressive. She has a love affair, contracts numerous debts, has another affair, and commits suicide. Such is the slim basis of the novel, which parallels in most respects the story of a certain Eugène Delamare, himself a health officer and former student of Gustave's father.

The category of health officer existed during the French Revolution, but was not rigidly defined by law until 1803. The government's original goal in establishing the category was to provide better health care to the rural population, but as the century progressed, the government saw that the goal was not being met, since at one point there were as many health officers in the cities as in the countryside, and an unfortunate rivalry had developed between them and regular doctors. The title was therefore abolished in 1892.

The program of study for the diploma of health officer lasted three years. Since a high school diploma was not needed for entrance into the program, health officers were less well-educated than doctors, and came from lower socioeconomic groups. The program ended with three examinations: (1) general anatomy and physiology, (2) internal and external pathology and obstetrics, (3) internal and external clinical practice, therapeutics and materia medica, followed by a composition on a subject chosen by lot from a number of predetermined topics. In the novel Charles follows this program precisely, passing his examinations by memorizing the answers to all the predetermined topics.

The life of a country health officer was far from romantic. His days were long, with consultations in his office in the morning, and the rest of the day spent on horseback visiting patients in outlying farms and hamlets. For all of that his prestige and income were far inferior to those of a doctor. Only in a region where there was no doctor could a health officer acquire some prestige, which was all he had to compensate for his low income. Since a health officer could practice only in the region *(département)* in which he had received his diploma, Emma's horizons are limited geographically as well as financially. The health officer was forbidden to perform major operations except under the supervision of a doctor, and was liable for damages in case of infraction. Charles Bovary's surgical practice in the novel is generally limited to the extraction of teeth and bloodletting, at both of which he excels. Afraid of killing his patients, he normally prescribes relatively innocuous treatments, such as soothing potions, foot baths and leeches.

How then is it possible, given the law and Charles Bovary's timid nature, that he undertakes to operate on a clubfoot? First of all, the term *major operation* was not defined in the law governing the status of health officers. Secondly, Emma, hearing of the idea from Homais the druggist, and dreaming of future glory for Charles, and of course herself, argues strongly for the operation, which Homais insists is minor. In fact, subcutaneous tenotomy, developed about 1833 by Delpech, was in its infancy, but had already caught the public fancy. An article appearing in the *Journal de Rouen* in 1841 told of recent advances in the surgical treatment of strabismus and mentioned in particular the success of Gustave's brother in performing the operation at Rouen hospital.

The surgical treatment of clubfoot was also popularized in the press after the publication of Dr. Vincent Duval's book *Traité pratique du pied-bot (A Practical Treatise on Clubfoot)* in 1839. Flaubert (as well as Charles) consulted this work and his notes have been found and published. An interesting coincidence is that a patient mentioned in Duval's book had consulted Dr. Flaubert Sr. for conjunctivitis. Since she had a clubfoot, Dr. Flaubert attempted to treat it according to traditional methods, namely, holding the foot immobile for several weeks in metal splints. He was unsuccessful and the patient later consulted Dr. Duval, who treated her successfully by means of surgery.

Dr. Duval's treatment consisted of cutting the appropriate tendon, depending on the type of clubfoot, and then enclosing the foot in a mechanical device to hold it immobile during the healing process. Flaubert's notes and the text of the novel follow closely the stages of the treatment as outlined in Duval's book: very little pain during the operation, a crackling sound as the tendon is cut, only two or three drops of blood, immediate immobilization of the foot. Flaubert even borrowed some of the terminology invented by Duval, such as *strephopody, strephocatopody, strephendopody,* since their exotic appearance aptly suggests to the reader Charles's incomprehension as he reads Duval's book. Flaubert noted, too, some of the blunders that an inexperienced surgeon might commit:

> 1. Too small an incision, producing ecchymosis, erysipelas, edema, abscess;
> 2. Too much pressure from the mechanical device producing eschar, and before that intense pain;
> 3. Poorly cut tendon, giving rise to tetanus, or at least serious convulsions;
> 4. He can, if he is completely ignorant, hit the wrong tendon, mistake the type of clubfoot, be bewildered by the talipes valgus and the talipes equinus and thus produce a type of clubfoot unknown to science.[5]

Charles commits all of the above errors, with the result that gangrene sets in and the leg must be amputated. This is a major operation and Dr. Canivet is called in from a neighboring town to perform it.

The clubfoot operation is a key scene of the novel. Well-documented, in accord with Flaubert's precept that fiction must respect the truth, the circumstances of Charles's greatest failure prove to Emma that Charles will never liberate her from the oppressive provincial atmosphere of Yonville, that he will never become a famous surgeon like Dupuytren. This realization turns her toward a self-destructive love affair with Léon and a series of extravagant purchases leading to bankruptcy and suicide.

Aside from that, however, the portrayal of the relationship between medical practitioners in the operation scene is of some significance in understanding Flaubert's attitude toward modern society. Curiously, regular doctors play almost no role, perhaps because for Flaubert they represented the exception rather than the average. Canivet's role in the operation scene is purely to amputate Hippolyte's leg, as suggested by his name (from the French word *canif,* "penknife"). He makes one other appearance in the novel, after Emma's suicide attempt, administers an emetic when it is too late and is roundly castigated by his colleague Dr. Larivière. The latter, whose portrait is supposedly based on Gustave's father ("He belonged to that great surgical school descended from Bichat, to that now defunct generation of philosopher-practitioners," *Madame Bovary*, p. 326), is the only character to be portrayed in wholly favorable terms, but he arrives too late to save Emma.

The scene of the clubfoot operation and other medical scenes in the novel concern Charles and/or Homais, the very bottom rungs of the medical profession. Charles is passive and timid, performing the operation only at the insistence of others. Homais is the motivating force, the instigator of the entire action, just as later on he will make the therapeutic suggestion that Emma, when she is recuperating from the catastrophic effects of the end of her first affair, go to the theater, which leads to her second love affair. From these events the reader might conclude that Homais's role is artificial, serving to turn the action of the novel in the directions in which Flaubert wants it to move.

Such a conclusion would be erroneous, however. Homais occupies too much space in the novel for that to be his sole purpose. It is not possible here to examine the complex relationship between Homais and his creator. Suffice it to say that Homais represents for Flaubert a natural spawn of modern democratic society. His effect in the novel is harmful, not only because his seemingly well-intentioned proselytizing on behalf of progress has by chance made a victim of Hippolyte, and indirectly of Charles, too, but more importantly because his influence is essentially pernicious. From his very first appearance Homais exists through his speech.[6] He is a veritable storehouse of sayings, commonplaces, quotations, little-known facts, stereotypes and prejudices, all coexisting in his mind without any apparent system or order. Add to this an overweening egoism and a desire to dominate, and we have a character who is clearly a demagogue. He becomes a true threat to society through his access to the columns of a newspaper, for he wields far more power there than he could in his drugstore in Yonville. Journalism was for Flaubert the lowest level of literary endeavor, appealing to the masses with half-truths, propaganda and lies, and Homais's journalism is of this sort. His reports on the agricultural fair and the clubfoot operations have little relation to objective reality. His malevolence shows when a salve of his invention fails to cure the scrofulous afflictions of a blind beggar who haunts the Rouen-Yonville road. The beggar tells everyone who passes of Homais's failure, and Homais uses his position as journalist to mount a campaign of vilification against the beggar until the latter is incarcerated. Encouraged by his successful battle, Homais becomes involved in public affairs and politics, receiving finally the cross of the Legion of Honor for his services. Homais has taken on the dimensions of myth, and Flaubert has for once forsaken his clinical observation for prophetic vision.

NOTES

1. Gustave Flaubert, *Oeuvres,* ed. Maurice Nadeau (Lausanne: Editions Rencontre, 1965), vol. 6, p. 260. Future references to the *Oeuvres* are given in my text.

2. See Benjamin Bart, *Flaubert* (Syracuse University Press, 1967), pp. 90–96, for a complete discussion of Flaubert's illness.

3. *French Studies* 10 (1956), pp. 322–43.

4. *Madame Bovary,* ed. Claudine Gothot-Mersch (Paris: Garnier, 1971), pp. 319–20, translation mine. Future references are to this edition. A good English translation is that of Paul de Man (New York: Norton, 1965), which also contains some earlier versions of the novel and critical essays.

5. *Madame Bovary. Unpublished drafts and fragments* (in French), ed. Gabrielle Leleu (Paris: Conard, 1936), vol. 2, p. 70.

6. See Robert Niess, "On Listening to Homais," *French Review* 51 (1977–78), pp. 22–28, for this aspect of Homais.

The Persona of the Doctor
in Céline's Journey to the End
of the Night
and Camus's The Plague

Germaine Brée

A Brief Panaromic View

The purpose of this paper is to study the specific ways in which the persona of the physician functions and becomes charged with meaning within the fictional world of two contrasting novels, *Journey to the End of the Night* (1932) and *The Plague* (1948). Many other novels might have been selected; for, whether in soap opera, popular fiction or literature proper, the medical doctor is one of the dominant motifs in our culture. The magic mountain of tuberculosis; the cancer or psychiatric ward; the plague or cholera epidemic; the clinic or nursing home offer, it would seem, privileged structures for fictional elaboration. They inevitably call forth the figure of the doctor. The two French novels I have chosen, beyond the fact that they have almost become classics in this country, have one feature in common: in each the story is narrated by a doctor, and the author uses the narrator's profession to establish the perspective and circumstances through which the story acquires meaning. Both novels inevitably raise a complex network of questions. Not the least among them are the lights they throw obliquely on the role—or variety of roles —the persona of the physician plays in the imaginary constructs of our time; the measure in which myth and reality blend in the process whereby the novelist makes use of the figure as a hermeneutic device guiding his reader toward the search for a deeper meaning beneath the surface flow of the story. Both novels belong to a time—the decades of the thirties and forties—when literature, understandably enough, was primarily concerned with the social and metaphysical question of man's fate.

In a very general way, as Susan Sontag eloquently demonstrated in her essay *Illness as Metaphor* (1978), we are still far from having discarded the centuries-old association of disease and sin. In most instances, at least among the more worldly-minded, the metaphor of a "sick world" has replaced the notion of a "sinful world." Metaphorically speaking, collective disturbances are easily compared to physical lesions, and so quite naturally for novelists preoccupied with the nature of contemporary society, the doctor took the place formerly occupied by the priest. It is not surprising that, as the medical establishment began to play an increasingly important role in our lives, the doctor also acquired some of the daemonic characteristics of the priest. The healers, the idealized "men in white" of popular mythologizing, who command respect and deal authoritatively with threatening ills, could also by association be perceived as death-dealers, accomplices of the invisible ills they uncovered. In the nineteen-twenties, in his play *Orpheus,* Jean Cocteau introduced Death on the stage in the guise of a beautiful aseptic woman surgeon "in white." The technological aspect of today's medical establishment is one of the factors that have of late transformed the doctor's image and thereby the functions he may assume in fiction.

More often than not in the nineteenth-century novel of horse-and-buggy days the doctor was not a figure of power or even authority. A local figure, kindly and somewhat down at the heels, a gentle skeptic in many instances, seen often as a good raconteur, more than a little fond of his bottle of wine, he was no longer the farcical character inherited from Plautus that Molière had put to such good use. He tended to be a marginal figure, rarely cast in the role of hero; the inept doctor lived on in one of the standard vehicles of a distinct genre—satire.

In France, in the wake of such prestigious figures as Claude Bernard and Louis Pasteur, the doctor acquired new dignity. Alongside the inept and bungling Charles Bovary, Flaubert introduced the wise and scientifically trained Dr. Rivière, a fictional embodiment, it has been suggested, of his own idealized father. It was no doubt Zola who, with his *Dr. Pascal,* projected an idealized image of the physician as hero. A humane practicing physician who visits his patients in good nineteenth-century style, Dr. Pascal is also a man who works in solitary and selfless concentration upon the problems of heredity, a man with broad moral and social views and indifferent to financial gain, who battles against ignorance and prejudice in the higher interests of humanity. The doctor, in fact, has acquired so solid a status in Zola's esteem that novelist and doctor merge: Zola endowed Dr. Pascal with the same high moral quality he also attributed to the "new experimental" novelist he wished to be. Dr. Pascal is a *humanly* exemplary figure, just as the knight had been in medieval time or the enlightenment "philosopher" in the eighteenth century.

In contrast I shall go outside France to take a look at a brief and macabre mid-twentieth-century play by Dylan Thomas, *The Doctor and the Devils;*[1] it dramatizes better than any other text I know the surreptitious process whereby the exemplary medical figure merged into another far less worthy of respect. Simultaneously it calls into question the moral and social values of the activities of the medical establishment as a whole. In this case, it is clear that the persona of the physician reflects the uneasi-

ness of the noninitiate confronted by what seems to him the inhuman
practices of modern medical research. Zola's Dr. Pascal had no laboratory. Conversely, Jules Verne's technologists did not experiment with
human bodies. *The Doctor and the Devils,* like Wiene's expressionist film
Dr. Caligari, is not unconnected with the survival in our contemporary
imaginations of the ambiguous figures of medieval alchemy, of Faust and
his pact with the devil.

The dark double of the benefic figure emerges with the fear and
questioning of his power: a bonus, of course, for the world of fiction.
Ostensibly in Dylan Thomas's scenario the devils are the body-snatchers
who steal the corpses from the local cemetery and sell them to the medical school in town for demonstration and experiment. Whereas awe and
respect surround the successful doctors, the body-snatchers are despised
and feared outcasts among the town-dwellers. But while the eminent
doctor and director of the establishment delivers uplifting lectures to his
students on the sanctity of the human body, the body-snatchers start to
dispatch the poor and the weak in order to fill their own pockets while
catering to the lab's needs. When the situation erupts publicly, the doctor
is looked upon with fear and reprobation for what is seen as his silent
complicity. But he emerges apparently unscathed. Briefly, doubt shakes
his high-minded righteousness as he wonders if he had set himself up
above pity, like a god over death. A potentially sinister figure emerges,
but not a strong one. Faith in the doctor's authority and in the sincerity
of his human concerns no longer sustains the doctor's image. The play
attacks the man's professional self-esteem. When the mask falls, the great
man turns into a kind of rather sinister buffoon. The shadow of the
records of medical men in concentration camps and gulags may well have
helped to corrode the exemplary image.

The doctor figure, with his growing importance and his fictional past,
and because of the nature of his work and the human relations it involves
—far more intimate than those, for instance, of the physicist or engineer
—can be put to a number of fictional uses. When the psychoanalyst
doubles with the physician or, differently, with the electronic technician,
the persona of the doctor can become heavily charged with the myths,
fears, dilemmas, conscious or not, that inhabit our psyches. He is readily
cast as the visible impersonation of the enigmatic. This is the image of
the doctor that in antithetical ways Camus and Céline demythicized,
returning the doctor to the dimensions of the common human condition
as portrayed in their fictional discourse.

Doctor and Writer: Dr. Destouches and His Quadruple Mask

The, in my opinion, much-maligned Dr. Destouches[2] (Céline was his pen
name) was a practicing physician and remained one all his life. He is not,
to be sure, the only doctor-writer in the annals of literature. But he is
certainly the one whose professional status as a doctor has been most

thoroughly obscured: first by violent reactions to his involvements in the political arena of the thirties and forties; and second by the literary medium he fashioned for his particular expressive needs. The personality of the man has been distorted by confusions between the doctor himself and the masks he used to detach his fictions from the realistic mode and to situate them within the satiric and fantastic. Céline, the writer; Dr. Bardamu, the narrator, the flow of whose idiosyncratic, highly colored, truculent and dazzlingly inventive and comic language hurtles us through the eight bulky volumes of Célinian fiction; Ferdinand Bardamu, the medical student, seedy doctor and protagonist of *Journey to the End of the Night;* and finally the nocturnal Robinson of that same novel, are four such masks. (Dr. Bardamu is the teller of the story of which Ferdinand Bardamu is the protagonist. We assume, though we cannot be sure, that they are the same character but at different stages in life.) Of the four masks, Robinson, like Céline, is not identified as a doctor. Granted that there are innumerable permutations among them, they are nonetheless distinct personae. To judge Dr. Destouches in terms of these personae is to confuse the man with the satirist, and the satirist with his masks. Since the confusion has been fairly prevalent and has obscured the quality of the work and its import, it is, I feel, useful here to take a look at the doctor, stripped of the man's questionable and not impartial legend.

Dr. Destouches, an acquaintance notes, was "a real doctor, not an amateur." And he presents the following testimony: "I penetrated into the intimacy of the practician when he tended my children and later amongst his patients at the Clichy dispensary" (in a working-class section of Paris). The doctor, he observes, was a man of "infinite patience, kindness, gentleness, whom nothing discouraged"; a man "without needs, without vice, without a car, without a servant . . . who drank only water and never smoked."[3] In regard to his patients, Dr. Destouches does not seem to have been professionally delinquent; rather, the opposite.

That young Dr. Destouches had great respect for his profession, the preface of his 1924 thesis indicates. There he explains his choice to "study a great doctor's work": "If our choice fell on P. I. Semmelweis, it is because medical thought, so beautiful, so generous, possibly the only really human thought that exists in this world, has set its easily deciphered imprint on every page of his life."[4]

The paradox then arises as to why L.-F. Céline, the writer, through the narrator and Ferdinand, projects in his work one of the more fantastically ferocious and farcical parades of doctors, patients, and medical institutions in our literature. This is more particularly true of *Journey to the End of the Night,* upon which I shall focus my discussion.

Céline deliberately chose an explosive literary mode: the satiric, picaresque narrative. Along with his satiric dismantling of the social pieties (the traditional enterprise of satire), Céline introduced, through his choice of the doctor as protagonist and narrator, a biological vision unique in its force and precision. From such minor disgraces as varicose veins, pyorrhea and bad breath, to the cancers "mounting upon you from behind meticulous and gory," to the syndromes of alcoholism and malnutrition, descriptions of the biological ignominies to which human beings are heir create a kind of "garden of human disintegration" worthy of Hieronymus Bosch, whom Céline admired.

Clearly Céline makes full use of Dr. Destouches's medical experience although, as J. H. Matthews sensibly notes, he does not write in his role as doctor, ministering to his patients. His choice of medium and the strange blend of the comic, lyric and horrendously realistic flow of his carefully controlled language define the mode of perception whereby, like Swift before him, he removes events and scenes from the level of the unbearably realistic to the fantastic. The novel is not only about the scenes and events that follow each other in loosely connected sequences. It is about what the flow reveals.

In the opening pages of *Journey to the End of the Night,* the protagonist Ferdinand describes the human beings his pal has dignified by the term "the French race" as "clods like himself; bleary shivering and lousy" prone to "hunger, pestilence and cold."[5] It is this contrast between the sedulous cultivation of high-minded images of humanity and the biological reality of the human organism that Céline exploits. And the journey he takes us on is surely linked to the physician's view of the reality we hide from ourselves. That we are not the only living organisms in this world is what *Journey* conveys. And it stresses the presence of the bacilli, the germs, the streptococci that batten upon us, organisms perhaps better equipped by now for survival than we ourselves. In Céline's work, disease is not a symbol or a metaphor. It is an organic lesion; and it is a sign, medical and social, proliferating in our modern urban city slums. Human beings, as Céline sees them, are an endangered species, fast losing their biological capacity for maintaining an organic equilibrium in a threatening environment. This is so because of the ignorance, stupidity and neglect so gleefully depicted in the narrative, a consequence of a general inattention to physical human needs. The doctors he depicts, including his Bardamu, are parties to this dereliction. He could not have made his point had he chosen as narrator and witness an exemplary figure. Literally and literarily speaking, Ferdinand is made of the same stuff as his patients. *Journey to the End of the Night* was surely born of a "medical thought," and perhaps even more pertinently of a sweeping medical imagination.

The Doctor's Testimony—Dr. Rieux as Chronicler of the Plague

If *Journey* with its medical personae was born of a doctor's concern, the fictional Dr. Rieux of Camus's *The Plague* was a latecomer in Camus's novel. In his role as chronicler of a fictional encounter between humanity and a pestilence, he had been preceded by a lycée professor of literature. It was the topic in this instance that generated the persona. But it is not primarily as a physician that, Dr. Rieux informs us, he undertook his task.

For it was only when the plague had loosened its grip on the city of Oran that the doctor "resolved to compile the chronicle." His purpose is not to provide a medical account of the epidemic, but to "bear witness in favor of those plague-stricken people; so that some memorial of the injustice and outrage done them might endure; and to state quite simply what we learn in time of pestilence: that there are more things to admire in men than to despair."[6] It is no secret that it was originally Camus's intent to use the traditional analogy of collective disaster and epidemic to come to grips with the grim experience of World War II. The Black Death, the most dreaded of the pandemics that swept the world in the past,[7] was the form of infection he selected. Understandably enough, the analogy only started to work to Camus's satisfaction with the adoption of the doctor-narrator. It was only through the doctor's perspective that Camus was able to free his narrative from those traditional views of illness as punishment, perverse choice, or fate that Susan Sontag considered in her essay. He was thereby able to renew the significance of the analogy in terms of a modern medical experience.

"Before proceeding further with disease history," writes William McNeill in *Plagues and Peoples,* "it is worth pointing out the parallels between the microparasitism of infectious disease and the macroparasitism of military operations. . . . Macroparasitism, leading to the development of powerful military and political organization, has its counterpart in the biological defenses human populations create when exposed to the microparasitism of bacteria and viruses. In other words, warfare and disease are connected by more than rhetoric and the pestilences that have so often marched with and in the wake of armies." In this view, Camus's analogy of plague and war could hardly be more apposite. Furthermore, the role of modern medicine, which has devised a therapeutic of defense against the invading bacilli by building up the inner defenses of the body against the invader and simultaneously acting on the outer environment, was particularly germane to the perspective Camus wished to adopt. Camus wished to bypass the current indictments of leaders and ideologies to explore what we might call the pathology of war, the conditions it creates and the toll it takes in human suffering. His choice of chronicler defines and circumscribes the area and frame of the fiction as it had done in the case of Céline. And the modern relation of physician to plague transforms the significance of the traditional analogy.

The outbreak of plague in Oran is contained within the city, localized. Although no cure is applicable, the nature of the disease is known. Within the narrative frame the doctor does not consider it as a manifestation of the wrath of God, a visitation linked to moral wrong doing; or as an inevitable happening. He sees it for what it is: a breakdown in the taken-for-granted immunity of a population to a particular bacillus. And he applies the therapeutic measures available in the emergency. But when the emergency is over, his role as doctor is superseded by a nonmedical reaction to the experience: anger. His language becomes emotionally charged as he thinks back over the past embattled months. The plague appears as "a sort of crime"; an "outrage and an injustice"; a hideous infliction of useless suffering. And paradoxically, as an instrument of revelation, not because of any virtue linked to its action but because it brings human beings a heightening of awareness of their real stature, of their capacity to endure and to refuse that the disease's rule should go unchallenged.[8]

The physician here joins the parade of Camus's "absurd" paradigmatic men; but he is humanized by the compassion that Camus diagnoses as the initial source of his choice of profession. It is that compassion, and not his skill as medical practitioner, which distinguishes him from other human beings. That he knows his skill is limited adds a certain human pathos to the character. He cannot dominate the plague. This is an essential factor in Camus's demythification of the popular image of the doctor as healer. It is natural, though, that the persona of the doctor-narrator in *The Plague* should take on the human qualities and high seriousness characteristic of the perspectives he establishes. As in the case of Céline's Ferdinand, he is cut out of the same literary material as the testimony he bears: the lucidity, the endurance, the untiring dedication, the sense of human solidarity and shared responsibility that in Camus's eyes define human values. In a sense he appears as the moral antithesis of Céline's Ferdinand. Yet if we remain within the frame of the fiction, Rieux and Ferdinand have something in common. Ferdinand describes the depredations of disease preying upon the masses of human beings in the normal course of life. Dr. Rieux is witness to the outbreak of a collective infection that strikes and destroys with dramatic suddenness. But for both, the depth of concern is first for the physical being, the suffering human body. The doctor's function in both novels is the same: to shake the reader out of a kind of callousness and indifference in that particular area. It is a departure from the trend toward abstract approaches to the understanding of human beings.

Within the Frame of Fiction

Ferdinand is initiated into the reality in which he is enmeshed on the battlefields of World War I. Dr. Rieux, for whom the epidemic is an invasion, is also cast in the role of combatant. As a professional man he is responsible for mobilizing all available forces in the fight against the invader. In this he is not seen as a lone figure. The appearance of the plague activates a network of forces. Rieux's colleagues in the town proceed as he does, noting the symptoms, tabulating and reporting the progress of the disease. The city bureaucracy establishes statistics. The medical association convenes in order to determine the course of action and meets with the city administrators to persuade them to apply the measures prescribed: the rules and regulations that, worldwide, record the current state of epidemiology. The doctor's job is to see that they are stringently adhered to. He is not engaged in a private undertaking; clearly theirs is a collective action professionally defined. Although the novel is focused on Dr. Rieux, it is clear that he represents a corps of medical men who are, as best they can, "doing their job"; an unglamorous and exhausting job. Camus has underplayed the human resistances they encounter. The city bureaucracy procrastinates but heeds their advice; the international organization heeds their signals, though the help sent is "too little and too late." But, once the diagnosis is established, the doctor's action is prescribed: his profession precludes choice. Camus sketches only two other doctor figures: Dr. Richard, who shows a professional reluctance to declare an emergency (for doing so would disrupt normal life) until there is no uncertainty as to the diagnosis; and the more fully depicted Dr. Castel, an old colonial physician who faces reality more brutally.

Once the impersonal machinery of treatment and prophylaxis starts to work (diagnosis, ambulance, hospital or quarantine camp, burial), the outer image of the doctor changes. Inflexible and tireless, to the patients he appears ruthless and inhuman. They are snatched from their homes, stripped of their identities, their private feelings negated. The ambiguous dark image dramatized in *The Doctor and the Devils* surfaces and is clearly adumbrated in one episode. A small boy is losing his personal battle against the plague. To make up for the lack of needed serum Dr. Castel had been developing a substitute as yet untried. Rieux and he decided to try it in a last attempt to save the child. It fails; but it greatly prolongs the child's agony. Dr. Castel, observing the struggle objectively, decides to try again. But to the nonmedical onlooker, doctor and plague appear as accomplices in the martyrdom of the child. But within the narrative no further doubt is raised as to the rightness of the doctors' action. Engaged in an unequal struggle they can neglect no chances. And their actions receive the support of the best men in the community, who rally around them. Rieux is surrounded by personal friends. He is universally respected for his moral and intellectual integrity. He is not glamorized by Camus.

In contrast, Ferdinand cuts a shabby figure. This is inherent to the literary medium chosen. Semiclown, semiknave, he acts as a kind of decoy. He, too, from the day of his projection onto a battlefield, is engaged in an unequal struggle. His strategy, as befits his literary role, is flight. This keeps him moving so that Céline can unfold the seamy side of society and the horrid realities beneath its surface.

In Ferdinand's constituency, Garenne-Rancy (Rancid Rabbit Warren), his empty pockets and shabby clientele authorize a bland reversal of perspective. As the doctor stumbles from one desperate case to another, he encounters a maze of ignorance and prejudice. One of the grim and baroquely comic effects is to change the relation of patient and physician, generating an ironic image of the doctor as victim of his patients. And indeed what they require of him is in fact not a cure but the ratification of their efforts to achieve financial security through medicare or other less innocent projects. The horror of Ferdinand's situation within the general pattern of dereliction is shown in a scene in which he is called to tend a young woman who has attempted an abortion on herself. He listens to the slow drip-drip of blood flowing from the bed to the floor while the family envisages her care in terms of standards of respectability. The girl will die, for the family will not sign the authorization the doctor needs to transport her to a hospital. Ferdinand's anger, despair and disgust are signs of his frustration. He fails to fulfill even the most elementary of his medical duties.

As a comic relief to this parade of horror, Céline, through Ferdinand, brings into play an entertaining gallery of medical eccentrics, semimountebanks, semi-self-seeking egotists, whose names indicate their comic function. There is, for example, the urbane Bestombes (Tomb-fucker), the magnificent fraud in charge of the rehabilitation center for soldiers evacuated from the front as cases of mental breakdown. Behind a hilarious rhetoric that justifies a therapeutic resting on a specious mythology of adjustment to the idea of death, the doctor is practicing the fine art of a double evasion: of his medical responsibilities and of the firing line, conniving with the military establishment who want the men back at the front. This is therapeutic comedy, not reality.

Then there is Dr. Parapine—a sexually charged name (*par rapine:* by rapine)—a harmless fossil lodged in the recesses of the Bioduret Institute (a caricature of the Pasteur Institute). A decrepit old man whose critical reputation rests on an obscure paper years behind him, he stagnates in his musty lab—amid his rotting experimental rabbits—nursing his hatred of the director and his obsessive attraction to the adolescent girls of the neighboring lycée. And there is Dr. Baryton (Dr. Baritone) who directs the lunatic asylum in which Parapine and Ferdinand eventually find refuge as technical assistants. A fraud, like Bestombes, Baryton is also a man who persuades himself by his own rhetoric of the validity of his inept therapeutic treatments. He too finally takes off, leaving his patients to the care of his assistants.

In all three cases it is the interplay of sordid reality and grandiose rhetoric, both of course comically exaggerated, from which Céline draws his burlesque effects. Distorted though these characters are, as befits the medium adopted, behind the satiric mask they are never diabolical. They are in fact all too recognizably human. And if devils there are, they are those shared by Céline's society-at-large.

It would be interesting for a historian of medical practices to explore the real targets of Céline's satire in the twenties and thirties; and to assess the pertinency of his attack upon the professional and state neglect of the vital needs of a modern proletariat crowding into the polluted, unsanitary, sprawling, working-class suburbs of Paris, undermined by the unchecked progress of alcoholism and tuberculosis. Céline fiercely points to the low standards of psychiatric care and the widespread evidence of inept medical practice, if not malpractice, dispensed to the poor.

The lampooning itself is only possible, curiously enough, because, however different their aesthetic intent, Dr. Destouches like Albert

Camus measures the distance that exists between the doctor's task and the resources at his command: thence the burden society puts upon the man. But whereas Céline's concern is medical and social, even, one might say, practical, Camus's is metaphysical and moral. Céline's cry of alarm is historically situated; Camus's fictional model is an illustration of man's fate as he understands it. But in both cases the doctor emerges as the figure most critically involved in the future of the human race.

NOTES

1. New Directions, 1953. A dramatization of a story by Ronald Taylor.

2. I here regretfully admit my complete disagreement with the analyses of my colleague Bettina Knapp concerning Céline. In my opinion a much more impartial evaluation of both the man and the work can be found in J. H. Matthews's study of Céline, *The Inner Dream: Céline as Novelist* (Syracuse: Syracuse University Press, 1978).

3. "Chez Gen Paul à Montmartre," by André Pulicani (Paris, *L'Herne* no. 3, 1963), pp. 37, 38. The translations are mine unless otherwise indicated.

4. The preface was first published in 1963 in the review *L'Herne* no. 3, pp. 163–64.

5. *Journey to the End of the Night*, trans. John H. P. Marks. (New Directions Paperbook No. 84, 1960), p. 4. All quotations refer to this edition.

6. *The Plague*, trans. Stuart Gilbert (New York: Knopf, 1961), p. 278. All quotations refer to this edition.

7. William McNeill has given a rather interesting account of their manifestations and effects in *Plagues and Peoples* (New York: Doubleday, 1976). There is a striking similarity between the conclusion of his account and that of Camus's narrative: "infectious disease which antedated the emergence of humankind will last as long as humanity itself, and will surely remain, as it has been hitherto, one of the fundamental parameters and determinants of human history" (p. 291). Rieux knew "that the plague bacillus never disappears for good . . . and that perhaps the day would come when for the bane and enlightenment of men, it would rouse up its rats again and send them forth to die in a happy city" (*The Plague*, p. 278).

8. A factor in this view of the relation of doctor to disease is certainly Camus's own experience of illness. The first bout of pulmonary tuberculosis he suffered at seventeen was followed by recurrent attacks in 1937, '42, '49, '50, '54, and '58. Tuberculosis, the young Camus said, was "metaphysical," an invisible and daily reminder of the human fate. It functions on the individual level as the plague does on the collective via an invasion of the biological organism; and in terms of the therapy available to Camus in those years, would at best be contained, though not cured, by the patient's concentrated effort. It is significant, within the larger frame of the fiction, that Dr. Rieux's wife dies of tuberculosis, which her husband cannot cure.

A Moral Image of Modern Man:
The Doctor in the Work of Martin du Gard
Mary Jean Green

In his fictional chronicle of the Thibault family, written in the troubled period between the two world wars, Roger Martin du Gard (1881–1958) examines the different responses to life of two brothers, Jacques and Antoine Thibault. Jacques, the eternal rebel, is a political activist. Antoine, less alienated from his society, is a doctor. Although Jacques dies bravely and selflessly in a futile effort to prevent the outbreak of the First World War, it is the figure of Antoine, as both doctor and dying patient, that embodies Martin du Gard's vision of human moral action in the chaotic and incomprehensible modern world.

Summing up the conclusion of Martin du Gard's Nobel prize–winning novels, Albert Camus wrote: "Of Martin du Gard's two central characters, the priest and the doctor, the former has all but disappeared. The Thibault series ends with the death of a doctor, alone among other doctors. It seems that questions are now asked only within the domain of humanity."[1] Camus's words, and Martin du Gard's novels, point to the modern displacement of the religious by the secular, a replacement of the ideal of sainthood by that of the doctor.

Dr. Antoine Thibault's world is clearly that of the twentieth century, with its advanced technology, its promise of material prosperity, and— as the war suddenly reveals to him—its unprecedented potential for mass destruction. Unlike his perpetually discontented younger brother, Antoine is a man with a healthy appetite for personal happiness and an active sensuality. It is his preference for the concrete over the abstract, a life of action rather than contemplation, that has drawn him to the study of medicine and its daily contact with physical reality. Medical science represents, in his eyes, "the greatest achievement of twenty centuries of efforts in all fields of knowledge, the richest domain open to the genius of man" (1. 1130).

Martin du Gard is so convinced of the importance of Antoine's work as a doctor that he devotes an entire volume of his series, *The Consultation*, to describing one afternoon in his character's medical practice. As Louis

Aragon has commented, "it has always amazed me that it was necessary to await the modern era and Martin du Gard to find in a novel a doctor who is really practicing medicine and not arranging marriages or setting up industries in mountain villages."[2] Antoine's overriding concern is the alleviation of human suffering, and he gives each of the cases before him an exclusive, sympathetic attention. Although he is not indifferent to the growth of his reputation as a specialist in children's diseases, Antoine does not allow his personal concerns to distract his attention from the welfare of his patients. Always sensitive to beautiful women, he nevertheless refuses to let a seductive mother prevent his careful diagnosis of her stepdaughter's spinal tuberculosis. And he spends more time treating an inflammation on the arm of a neighborhood orphan than attending to his richer clientele.

Since many of his patients are children, Antoine finds himself vaguely troubled by the metaphysical implications of the cases he sees before him. The repeated evidence of the suffering of innocents seems to call into question the very order of the universe. But Antoine's inability to understand the overarching structure of reality cannot threaten his conviction that his own activity within it is of some value.

Indeed, a superabundance of work leaves him little time for adequate meals, let alone metaphysical speculation, and he must develop his ethics in response to the demands of the moment. Without the support of the traditional religious world view, which had died with his father's generation, Antoine, like many other men of his century, must discover values and principles of action through his own experience. His medical duties themselves, as he tells a friend, provide him with a rule of conduct. As a doctor of integrity, he is always careful to make an honest diagnosis, even when such a diagnosis may cost him personal advancement. This actually happens later in the war, when the military medical command refuses to admit the existence of typhoid at the front, despite abundant evidence to the contrary. But Antoine is able to bend his principles when strict honesty would cause needless suffering: in *The Consultation* he lies without remorse to reassure a guilt-ridden father who blames his son's retardation on his own youthful exposure to syphilis.

Antoine's operating principle, that departure from conventional moral principles may be justified in the effort to relieve suffering, is put to a severe test in the case of a friend's dying child, for whom he can do nothing. Yet he refuses the silent supplication of the father, as well as the more articulate exhortation of a young medical assistant, to put the child out of her misery with a merciful overdose. Stammering something about "respect for life" and, more significantly, "a limit to our power" (1. 1117), he is bothered by his inability to fully articulate his intuitive rejection of this appeal. Not long afterwards, however, Antoine is confronted with a similar situation, and this time the patient is his own father, who is dying a long and difficult death from renal failure. Martin du Gard's detailed symptomatic description of the father's condition has drawn him the unqualified praise of medical critics, some of whom have devoted entire theses to his works.[3] As the physical degeneration progresses, the old man has time to make his preparations for an imminent death before sinking into a state of delirium broken by periodic crises. After nights of helpless observation of his father's suffering, and unable to bear the strain any longer, Antoine finally administers a calming—and fatal— injection. What he had not been able to do *as a doctor*, who, he believes, must impose severe limitations on his sometimes godlike power, he can now do in good conscience as a son faced with a suffering, terminally ill father.

The provisional morality that Antoine develops through his experience as a general practitioner must soon confront two major challenges: his inheritance of the family fortune and the outbreak of the First World War. Each of these situations, of course, reflects a more general characteristic of the modern world: a preoccupation with material prosperity and the possibility of mass destruction. The inheritance of wealth is by far the less serious challenge; yet it threatens to distract Antoine from his meaningful life of service to patients. He uses his inheritance to pursue his dream of making his name immortal by setting up his own luxurious private research laboratory. Martin du Gard is not criticizing Antoine's desire to participate in medical research, but rather his preoccupation with personal glory, which threatens to turn him away from his original concern for human beings and his contact with patients. Although Antoine plans to take the credit for discoveries, the actual research is to be done by his three young research assistants, whose services he has bought. Progressively cutting himself off from real work and from real human beings, Antoine demonstrates the dangers of an all-consuming commitment to personal glory and material wealth, temptations inherent in the career of a modern doctor.

Antoine is so taken up with his own concerns that he is deaf to the noise of the world around him, and even the urgent warnings of his politically conscious brother Jacques fail to rouse him from the illusion that he exists independently of his social environment. But the year is 1914, and Antoine is soon forced to acknowledge his participation in the common destiny when he is ordered to join his medical unit at the front. On the battlefield he rediscovers the importance of his original vocation of active service to patients, and he sees the worthlessness of his vain ambitions, to which the war has brought a decisive end.

Yet the war, with its involvement of previously inconceivable numbers of troops, its use of modern weaponry, its manipulation of the media for mass propaganda, raises other problems. In this new situation Antoine must seek a model of individual action that can most effectively preserve his basic humanistic values. He is momentarily tempted by his brother Jacques's political action, just as Martin du Gard himself was attracted by political involvement in the troubled years that preceded World War II. But Jacques's suicidal attempt to prevent the war proves futile: badly injured in the crash of a plane from which he had planned to drop pacifist leaflets, he is shot in the panic of the initial French retreat.

The nineteenth-century ideal of individual heroism is symbolically over-whelmed by the mass catastrophes of the twentieth. Individual action seems to have little significance in modern history. In Martin du Gard's historical analysis, even great men like Jaurès and Clemenceau fail to dominate events. But, although individuals cannot change history, they can continue to combat its destructive consequences. Here again the model is a doctor, in the person of Antoine's revered teacher, Dr. Philip. Philip has effected one of the major life-saving enterprises of the war by reorganizing a medical service ill-prepared for the massive casualties. Antoine, too, performs a life-saving service, more humble but equally valuable, risking his life under enemy fire in the most primitive of condi-tions. The wartime doctor thus embodies a moral image of modern man, fighting to preserve human values in the midst of chaos.

At the end of the war, as he lies dying in a clinic for victims of poison gas, Antoine finally has the time to face the ultimate questions always pushed aside by the demands of the moment. In this meditation of a dying doctor, which forms the substance of the last novel in the Thibault series, Martin du Gard comes to a new and more profound understanding of the meaning of the medical profession. Writing in his journal, Antoine realizes that his profession has provided him with the foundations of an entire philosophy of life, which has proven capable of steering him through the menacing and unpredictable world born of the war.

The doctor, with his experience of life and death, is accustomed to facing unpleasant facts without illusion. Antoine must carry this painful lucidity to its logical conclusion when a consultation with Philip forces him to recognize that his own condition has become incurable. As a doctor, he cannot delude himself with hope for a miracle, and he has always known that all his therapeutic successes were only temporary victories in the long battle with death. But, like the doctor who continues his efforts despite this knowledge, the individual must go on with his own struggle in a world that provides little reason for optimism.

The world view he has adopted as a man of science, accustomed to dealing only with the facts before him, leaves Antoine no room for belief in immortality, or even in the comforting historical theories of modern political doctrines. These he dismisses as illusory consolations that inter-fere with lucid analysis. As he tells his nephew, a "man of value," like a doctor, must preserve his freshness of vision: "Each disease—like each social crisis—presents itself as a case without identical precedent, as an *exceptional* case, for which a new therapy is always to be invented" (2. 982). Any solution adopted must be regarded as provisional: "we must re-nounce the notion of a stable truth, we must hold something to be true only with great reservations and only until such time as we have proof to the contrary" (1. 1386). Antoine sees life as a continual process of re-search, like that of a doctor who adopts new treatments and submits them to the test of experience. He offers as an instructive example the early use of antiseptics, when a too thorough application of the new remedy killed living cells as well as bacteria.

Although science cannot be expected to solve all human problems, the progress of medicine, extraordinary in this century, provides a realistic example of what it can do. In the modest hope of contributing to this progress, Antoine refrains from ending his suffering with a fatal injection in order to keep a daily record of his own terminal case. But the First World War has also provided a vivid illustration of the destructive potential of technological progress. As Antoine, himself a victim of this technology, contemplates the vastness of the starry universe, he finds a certain consolation in this evidence of human finitude and realizes that the study of science, if understood properly, can also help man to accept his own limitations. His medical practice, as distinct from its theory, has brought Antoine into daily contact with human beings, and it is the knowledge drawn from this experience that provides him with a modest optimism. Seeing himself and his contemporaries as the most recent links in a chain stretching back into time, he affirms the continuing existence of a human moral consciousness that provides some foundation for a realistic faith in human progress, even if only in a distant future.

Through his close observation of Antoine Thibault's life as a doctor, Martin du Gard has given us a model of individual ethical action in the modern world. In his consultations with patients, his heroic service on the battlefield, and, especially, in his courageous confrontation with his own death, Martin du Gard's Dr. Antoine Thibault has consistently exemplified the highest ideals of the medical profession; and his example becomes, by extension, a model for all human action. Despite his lucid skepticism, he affirms the creative, life-sustaining power of human science in a world dominated by death and destruction; the strength of human fraternity against the inhuman forces of disease and war; and the value of individual ethical endeavors in the context of a modern mass society.

NOTES

1. Albert Camus, Preface to *Oeuvres complètes de Roger Martin du Gard* (Paris: Gallimard, Bibliothèque de la Pléiade, 1955), 1, p. xvii. All quotations from Martin du Gard's works refer to this edition; all translations are mine. Stuart Gilbert has translated *The Thibaults* (New York: Viking, 1939).

2. Quoted in Michel Laparade, *Réflexions sur quatre médecins de roman: Essai de définition d'un humanisme médical contemporain* (*Reflections on Four Fictional Doctors: Toward a Definition of a Contemporary Medical Humanism*) (diss., Faculté Mixte de Médecine et de Pharmacie, Bordeaux, 1948), p. 14.

3. Although not a doctor himself, Martin du Gard had, at various times, sat in on courses in both medicine and psychiatry and always consulted medical friends about Antoine's cases. For analyses of his work by medical students, see Laparade's thesis and Gilbert Almeras, *La Médecine dans "Les Thibault" de M. Roger Martin du Gard* (*Medicine in Martin du Gard's "Thibaults"*) (diss., Faculté de Médecine, Paris, 1946), p. 45 ff.

The Healer in Shakespeare
Marjorie Garber

Disease in Shakespeare's plays is almost always a metaphor, a sign of some moral failing in the society, the state, or the individual. John of Gaunt makes this explicit in *Richard II* when, speaking from his own deathbed, he insists that Richard and not he is the dying patient: "Thy deathbed is no lesser than thy land, / Wherein thou liest in reputation sick; / And thou, too careless patient as thou art, / Commit'st thy anointed body to the cure / Of those physicians that first wounded thee" (2.1.95–99).[1] The "physicians" are flatterers and favorites in the court, who have led Richard away from kingliness and toward profligacy and self-indulgence.

A similar illness afflicts the Scotland of Macbeth, as he himself acknowledges, asking a doctor to "cast / The water [i.e., analyze the urine] of my land, find her disease, / And purge it to a sound and pristine health" (5.3.50–52). But he himself is the disease of which his land is sick, and it can only be cured by his overthrow and death.

In *Henry IV Part 2* and *Henry V,* venereal disease—or, to use our apt modern euphemism, "social disease"—becomes a metaphor for the dissoluteness and morbidity of Falstaff's tavern world. Shakespeare's other term for this ailment is "malady of France," and France is also the country with which England is at war. In effect England is suffering from *two* maladies of France, one spread from within her own corrupt society, the other caught from the enemy without.

Occasionally the pertinence of the disease metaphor is observed and commented upon by characters within the plays. When in *Julius Caesar* Brutus remarks that Caesar has "the falling-sickness," epilepsy, Cassius turns that fact into a bitter pun. "No," he retorts, "Caesar hath it not; but you and I, / And honest Casca, we have the falling-sickness" (1.2.253–54). As underlings they are falling as Caesar rises, declining in political power as he grows in strength. Likewise when King Lear prefers the flattery of his elder daughters to Cordelia's loving silence and disinherits his youngest (and erstwhile favorite) child, Kent admonishes him in ironic terms: "Kill thy physician and the fee bestow / Upon the foul disease" (1.1.163–64). The king's action is a choice of sickness over health—as Lear's subsequent madness will confirm.

Madness—real, feigned, or falsely diagnosed as such—is one of the diseases that rages throughout Shakespearean drama, from *The Comedy of Errors* and *Twelfth Night* to *Hamlet* and *Lear*. Another, and perhaps the most common Shakespearean malady, is insomnia. For those many characters afflicted with it, sleeplessness is a symptom of a troubled conscience. Thus Richard III lies "guiltily awake" in his tent at Bosworth Field, while his rival, Richmond, sleeps peacefully through the night (5.3.147). King Henry IV, wandering through his palace in the small hours of the morning, asks painfully "Sleep, O gentle sleep, / Nature's soft nurse, how have I frighted thee?" (*2 Henry IV*, 3.1.5–6). Brutus muses that "Since Cassius first did whet me against Caesar, / I have not slept" (*JC* 2.1.61–62). Iago gloats over the spectacle of Othello tortured with jealousy: "Not poppy nor mandragora, / Nor all the drowsy syrups of the world, / Shall ever medicine thee to that sweet sleep / Which thou owedst yesterday" (3.3.327–30). The witches predict of Macbeth that "Sleep shall neither night nor day / Hang upon his penthouse lid" (1.-3.19–20); Lady Macbeth tells her husband that he "lack[s] the season of all natures, sleep" (3.4.141), and then she herself falls prey to sleepwalking and nightmares. The mad King Lear, rescued by Cordelia, is placed under the care of a doctor and sleeps, to awaken sane once more. Leontes, like Othello consumed with jealousy, complains that he has "Nor night nor day no rest" (*WT* 2.2.1). The loyal courtiers in *The Tempest* fall instantly to sleep to Ariel's music, while the traitors among them remain awake.

Much has been written about "disease imagery" in the plays, and about the relationship between the sick king and the suffering land. Not only in the great tragedies—*Hamlet, Othello, Macbeth, King Lear*—but also in the comedies and romances the illness or obsession of the protagonist afflicts the entire society of the play, as well as its language. In *The Winter's Tale*, for example, Leontes's unfounded jealousy leads to the languishing and death of his young son, and also to a proliferation of words like "sickness," "disease," and "infection" to describe the moral and social climate of the Sicilian court. Sicilia becomes a waste land without life, love, or an heir to the throne, until Leontes accepts the guidance of Paulina as his "physician" (2.3.54) and counsellor, and is reunited with his wife and daughter.

But—as this last instance suggests—there is another, less frequently noted aspect to the metaphor of illness as it affects Shakespeare's dramatic world. The plays present a number of physicians, doctors and healers, whose ministrations are often as metaphorical and symbolic as the diseases they attempt to cure. Shakespeare is not particularly interested in physical ailments of a literal kind. When, as frequently happens, one of his characters is wounded, whether in a duel (Mercutio in *Romeo and Juliet*), in battle (the bleeding captain in *Macbeth*), in a treacherous attack (Cassio in *Othello*) or as the result of an unwise word or jest (Sir Toby and Sir Andrew in *Twelfth Night*), there is an immediate outcry to "fetch a surgeon"—but in no play does a surgeon ever appear. Instead the call for a surgeon serves as an exit line, signaling the departure of the injured man from the stage. A surgeon's work in Shakespeare's time would have been limited to the most basic manual skills, as Falstaff indicates in his famous lines on honor: "Can honor set to a leg? No. Or an arm? No. Or take away the grief of a wound? No. Honor hath no skill in surgery then? No." (*1 Henry IV* 5.1.130–33). There is not much scope here for metaphor or philosophy. In fact, the only "symbolic" role played by a surgeon in Shakespearean drama is achieved through the absence of one—when Shylock refuses to supply a surgeon to stanch Antonio's wounds as he prepares to exact his pound of flesh. The surgeon here becomes an emblem of that quality of mercy that Shylock cannot find in the letter of the law.

Although there are no surgeons among Shakespeare's dramatic characters, there are medical doctors, and also amateurs of medical practice. Friar Lawrence in *Romeo and Juliet* is skilled in the distillation of plants and herbs, and observes with some sophistication that the same flower may provide both poison and succor: "For this, being smelt, with that part cheers each part; / Being tasted, stays all senses with the heart" (2.-3.25–26). Based upon this knowledge he concocts a sleeping potion for Juliet that will counterfeit the symptoms of death for a period of forty-two hours, after which she will "awake as from a pleasant sleep" (4.1.106). In the same play Romeo locates a poor apothecary whom he has observed "culling of simples," (5.1.40), or gathering medicinal herbs, and buys from him a dram of lethal poison. In *Hamlet* we find that Laertes possesses a similarly lethal drug, "an unction" he bought from a "mountebank" or quack (4.7.141), so virulent that there is no remedy once it enters the bloodstream. And Claudius, too, has poison in store, ready to drop into Hamlet's cup in the duel scene. A more benevolent compound is used by Puck in *A Midsummer Night's Dream:* the juice of a flower called "love-in-idleness," which when placed on the eyelids of sleeping men or women makes them "madly dote" on the next creatures that they see.

Each of these drugs is part of the pattern of symbolic meaning for the play in which it appears. Friar Lawrence's wisdom about the ambiguous powers of herbs does not extend, as it should, to an assessment of human frailties, and his plan for the "death" and restoration of Juliet would have been viewed by the Elizabethan audience as dangerously close to sacrilege: a resurrection intended by man rather than God. It is no surprise, therefore, that his stratagem miscarries, and leads ultimately to Juliet's real death. Romeo, paying the apothecary in gold, observes that it is the gold and not the poison that is truly malign: "I sell thee poison; thou hast sold me none" (5.1.83). His remark, typical of the lovers' idealism as contrasted with the materialism of their elders, is also part of a more extended pattern of symbolism in which gold becomes an emblem of failed understanding and false love. The poisoned cup and rapier of *Hamlet* are signs, not only of the rottenness and disease pervasive in Denmark, but also more specifically of poisoned sexuality: the cup is a traditional symbol for the female, the sword for the male. And the magic love juice of *A Midsummer Night's Dream* is a metaphor for the irrationality of love itself.

When we turn to those characters who are explicitly identified as doctors we find a significant pattern of similarities, one that might be thought to include the ministrations of the amateur medical practitioners we have just observed. In *Macbeth* a Scottish doctor attends on the sleep-walking Lady Macbeth and is horrified by what he sees and hears. When Macbeth irritably asks him "Canst thou not minister to a mind diseased, / Pluck from the memory a rooted sorrow, / Raze out the written troubles of the brain . . . with some sweet oblivious antidote?" (5.3.40–43) the doctor replies, "Therein the patient / Must minister to himself" (45–46). There is nothing he can do.

Gerard de Narbon, Helena's late father in *All's Well That Ends Well,* is said to have been "famous in his profession" and rightly so: "He was skillful enough to have lived still, if knowledge could be set up against mortality" (1.1.31–32). But knowledge cannot make a man immortal, and Gerard de Narbon is dead. Moreover, the king's present physicians in the same play, demonstrably less able than de Narbon, have given up on their patient, admitting that there is no way to save him. Like the Scottish doctor in Macbeth, these doctors are associated above all with a sense of their own limitation as healers. There are some cures they cannot effect, some knowledge they lack. Above all they lack a miraculous power over life and death.

The same point is made tellingly in the figure of Lord Cerimon, a physician in *Pericles* who appears in only one—but a very important—scene. Like Friar Lawrence, Cerimon has studied the healing properties of herbs. As he explains, "'Tis known, I ever / Have studied physic, through which secret art, / By turning o'er authorities, I have, / Together with my practice, made familiar / To me and to my aid the blest infusions / That dwell in vegetives, in metals, stones; / And I can speak of the disturbances / That nature works, and of her cures" (3.2.31–38). His skills and his generosity, says one of his aides, have built him a renown "that time shall never raze" (48). In the course of the scene that follows we will see Cerimon revive Thaisa, the wife of Pericles, who had been thought dead and cast overboard in her coffin. But—as with Friar Lawrence—this act of apparent "resurrection" is severely mitigated by the dramatic context.

The scene in which we encounter Cerimon begins with a conversation between him and a servant who has come for medicines to aid his master. But the doctor is uncompromisingly pessimistic: "Your master will be dead ere you return," he says. "There's nothing can be minist'red to nature / That can recover him" (3.2.7–9). With this gloomy prologue, an acknowledgment that he cannot restore the dead to life, the chest containing Thaisa is discovered, and under Cerimon's care she awakens. "They were too rough / That threw her in the sea," he says (79–80), again stressing the fact that his powers of healing are natural, not supernatural; she was never dead, only asleep. Furthermore, when the scene ends Cerimon closes it with a pious wish: "Aesculapius guide us!" (112). This may seem merely a conventional appeal to the hero-god of medicine, but the story of Aesculapius has a particular relevance here. Through his powers Hippolytus was raised to life again, at the request of the goddess Diana (Virgil, *Aeneid* 7.765–79). But when Zeus, the king of the gods, heard of this restoration, he was enraged that the natural sequence of life and death had been violated. In retribution he killed Aesculapius with a thunderbolt and sent him to the lower world. The warning—that physicians, however gifted, are mortal and therefore limited in their powers—is one that is repeatedly emphasized in Shakespeare's plays.

This firm dividing line between the professional healer and the miracle worker or god is bridged by one medial figure in the plays: the English king, Edward the Confessor, who is described in act 4 scene 3 of *Macbeth*. Edward's touch was said to be able to cure scrofula, a disease therefore known as "the king's evil."[2] We learn that he is beseiged for help by "wretched souls" whose sickness is beyond "the great assay of art"—the skills of the ordinary physician (141;143). "Strangely visited people, / All swoll'n and ulcerous, pitiful to the eye, / The mere despair of surgery, he cures, / Hanging a golden stamp about their necks, / Put on with holy prayers" (150–54). Edward is a holy king who cures, as opposed to the unholy Macbeth, who infects his land and subjects. And Edward's holy medicine of prayers also balances and contrasts with the unholy medicine of the witches, whose bubbling cauldron of "hell-broth" is (4.1.19) distilled from such ingredients as eye of newt, toe of frog, nose of Turk, and "finger of birth-strangled babe" (30).

But King Edward, later to become a saint, is a figure importantly different from the other mortal healers we have observed. Moreover, since he never actually appears upon the stage, but is instead only discussed by his admirers, he remains a sign rather than a dramatic character, an emblem of healing in a play preoccupied with disease. Yet there are some Shakespearean characters who do appear onstage and perform acts of restoration and healing seemingly beyond those of professional physicians. Perhaps significantly, all of these powerful figures are women.

One such healer is Helena, the daughter of the famous doctor Gerard de Narbon in *All's Well That Ends Well.* The king in that play suffers from a fistula and has "abandoned his physicians" in despair of a cure (1.1.14). As we have already noted, the doctors give him no hope, so that we are offered from the outset another reminder of the limited power of medicine. It cannot cure those who are doomed to die. But Helena has inherited her father's "receipts," or formulas, and adds to them her own faith and love. She is willing to forfeit her own life if she fails to cure the king, and this energetic certainty appears to act upon him more directly than any medicine. Like Antonio in *The Merchant of Venice* and Antipholus of Syracuse in *The Comedy of Errors* the king seems to be suffering from melancholy and resignation; when he is told that his subjects love him and want him to live, he replies despondently, "I fill a place, I know't"

(1.2.69). In effect he is waiting to die. But when Helena (called by one admiring courtier "Doctor She") enters his life, she offers him something that might be described as "the will to live." The subsequent "miracle" (2.3.1) owes something to the medical skills of Gerard de Narbon, and something to heaven, to which Helena ascribes her power; but a crucial third element is Helena's own resolute energy, determination, and hope. Having lost her own father, she becomes a kind of foster daughter to the king, and earns from him a dowry, the right to choose a nobleman for her husband.

There are several other versions of "Doctor She" in the later plays. Marina, the daughter of Pericles, is asked to use her "sacred physic" (*Pericles* 5.1.76) on a "kingly patient" (73) who will turn out to be her long-lost father. Thinking that his wife and child are dead, Pericles has fallen into a melancholy so extreme that he has not spoken for three months, and eats only "to prorogue his grief" (27), keeping himself alive that he may continue to mourn. Once again the doctors have despaired of a cure, but Marina, pledging to "use / My utmost skill in his recovery" (78–79), ministers to him not with medicine but with music. It is her own story that finally rouses him from his self-absorption, as he recognizes in its outlines the story of his own lost child. Filial love, accompanied by the soothing strains of music, restores him to language, life, and health.

In fact, music is a frequent accompaniment to these "miraculous" revivals. The doctor in *King Lear,* for example, calls for music to be played louder as he awakens the sleeping king. Cordelia, who stands by him, leans forward to kiss her father, and like Marina she speaks of herself as his physician: "O my dear father, restoration hang / Thy medicine upon my lips" (4.7.26–27). Once again the real cure, the real medicine, is filial love, the love of a daughter whom Lear had thought lost beyond recovery.

In *The Winter's Tale,* too, music is combined with the restoration of a lost daughter and wife, as Paulina awakens the supposed statue of Hermione, and reunites the grieving king Leontes with his family. Much earlier in the play—sixteen years earlier, according to its chronology—Paulina had tried to achieve this same reunion, at a time when Leontes, having falsely accused his wife of infidelity, found himself unable to sleep. Calling herself "your loyal servant, your physician" (2.3.54), she attempts to show him his newborn daughter, who closely resembles him. "I come to bring him sleep" (33), she declares. "I / Do come with words as medicinal as true, / Honest as either, to purge him of that humor / That presses him from sleep" (36–39). But Leontes rejects her ministrations, and must wait for the "miracle" of his daughter's return and his wife's apparent rebirth.

All of these situations present women in healing roles, ministering to patients whose suffering is spiritual as well as physical. The "arts" they use—and *art* is a frequent Shakespearean term for the skills of the physician—are "arts" in another sense as well: music and language—the story of the past, and a promise of love and nurture in the future. Pericles calls Marina "Thou that beget'st him that did thee beget" (5.1.199), and there is a way in which these healing women are indeed mothers, giving new life to men who are suffering a condition of living death. Like the holy king Edward, they offer a "healing benediction" (*Macbeth* 4.3.156) that revives the hopeless to hope, and cure a "king's evil" of a spiritual but no less deadly kind.

"Canst thou not minister to a mind diseased?" Macbeth asked his wife's physician, and received a negative reply. But through their art the healing women of Shakespeare's later plays do exactly that. Lear is restored from madness, Pericles from grief, Leontes from jealousy and remorseful guilt, the King of France in *All's Well* from physical illness, but also from melancholy and despair. The limitations that Shakespeare is so careful to point out in the powers of professional doctors and their medicines do not apply to such cures of the soul. Paulina does not literally bring Hermione back to life, any more than Cerimon can literally restore the dead. But in awakening the "statue" of Hermione she awakens Leontes, her real patient, and brings about a metaphorical rebirth of the spirit that is equally remarkable in its own way. Muses as well as mothers and daughters, these women practice an art that is in the truest sense restorative—an art that, like that of the playwright, transforms all those it touches.

NOTES

1. References are to *The Complete Signet Classic Shakespeare*, gen. ed. Sylvan Barnet (New York: Harcourt Brace Jovanovich, 1972). Citations to the plays by act, scene, and line number are given in parentheses following each quotation.

2. The "king's touch" was thought to be inherited by Edward's successors, including James I, the monarch before whom *Macbeth* was presented. The last English ruler said to heal people in this way was Queen Anne (the daughter of James II), who reigned from 1702 to 1714.

Part Three:
Disease as an Altered— or Heightened—State of Consciousness

Like two angels in the throes of torture
Of an implacable calenture,
Let's follow into the crystal blue
Of morning the mirage in distant view!

> Charles Baudelaire,
> "Lovers' Wine" in *The Flowers of Evil*,
> trans., Enid Rhodes Peschel

I have seldom written poetry unless I was rather out of health. . . .

> A. E. Housman, *The Name and Nature of Poetry*

All interest in disease and death is only another expression of interest in life.

> Thomas Mann, *The Magic Mountain*

Literary Insights
and
Theories of Person
Andrew E. Slaby and Laurence R. Tancredi

Literature, as well as other forms of the creative arts, has an important humanizing influence on the physician. It contributes to shaping the physician's sensitivity to the full range of human behavior and potential, extolling the merits of flexibility and expansiveness in the intellectual and emotional understanding of patients.

For some time literature has been used to introduce aspiring physicians, psychiatrists in particular, to various manifestations of psychopathology. Some of the most graphic descriptions of mental illness prior to the nineteenth century are found in the work of great authors. William Shakespeare's *King Lear,* for instance, traces the King's psychological deterioration as he is betrayed and cast out by Regan and Goneril, his two hypocritical daughters who pretended great love to receive the power and rank of his title. Finally he goes mad while shelterless in a storm. In such instances, literature is an adjunct to the person of the physician, to heighten sensitivity to the full creative potential of human beings and to the complexity of psychological and physical forces that militate to destroy them. Literature allows the more usual of us to share to some degree the ecstasy of the creative experience as well as to feel the pain of existential *Angst.* The routine and technical aspects of medicine sometimes numb the sensitivities of the physician to the plight of patients and their families. Literature teases at the edge of the spirit. It asks questions and inspires hope. Sometimes it saddens. But in all instances, well-written literature enhances the reader's sensitivity to the complexity of the human situation in sickness and in health.

An often neglected function of literature is the role it plays in the expansion of what is known about human personality and the workings of the mind. It is this function of creative expression in written word that we wish to address—the role literature plays as the cutting edge for psychiatric theory.

Writers whose fictional presentations of individuals in various situations are alive to us, are "real people," reflect in their work basic psychodynamic assumptions. There is a consistency to the behavior of characters in good novels, plays, and poetry just as there is to behavior of people in real life. If behavior changes, it does not come unexpectedly if you know anything of the individual's past. Literature that is less an expression of art than an articulation of a predominant social ethic seems less real: The rake does not become a true gentleman with the attendant attributes of culture and social sophistication. Thus, the novels of Horatio Alger, Jr. (such as *From Canal Boy to President, Ralph Raymond's Heir,* and *Sam's Chance and How He Improved It*) did more to provide hope for the downtrodden masses of early twentieth-century America who aspired to rise from poorly paid factory and mining jobs to fame and fortune than they did to provide understanding of the complexity of human motivation or, for that matter, to earn for Alger a place in literary history as a great writer. *Sam's Chance* was a sequel to another of Alger's works entitled *Young Outlaw* and was designed (as articulated by the author in the preface) to show how the young man was induced to give up his bad habits, and how he deserved his ultimate prosperity. The goal of the author is obvious and consistent with the social philosophy of the immigrant nation of the early twentieth century that hard work and good clean living in America hold promises of both financial and social rewards. Bad habits lead to self-destruction and ruin. In contrast to this are the autobiographical writings of St. Augustine and Marcel Proust. In Augustine's *Confessions* we see that the roots of his greatness and ultimate major contributions to religion and an understanding of the human mind lay not in good clean living and hard work. Augustine led an early life of debauchery and, in fact, fathered an illegimate child. His exceptional psychological sensitivity and the ever-present influence of his mother, St. Monica, are themes throughout his confessions; his ultimate conversion to his mother's religion and the prominence he achieved in matters of religion and saintly life are not unexpected. Comparably, Proust's ever-present childhood craving to enjoy his mother's love and be rid of his father is elucidated in his writing and helps to explain much of what we know of him through his art and of him as a person through his biographers.[1]

    D. H. Lawrence's *Sons and Lovers* portrays in fiction, through the characters of Paul Morel and Paul's mother and father, his own early life in the mining community of Eastwood, Nottinghamshire. Paul Morel is the young Lawrence in a painful ambivalent relationship to the mother whose love and sacrifice give sensitivity but whose bonds bind and serve as impediments to further growth without the pain and guilt of separation —a situation familiar to many men. The characters in *Sons and Lovers* are alive, we feel we know them because, in their essence, they touch upon something we are and know, just as they touch upon the life of the author, who wrote articulately in fiction about that which he knew best—himself. Comparably, the character of Stephen Dedalus in James Joyce's *A Portrait of the Artist as a Young Man* and in *Ulysses* resonates with the real person of the author as we know him through his biographers. In the works of both authors there is an historical and psychodynamic consistency to the characters, particularly to those modeled on the authors themselves— Paul Morel and Stephen Dedalus. They love, they hate, they are ambivalent at times, anxious at others and not infrequently a bit melancholic. Their relationships to their mothers and fathers, like Lawrence's and Joyce's, or our own, if we are sensitive enough to cut through the distortion of convention, are complex. The Lawrence novel deals with the intensity of a developing man's love for his mother. This is a flesh and blood emotion; they are in a sense "lovers." Only when Paul Morel's mother dies is he truly free to enjoy the love of another woman. In *Sons and Lovers,* the reader is shown by example the nature of oedipal love and its power as a force in determining adult behavior. The way that a man's relationship to his father colors adult values and feelings is brought out in Joyce's Dedalus. The novels in which Stephen Dedalus figures prominently are colored by the ambivalent feelings the author, like Dedalus, has toward the Catholic Church and Ireland. Dedalus struggles with feelings toward the insensitive father, from whom he would like approbation, warmth, and interest. *A Portrait of the Artist as a Young Man* begins with a story that the father is reading his son. The novel ends with the words "old father, old artificer, stand me now and ever in good stead." The constant struggle with the fatherland, Ireland, and the authoritarian, dogmatic and unfeeling image conveyed of the Irish Church parallel that of a father who knows not his son's sensitivity and could sell his books without knowing the symbolic impact of such an act. Many of us know of similar pain but perhaps not in the way or degree Lawrence and Joyce experienced it, enhancing their sensitivity as human beings, their capacity to feel and their ability to create.

Other writers deal less obviously with the forces of unresolved childhood conflicts on adult life than they do with the tendency of all human beings to select out, albeit unconsciously, friends and lovers who draw out hidden and unactualized aspects of themselves. This is well demonstrated by Willa Cather in her novel *The Professor's House.* It is an introspective study of a scholarly man, Professor St. Peter, who is passing through the critical period between middle age and old age. He is reluctant to move into a new, more comfortable house and remains in the old room he has been used to working in, despite the protestations of his wife and daughters.[2] Into his reflective musings come memories of a former student, Tom Outland, whom he had taught several years before. Outland was a brilliant young scientist and inventor who had never known his parents and was raised by a family in the West. One learns from the professor's reflections about Outland's passionate sensitivity for Indian artifacts with their mystical link to centuries of unrecorded stories of human life; and about his lust for adventure, which led to his death in his twenties in Flanders fighting with the Foreign Legion. Cather effectively uses the house, with its familiar and comfortable (but uninspiring) accouterments, as a symbol of Professor St. Peter with his close-trimmed Van Dyke, who is also comfortable but uninspiring. Tom Outland is a symbol of something outside of the professor's experience (hence the name *Outland*). The professor's only adventure into the unfamiliar is through his work on Spanish adventurers in North America. His preoccupation throughout the novel—with the story of a young man whom he knew years before—is the struggle of a middle-aged man with that element within him, as in all of us, that urges him to be something more exciting, more explorative and, alas, more creative and adventurous. Tom Outland is the professor's own, unactualized self. But the world of the explorer, the adventurer and the creative person is not one of comfort and familiarity, by definition. It is filled with anxieties and risk. Cather's story is a lesson to the reader on midlife crises, the struggle to draw into perspective one's ideal goals and the reality of one's achievements.

In the works we mentioned by Lawrence, Joyce, and Cather, we see reflected fundamental psychodynamic assumptions developed by Sigmund Freud, Erik Erikson, and others. Personality unfolds in an orderly and predictable manner. The genesis of the adult personality lies in the past. Just as Erikson consciously used his conceptual model of developmental stages[3] and identity[4] in psychobiographies of Martin Luther and Mohandas Gandhi,[5] so too—but less consciously—do skilled writers reflect these same principles in their writing. In the words of Wordsworth, "The Child is father of the Man."[6] The genesis of adult personality, drive and conflict lies in early development. Motivation is not always conscious. A number of subterranean conflicts and feeling states determine what we do. Even the most sensitive and intelligent of us are driven by demons we know not. If we are arrogant enough to think we always understand what we feel or lack the humility to know that our motivations are not always holy, we may be destroyed by pride just like the protagonist in a Greek tragedy.

Another function literature serves is to allow the sacred privilege of entry into the world of the neurotic and even the psychotic mind. Accounts of mental illness in literature are generally not only better written than clinical case histories, but often much more complete. The novel *I Never Promised You A Rose Garden,* written by Hannah Green, the play *Equus* by Peter Shaffer, and the film script *Face to Face* by Ingmar Bergman, all contain portrayals of psychosis. Bergman's work is particularly disarming because the protagonist seems so much like all of us, yet in it, as in so much of Bergman's other work, is a cutting through mythologies —the delusions of convention and routine. He, like a good psychotherapist, asks the unholy questions and receives uncomforting answers. Life is not always what it seems; storms may be contained until the organism is overburdened.

In addition to explicating for the reader aspects of normal and abnormal development, the novelist can explore aspects of psychological functioning before they are known to medicine and before it is socially acceptable to discuss them in other forums. It is in this role that the writer serves the critical function of expanding what is known in psychiatric theory or accepted by the psychiatric establishment. Virginia Woolf in *To the Lighthouse* (1927) and James Joyce in *Ulysses* (1914) explored through the medium of the written word free association as a key to an understanding of the principal characters. The peregrinations of the mind uninhibited by the forces of censorship were so shocking in the early twentieth century that *Ulysses* was banned. Like neurotic individuals who use suppression and repression of unacceptable thoughts and feelings, society capped Joyce's work. People were not yet ready for it. Psychoanalysis was in its nascent phase and if such material ever came to the fore, it most certainly was to be retained in a physician's consulting rooms and not incorporated into theory and open practice. Woolf, in a somewhat more acceptable manner (and over ten years after the publication of *Ulysses*), and Joyce acquainted many readers who were still distrustful of psychoanalysis with the evolving psychoanalytic technique of free association by using, in their novels, the stream of consciousness technique. These authors in their creative work were forging new paths to understanding of the mind and how it functions.

In a similar manner, authors have teased away at conventional concepts of sexuality and its role in self-actualization. To present-day students of behavior, it seems strange that society and the medical profession would fail to see how a woman's extramarital liaisons may lead to growth and self-actualization, yet at the time publication of Flaubert's *Madame Bovary* (1857), Tolstoy's *Anna Karenina* (1876), and Lawrence's *Lady Chatterley's Lover* (1928), all three works were condemned for immorality. They presented the option to women to look outside of marriage for fulfillment, and they explored the consequences. In the first two instances, the affairs were tragic; in Lady Chatterley's love for the gamekeeper, Mellors, she found renewal and a means of self-actualization. Banned in England and the United States, this novel was circulated privately for years.

Traditional concepts of extramarital liaisons have since fallen into historical perspective as divorce rates rise rapidly and newly married couples "contract" into their marriages freedom for sexual liaisons outside of their union. Today psychotherapists speak no longer of "marital stability" but of "growth," "self-actualization" and realization of full potential. Comparably, when D. H. Lawrence in *The Fox* (1922) and E. M. Forster in *Maurice* (1914) first wrote of homosexual love in gentle and human terms, such love was seen as illness or perversion to be treated by psychoanalysis, conditioning or some other therapeutic modality. Today, changing societal attitudes and license to experiment with different types of relationships are making it apparent that identity on any level, of which the sexual is only a part, is dynamic and ever-changing.

The Eriksonian concept put forth in *Childhood and Society* (see note 3) that somewhere in adolescence there is a state in which the issues of identity versus role diffusion are worked through so that the individual can go on to struggle successively with such matters as intimacy versus isolation, generativity versus stagnation, is being reconsidered. Traditional concepts of identity, like those of relationships, are being reevaluated, and reassessment may occur at many times in one's life.[7] Divorce, in particular, may lead to a review of what one is doing and who one is. Questions are raised that sound like echoes of questions asked in adolescence, when presumably these questions were answered and laid to rest, enabling the individual to move on to intimacy, marriage, children and career—a path once thought to spell health. Again, the antecedents for these revisions in the way psychotherapists conceptualize behavior can be found in literature written decades before psychiatrists and allied mental health professionals questioned traditional boundaries of both sexual and personal identity. D. H. Lawrence in *Women in Love* (1920) explored the nuances of relationships among four people, two sisters and the men they loved. The book is believed to be a semiautobiographical account of the dynamics of the relationship between Lawrence himself in the character of Birkin; Lawrence's wife Frieda Von Richthofen Weekly in the character of Ursula; and Lawrence's good friends, the writers John Middleton Murry and Katherine Mansfield, in the characters of Gerald and Gudrun. In it Birkin struggles with a thinly veiled love for Gerald. Birkin is clearly passionately in love with Ursula and the love is reciprocated, but still there is a part of him that seeks something more. He wrestles naked before the fire with Gerald. The scene is sensuously portrayed and the question is raised of some sort of bonding, a *Bruderschaft.* The novel ends after Gerald's death with a discussion between Birkin and Ursula, who is now his wife, about Birkin's desire for both union with a woman and "external union with a man; another kind of love." Ursula calls it a "perversity" and states "it's false, impossible." The novel concludes with Birkin's stating "I don't believe that." Lawrence raises the question in the third decade of this century of whether a fulfilling heterosexual love can be compatible with a parallel homosexual love. It is a statement of the possibility of healthy bisexuality, a concept that has been and still is to some degree heresy within psychiatry.

This type of thinking not only challenges the concept of orderly solidification of sexual identity, but gets at the very roots of how the adult personality is formed. A challenge to gender identity is a challenge to all concepts of how personality is formed. In a more sophisticated manner, Virginia Woolf in her novel *Orlando* (1928) brilliantly toys with the elements of the identity of the adult. The degree to which greater understanding of self is prevented by convention and social mores—even by psychiatry, which, like the society of which it is part, is bound by convention—is only beginning to be understood. The creative person in literature and other art forms challenges, often without conscious intent, many assumptions of psychological theory in the unceasing struggle for self-honesty and the authentic in creative expression.

In the great works of art we find recorded the world as it is *felt* to be by the artist. We look to the bas reliefs, murals and statuary of the ancient Romans for clues to how they lived and what they valued. The stained glass of the great cathedrals of Europe taught the illiterate the stories of the Bible and the lives of the saints. Literature provides us with descriptions not only of what people have been and are but also of what they can be, even before the more empirical mind of the behavioral scientist dares think such thoughts aloud or even quietly entertains them in the privacy of the soul. Literary license allows exploration of aspects of the human spirit in the written word from which we all may heighten our sensitivity to the complexity of our own being and obtain insights for the advancement of the art as well as the science of medicine.

NOTES

1. See, for example, G. D. Painter, *Marcel Proust: A Biography* (London: Chatto and Windus, 1959).

2. We are grateful to Margaret Wimsatt for drawing our attention to this interesting work by Cather, a subject of her own research.

3. E. H. Erikson, *Childhood and Society* (New York: W.W. Norton, 1950).

4. E. H. Erickson, *Identity: Youth and Crisis* (New York: W.W. Norton, 1968).

5. E.H. Erikson, *Young Man Luther: A Study in Psychoanalysis and History* (New York: W.W. Norton, 1958); and E. H. Erikson, *Gandhi's Truth: On the Origins of Militant Nonviolence* (New York: W.W. Norton, 1969).

6. W. Wordsworth, "My Heart Leaps Up When I Behold" in Wordsworth, *Selected Poetry*, ed. M. Van Doren (New York: The Modern Library, 1950).

7. See D. Levinson, *The Seasons of a Man's Life* (New York: Alfred A. Knopf, 1978).

Proust's Asthma:
A Malady Begets a Melody
Diana Festa–McCormick

Proust was nine years old when he was seized with his first asthmatic attack. He gasped, struggled for breath, vacillated before the eyes of his dismayed mother. The sensitive and delicate child of yesterday was transmuted from that moment on into a sick, highly vulnerable and, most important, special being to whom favors were to be accorded, unremittingly, at the bidding of his illness. Bedtime, meals, walks, readings, all the rituals of bourgeois life were suspended for this boy, replaced by the tyrannical demands of crises always threatening.

Proust lived the rest of his life under the apparent domination of his illness. Doctors, who were mostly loath to recognize any physiological illness in him, were systematically avoided and ridiculed by the future writer. He continued undaunted to wear layers of woolens and scarves, to pile blanket upon blanket on his bed, to seal windows and to be afflicted by the very sight of an open door. He prescribed his own remedies, took stimulants and tranquillizers in turn, constantly oscillated between states of nervous activity and sloth. His letters (of which the fourth volume, recently published by Professor Kolb, only goes as far as 1904, with yet eighteen years before the end) are replete with almost audible sighs and endless lamentations about perennially sleepless nights, ill-arranged hotel rooms that forced him to assume uncomfortable positions, the inconsideration of servants leaving doors ajar, the inability to eat, the pain of digesting, the impossibility of attending some function or other because of aches or the agony of suffocation. A morbid concern not with health but with illness permeates the many hundreds of pages of correspondence now available to us, an obsession that slowly emerges as the reason for being—and the very definition—of the man and the genius at the heart of *Remembrance of Things Past.*

One need not go into Freudian analysis to understand that Proust sought not merely refuge, but also identity, in malady. What began no doubt accidentally or, at any rate, with no clear premeditation, was soon transformed into a weapon in the hands of the young man. What is of interest here is not so much Proust's basic pusillanimity but, indeed, the strength he was able to derive from an illness to which he instinctively clung from a tender age to his dying days. The asthmatic crises that figure as a leitmotif during his school years and later in his life as a young dandy, up to his mother's death in 1905, never seriously hampered him from attending the elegant reunions in fashionable homes that were so important to him. Proust was a snob and a social climber, and no amount of tortured nights in the grip of wakefulness or the oppression of what he indifferently called emphysema or asthma could detain him from dinner parties at the Ritz or at the home of Madame de Noailles; or from rushing, flattered and full of zeal, at the behest of Count Robert de Montesquiou or Duke Armand de Guiche. Interestingly enough, however, illness became the sustaining force when Proust needed total silence and abstraction from society in order to pursue his creative vision. Asthma was the valid explanation for a phobia of the outside as the writer became enmeshed in the tentacular world of *Time Past* and the need to shape it.

A year before dying, commenting on Paul Valéry's statement that all enlightened action abridges nature's work—for an artist is worth centuries in himself—Proust wrote, "These harmonious or thoughtful artists, if they represent a thousand centuries in relation to the blind work of nature, do not themselves constitute, the Voltaires for instance, an unlimited time in relation to someone sick, a Baudelaire, even better a Dostoevski, who in thirty years, between their epileptic and other crises, create something of which not a single paragraph could have been accomplished by a whole line of a thousand merely healthy artists."[1] Proust expressed here as an axiom what he had already incorporated into his work: the notion that illness and creation are often indissoluble, essential to the struggle against the limitations of a life span. His own seemingly long years of retreat in the shadow of pain and solitude could thus bring to light what twice or thrice that time in health and cheer would not have yielded—a victorious fight against the ponderous progression of time and ineluctability of death.

It is not within the limited scope of this essay to attempt a systematic analysis of the role of illness in Proust's work, of the relation between his own weak constitution and nature and the slow maturing of a vision that was to be translated into art form. Nor can fear, the very breath of his illness, be traced from its vague and cradlelike contours—fear of the dark, of solitude, of sleepless nights, of oppressive days, of the absence of loved ones, of the deprivation of a good-night kiss—to the anguished and compelling force that urged the crystallization of its very existence: a fear that, fixed in memory, struggled against its own paralyzing confines. What can be attempted, however, is to offer a glimpse of a few passages through the *Remembrance* in which illness, beheld under many miens, emerges as the secret of its conception and its hidden heartbeat. "Like lovers when they begin to love, like poets at the time when they sing, sick people feel closer to their souls."[2] We do not know if "soul" is indeed what Proust reached for, or if it was a narcissistic complacency slowly transmuted into a "oneness"—in which the outside world was uniquely blended with a peculiarly individual savoring of existence. What is unquestionable is that, as a recluse in the stratosphere of daily bouts with the sheer act of survival, Proust began to perceive within the four walls of his cork-lined room a deep opening onto the universe of man, with all the recondite wishes, thoughts and pretenses, the devious profferings of love, and the accidents of life and death.

Fittingly, the first important statement about illness in the novel is made by Bergotte, the fictional writer who was probably inspired by Anatole France. To the narrator Marcel—a purified autobiographical rendition of Proust himself—who is often ill, Bergotte says:

> "Are you well attended to? Who takes care of your health?" I told him that I had seen and would no doubt see again Cottard. "But that is not what you need!" he answered.—"I do not know him as a doctor. But I have seen him at Mme Swann's. He is an imbecile. Supposing that does not prevent him from being a good doctor, which I have difficulty believing, that does prevent him from being a good doctor for artists, for intelligent persons. People like you need suitable doctors, I should almost say particular regimens, medicines. Cottard will bore you, and boredom by itself will prevent his cure from being effective. And then, the cure cannot be the same for you as for any other person. Three-fourths of the illnesses of intelligent people come from their intelligence. They need to see a doctor who understands that kind of illness."[3] (1. 570)

Cottard, who has risen from anonymity to the dignified position of a professor of medical science full of self-importance, and is sought after in the elevated spheres of Parisian society—who is gently ridiculed throughout the novel as ineffectual in his obstinate prescribing of remedies for the body that take no account of the soul—can be seen as the embodiment of the world of medicine for Proust. He is here summarily dismissed as an "imbecile"—lacking the sympathetic and intelligent discernment that alone can help the artist in his fight against illness. *Intelligence* is the key word in this passage, and is to be taken in the full Proustian sense, meaning perception and sensitivity, the art of divining what is hidden to the eye. Unabashedly, the implication is that the artist on his sickbed is to be humored by an enlightened doctor: special diets would assuage digestion in the wake of poetry, and gentle sleep would fly on the wings of catered dreams. His maladies, inseparable from the workings of his imagination, are firmly tied to his anguish, his fears, and his struggle for expression. The ideal doctor would be one who could understand all that and would begin his work of redress within the very alcove of pain: where the soul pines in search of a melody.

Proust's father and his brother were doctors. It is easy to speculate —and it has been done many times—that the emotional world in which he lived was not shared by either of them, and that the strong identification he nourished with his mother made him feel at odds with the masculine segment of his family. From that may have derived his dislike for the world of medicine and all its practitioners who liberally dispense healing formulas. Medicine was at the very least considered by Proust to be an embryonic science, amorphous and transitory in its assumed principles and popular practice. What doctors pronounce today as solemn truths will inevitably be found erroneous or inadequate tomorrow, he was convinced. "To believe in medicine," reflects the narrator of *Remembrance,* "would be the supreme madness, if not to believe in it were not an even greater one, for from this heaping of mistakes have come out in the long end some verities" (2.298–99). The presence of doctors is hence sought only in the ancillary hope that, somehow, following accumulated blunders, they might miraculously hit upon a beneficial course. They insist on curing the body, but illness is not of the body alone. For sensitive people, at any rate, its origin resides deep within the longings of the spirit—since that very same imaginative power from which all greatness derives often victimizes sensitive people with the creation of their own illnesses.

When Dr. Du Boulbon—recommended by the writer Bergotte as a more sensitive medical man by far than Dr. Cottard—is called to the bedside of the ailing grandmother, he unhesitantly diagnoses a malady born of a languishing spirit. The poor lady has been having aches and pains, running temperatures and suffering from a feeling of oppression; but the man who should be giving her thaumaturgical potions declares that she alone can cure herself if she can make herself believe that she is not ill. "Neurosis is an imitator of genius," he adds. "There is no illness it cannot perfectly counterfeit. It imitates the very dilatation of those afflicted by dyspepsia, the nausea of pregnancy, the arrhythmia of the cardiac patient, the fever of the tubercular. Capable of deceiving the doctor, how could it not deceive the invalid?" (2.305). But can faith in health be attained when one is afflicted with discomfort and is in the throes of agony? If the question itself remains unformulated, however, an answer is proffered: "It is in illness that we realize that we do not live alone, but are chained to a being of a different kingdom, from which abysses separate us, which does not know us and by which it is impossible to make ourselves understood: our body" (2.298). If physiological illnesses cannot be clearly extricated from their causes, it follows that the ills of the body acquire a life of their own, become an alien force, and cannot be abjured at will. A vicious cycle is thus established in which one feeds upon the other; inner tensions work to the detriment of the body, while the imbalance of physical health injures the spirit, each exacting comfort from the other, at the price of anguish and solitude.

Proust saw doctors as mere servants who look at their masters' lineaments before diagnosing an illness. He refers to them as "third parties" (2.317). Undetected by them, violent battles are waged within, between the two essential contestants: the body and the soul. The face is but a pale mirror of that struggle—vaguely reflecting its uneven progression, showing a quiet acquiescence to illness or an ephemeral gain against it. The grandmother is slowly dying, gradually relinquishing all vital energy, each day heeding more closely the call of the grave. "It is rare," observes Marcel, "that these great maladies, such as the one which had just hit her fully in the face, have not been burrowing within the sick person before killing, and that during that time they did not become known, fast enough, like a neighbor or a 'friendly' tenant. It is a terrible knowledge, less for the suffering it brings than for the strange novelty of the definitive restrictions it imposes upon life" (2.316).

After Cottard and Du Boulbon, a last doctor is called for consultation. Professor E. is peremptory: "Your grandmother is lost" (2. 318), he pronounces. Uremia is not necessarily fatal, but in this case there is no doubt: the old lady's pale face and spent eyes must have dictated to the man of science his final decree. When the soul is vanquished, the reader of Proust cannot but conclude, medicine is powerless. But of what use then are men of science, except that they sometimes embody man's hope and sometimes, mysteriously, assume the shape of his faith? Aren't the ways of illness beyond their control as much as they are beyond the sick person's? Can they heal if they lack persuasion, can they ever shake a patient's mind away from the contemplation of his supine body, and break—from without—the bondage that grows between man and his illness? Proust does not ask these loaded questions. Yet they emerge, page after page, as he stands witness to discomfort, pain, anguish, that appear only fleetingly relieved by the world of medicine.

The grandmother's consuming illness in the novel was clearly patterned after Proust's mother's illness and the recurring crises that led to her end. Her husband had died two years before; it is speculated that she lost the will to live. Interestingly, Marcel himself was to die as soon as his *Remembrance* was completed and not before—and not of asthma, but of a pulmonary infection. Proust's mother suffered loneliness and torment because of her son's existence. Marcel's homosexuality was never discussed between the two, each sheltering the other from a knowledge that could only exacerbate their inner sorrows. The times were not ripe for a clear confrontation with a reality too painful to accept. Only after his mother's death could Proust pour into a work of art all the afflictions that had weighed upon his life. What had paralyzed him from action in the traditional world of man, making him incapable of both acquiescence and independence, what had compelled him into false attitudes of pride, into hiding and sham—his sexual propensities and his Jewishness, the two secretly linked in his mind as fatalities sealed in blood, pervasive and ineluctable—had found a kind of comfort in the manifestations of asthma. That malady, so undefinable and yet exacting, became a focal point for all his movements and, eventually, for his creation. It is in it that all his fears and hopes had first found a faithful testimony, and it is within its contours that his work of art finds its initial delineations. "Like a neighbor or a friendly tenant," his illness had stood sentinel by him, as if it were an entity outside of himself, recognizable and yet alien, with which he had slowly established familiarity, before he and his illness could exist harmoniously side by side.

In the realm of psychoanalysis that was then beginning to assert its sway, findings parallel to Proust's were being made. Illness is not always a scourge, it was being advanced, but indeed is at times a desirable presence. "The physician knows that there is not only neurotic misery in the world, but irremovable suffering as well," wrote Freud. "Whenever a neurotic is faced by a conflict, he takes flight in illness. We must allow that, in some cases, that flight is fully justified."[4] In Czechoslovakia, another unhappy writer tenaciously held in the grip of malady was writing, "I consider the therapeutic part of psychoanalysis to be a hopeless error. All these so-called illnesses, sad as they may appear, are matters of faith, efforts of souls in distress to find moorings in some maternal soil."[5] Through the character of Charlus—into whom Proust poured so much of himself, both dissecting his ills and compassionately tendering the fragility of that personality in disarray—Proust asserts, "There are illnesses of which one must not try to be cured because they alone protect us from more serious ills" (2.291). Asthma was for Proust the safeguard from the labyrinthine trails of Sodom and Gommorrha, his exit from inertia onto the path of art. What he had no doubt nurtured for years as a protective mechanism against the pressures of normal existence—the routine of work, the commitments and responsibilities of affection, all of which he had systematically avoided—was transmuted, within the confining walls of his room, into a gestative and illuminating vantage ground. "Within the detachment that suffering gives, in life, and the sentiment of painful beauty, in the theatre," he understood, "other men's destinies and our own finally allow our attentive soul to hear the eternal and unexpected word of duty and truth" (*Les Plaisirs et les jours,* p. 200). Duty here is none other than the necessity to abide by the dictates of art, to allow visions of years past to unfold before the eye as in a theatre, to seize them in passing, and to hold them fast within the magic resonance of words. "I have awakened the sleeping bee and I feel its cruel sting more than its powerless wings," Proust wrote to A. Bibesco on December 2, 1902. Not dreams, but suffering, he knows, will carry him onto the pinions of beauty.

It is difficult to establish whether Proust's asthma colored all aspects of life for him, or if his morbidly sensitive personality was at the root of his malady; possibly, they sustained each other, each heightening the other. What is known is that the writer's whole philosophy was one tempered by illness, that his vision of life, love, death, art, was inextricably bound to that prison of contemplation that was his solitary room and sickbed. Only there could he fully savor a vision of life. Outside reality seemed pale to him when measured against the world envisioned within the darkness of his room. But there, too, the torment of doubt and jealousy would take shape, molded by the immutable presence of illness. Love is much like a sickness for Proust, a consuming force that aims at once at the possession of the loved one's innermost secret, and at vanquishing love itself—the desire to hold, not in order to keep, but so that one may be rid of the slavery of sentiment. Like a malady, love is to be overcome if one is not to be overpowered and held prisoner by it. "Love is an incurable illness, such as those diathetic areas where rheumatism only allows a little respite in order to make room for epileptiform headaches" (3.85). As with an ailment with which one has "grown familiar" —and where a kind of symbiotic relationship is established between the patient and the malady—the antagonists in love too confront each other in helpless torment. "And, finally, how does one have the courage to wish to live, how can one make a movement to preserve oneself from death, in a world where love is only provoked by a lie and only consists in our need to see our sufferings appeased by the person who made us suffer?" (3.95). Only within the tension established between the lover and the object of desire can love truly be found: a kind of fever oscillating between the two, which prostrates and consumes, but through which a deeper perception is granted into the hearts of men and women. For desire itself is linked to "suffering and not at all to joy." To love is to die a little and to be vivified at the same time—for love, like all illnesses, allows a storage of emotions to be built up, from which light may one day emerge.

"How does one have the courage to wish to live?" asks Marcel, caught in the vise of a suffering from which no relief seems available. The answer to that agonizing cry is the work itself, the volumes written in the penumbra of candlelight in his cork-lined room—where the only echo ticking through the hours is dictated by accumulated emotions, and the only breath of life given by recollected sensations. "When I was only a child," he remembers, "the fate of none of the characters in the Scriptures seemed to me as miserable as that of Noah, because of the deluge, that kept him shut inside the Ark for forty days. Later, I have often been ill, and for long days I too had to remain in the 'Ark.' I understood then that Noah could not see the world well except from the Ark, although it was shut and it was dark upon the earth" (*Les Plaisirs et les jours,* 13). Creation feeds on suffering and solitude. Within the recesses of darkness and pain, within that Ark that sails on the sea of his imagination, a seer is slowly molded who learns to decode the mysteries of the world, so as to reshape them in a personal language that speaks with the voice of eternity. Immobile, watching dispassionately his tyrannical companion— that illness that breathes with his breath and will only cease in death— he perceives light on the wings of horror. ". . . I, that strange human creature who, while waiting for death to release him, lives with shutters closed, knows nothing of the world, remains motionless like an owl and, like the owl, only sees a little clarity within darkness" (2.982). From that dark chamber of illness, a spark slowly takes flight. A melody begins to live: *Remembrance of Things Past.*

NOTES

1. Marcel Proust, *Chroniques* (Paris: Gallimard, 1927), pp. 216–17. All translations of Proust are my own.

2. Marcel Proust, *Les Plaisirs et les jours* (Paris: Gallimard, 1924) p. 10.

3. All quotations from *Remembrance of Things Past* are taken from the Pléiade edition (1954) of *A La Recherche du temps perdu.* The volume and page number will be given in parentheses.

4. Sigmund Freud, "The Common Neurotic Stage" in "Introductory Lectures on Psychoanalysis," *Standard Edition of the Complete Psychological Works,* vol. 2, ed. James Strachey (London: Hogarth Press, 1963), p. 382.

5. Franz Kafka, *Letters to Milena* (New York: Schocken Books, 1962), p. 217.

Medicine and the Biographer's Art
Stanley Weintraub

Of the literary genres, biography has the most to learn from medicine. Largely because of Freud, biographers have become sensitive to some of the deepest wellsprings of motive and behavior, but in the process of utilizing psychology, writers often ignore the ills of the flesh for those of the psyche. For one thing, it is easier. We have a vocabulary of psychiatry and psychology accessible on at least a superficial level to the educated reader, while few biographers can acquire the perspectives, let alone the special knowledge, of the M.D. Yet let us look at some of the possible misinterpretations of lives resulting from the inability of the biographer to sense a medical approach to a biographical problem, or to examine the interaction of physical and psychological illness.

One of the great orators and parliamentarians of the latter decades of Victoria's reign was Lord Randolph Churchill, an ambitious, impetuous politician whose fall was as rapid as his rise. No one doubted that he was a future prime minister, but he was to many "a reckless and unprincipled mountebank," a dangerous man—a Conservative in name but a rebel against his class. His letters and speeches show that he sensed the social upheavals that would alter the structure of the world he would not live to see. Outmaneuvered in the cabinet, he was forced to resign in 1886, when he was in his midthirties, but everyone expected a comeback. It was not to be. From 1891 to 1895, he was in obvious physical and mental decline, and it was possible that even his impulsive miscalculation in December 1886 was the result of his already being gripped by the disability that would slowly wreck his nervous system. In his last year his wife Jennie hauled the stumbling and insane hulk on a horrific overseas trip as much to get him out of the public eye in England as for his irreversible decline. In England it was said that his condition was the inevitable result of his loose conduct as a young man, and when death mercifully but belatedly came, the opinion of his doctors was that he had succumbed to General Paralysis of the Insane, a euphemism then in use for syphilis. Ralph Martin in *Jennie* puts it bluntly—"died of syphilis, raving mad."[1] A turbulent and disturbing personality, Churchill was easily labeled with the most loathsome disease the symptoms suggested in an age when only a reference to it in Ibsen's *Ghosts* (medically unsound as it was, as the play was predicated on syphilis's being inheritable) was enough to have the play banned as obscene. There was no autopsy, but the evidence of his symptoms available to us suggests that—although the possibility of syphilis remains—he may have been suffering from a brain tumor, which would account for his instability in life as well as his agonizing death.

However indeterminate and obscure motivational factors may be in even the simplest of cases, organic causes other than syphilis could have produced the same clinical picture. Still, not only was Lord Randolph Churchill's reputation besmirched, but by implication his causes; and his behavior as well as his motives have never emerged from opprobrium. Yet this febrile, tense personality had created by his life and his death the conditions that impelled his younger son to an impetuously ambitious literary and political career to rescue the Churchill name. Young Winston could not erase the stigma of syphilis from his father's death certificate, but he would make another Churchill the leading English orator of his time—and prime minister.

It was easy for Victorian medical practitioners to talk of General Paralysis of the Insane, yet there was no test for syphilis before 1905, a decade after Lord Randolph died. But a lot was unknown to earlier physicians, let alone to writers. For all practical purposes, germs were unknown before 1870, although the microscope had been in use for centuries. Temperatures were not taken before about 1850, nor was the stethoscope widely used before then. Antiseptic practices, and anesthesia, which finally made surgery practical, were unknown before 1800; and many physicians now will confide that it is only in the last generation that we have come out of the witch-doctor era, despite the universal admiration of practitioners of medicine before then. The evidence of treatment, then, need bear little relation to what was actually wrong with the patient. And this may still be true. Further, since the biographer is usually dealing with a subject who is no longer with us, we have to admit that there can be no certain medical diagnosis in the absence of the patient's body. All we have to go on, usually, is the evidence of observation—that of the subject, or of a witness. And we know how unreliable that can be, especially before the era of the X-ray, the tissue analysis, the modern hard data beyond the ability of the biographer to interpret for himself.

Jennie Churchill's closest female friend after her widowing was the novelist Pearl Craigie, thirteen years younger but less beautiful, who wrote under the name of John Oliver Hobbes. Mrs. Craigie, who had been emotionally scarred by a notorious 1895 divorce case in which she was an innocent party, exorcised her demons through writing and traveling, and complained constantly of vague illnesses fashionable among Victorian women. "Art must indeed be a disease," she once wrote to one of her confidants, Father William Brown. "My own sufferings baffle description." In the later nineties she spent days in bed with exhaustion, often after a dramatic collapse. After heart stimulants taken by day, she switched to trional and veronal to enable her to sleep at night. Henry James may have seen even more than he realized when he put some part of her into the heroine of his *Wings of the Dove* (1902), in which the heroine, Milly Theale, heretofore has been seen as the master's nostalgic elegy for a dead cousin. Mrs. Craigie recognized herself, complete to idiosyncratic clothes and her mother's townhouse at Lancaster Gate. But, she wrote to a friend, James "makes me out to be suffering from some mysterious incurable malady (a popular delusion) and makes much of the fact that I *look* well: I have no air of the invalid."

Her novels and plays were filled with sophisticated, cynical women who reflected her own outlook. "I don't believe I shall live much longer," she wrote a friend early in 1905, noting her concern about her irregular pulse. "For some years I have been trying to cheat exhaustion; my mind is as active as ever but I can't struggle against this fatigue. My life has been sad and eventful. I have lived two lives in one: I take everything to heart and I have thought far too much. . . . My knowledge of the world has not embittered me, but it has *tired* me." To another friend she claimed that her ailment was (to use modern terms) a tubercular pericarditis that flared up as a result of nervous exhaustion, affecting her pulse and feeling like a dull, painful swelling in her chest. An unidentified specialist had confirmed that diagnosis, but on what basis we do not know. His response had been to prescribe "powerful drugs," which alleviated the symptoms on each recurrence, and until they took effect she was "fit for nothing." That he may have been more concerned with the symptoms than their origins is hinted at in a letter in which she confided that she had been "most unwell. There is *never* anything organically wrong with me, but my pulse goes wrong." One might expect this in a life punctuated by a domineering father she adored, a mother so eccentric that in a less wealthy woman insanity might have been diagnosed, probable sexual frigidity leading to a notorious divorce trial, and subsequent suitors whom she encouraged but from whom she withdrew when they grew too ardent. Yet in Pearl Craigie's life one is never certain which is cause and which is effect.

Lecturing and writing were her reasons for living, but in March 1904 she canceled the remainder of a lecture tour in America to return to England and her bed, writing a friend, "Please don't think I want a long illness and horrors. I want to die in harness and at work." Although she was now failing rapidly, no one seemed to notice any change because for years her life had been one of frenetic activity followed by exhaustion and collapse. She had even encouraged the romantically tragic idea that she had been a victim of heartbreak, and her friends and her public saw her behavior as acceptable affectation or regrettable world-weariness. Still, she wrote a confidant, "[Doctors] told me some years ago that I should go out like a candle: my heart was broken by grief long ago, and although it is sound physically, and I *ought* to live by all the rules of the physical game,—the laws of the spiritual game are more determined—if more elusive." In 1906, to speed her dissolution, she slashed a wrist, which was hardly in keeping with Roman Catholic principles about self-destruction. Like most such attempts, the result was a messy failure, and she appeared in public as guest speaker at a dinner honoring Ellen Terry as elegant as ever, wearing a lace sling. To escape the August heat two months later she began packing at Lancaster Gate for a motoring trip in Scotland with her son, who was home from Eton. The next morning a maid found her dead in her bed, a rosary in her hand. She was thirty-eight.

Despite the opposition of her father, an inquest was held, which ascribed the death to cardiac failure, a diagnosis that proved little. To make matters worse, however, her father insisted that she never took drugs of any kind, and denied all knowledge of cardiac problems. Both statements were true as far as they went, since she had told him nothing, but one-time suitor George Moore suggested privately that she had taken a drug overdose in a suicide attempt. Why else would she have expired alone, clutching a rosary? And why else would she write into her will (contrary to Church policy) instructions for her cremation? Still, it was easier to think of the author of *The School for Saints* and *Some Emotions and a Moral* as having died of a long-broken heart than to assume that she had taken her own life, and one can look back upon her work and her life from either standpoint. In a sense Pearl Craigie had been right about herself all along, we can now guess with some confidence. Possibly she was weakened by an interatrial septal defect that would permit her to reach adulthood, although with recurrent and increasingly serious problems of exhaustion, and that would eventually cause right-sided heart failure and death in the fourth or fifth decade. Whether or not there was any romantically tragic affectation in her books, the mysterious, incurable malady she had suffered may have been literally a broken heart.[2]

Another creative personality who is difficult to understand without examining his medical problems is Dante Gabriel Rossetti. A poet and painter whose idealized women are characterized by lush hair and impossible lips, Rossetti demonstrated great restraint. He painted only one nude in an era when nudes circumspectly covered with the filmiest of draperies and given classical titles to render them respectable for prurient heads of Victorian households were certain to sell. For Rossetti, no framed canvas substitutes were necessary, as he kept a mistress both before and after the death of his frail young wife, but questions remain about his relationship with the woman with whom he fell deeply in love when he was in his forties, Jane Morris, his favorite model and the wife of his best friend. Perhaps the extent of their embraces (by this time his mistress, Fanny Cornforth, was largely a housekeeper and companion) was limited by a problem that had by then become painfully chronic for Rossetti—a bulky hydrocele.

Although the sac was drained several times, the agonizingly enlarged testicle not only would have made sexual intercourse awkward for Rossetti, it was also likely to make the act esthetically less than attractive for any of his partners. It is probable, from the evidence of Rossetti's writing and painting, that amorous indulgence largely took other forms, even when his nights were sleepless with guilt. Having violated his dead wife's body by having her coffin exhumed to recover the manuscript poems he had buried with her, he had then published them together with newer poems clearly written to and about Jane Morris. Sexually, he had sinned in the word if not in the deed.

Whether the reasons were physical (the hydrocele) or psychological, Rossetti spent so many sleepless nights that he resorted to a traditional Victorian soporific, chloral hydrate, which he chased down with whiskey. The combination was literally deadly, as he kept increasing the dosage, and his work became technically poorer as his control over his hand and brain weakened. The results leave one to wonder—as in any case of drug addiction in the writer and artist—how much of the product is genius (or its opposite) and how much is beyond the control of the individual. The results also leave one to wonder about the aesthetic inferences of critics with respect to the work, when the work has clearly gone beyond the control of the artist.

Unlike other artists and writers (the classic example is Coleridge's opium-stimulated "Kubla Khan"), Rossetti never put his hallucinations into his "creative" work. But he had them, for a tendency to hallucinate before sinking into stupefaction was a characteristic of use of chloral. For the rest of his days, Rossetti imagined that an organized conspiracy existed to publicly execrate him as an evil influence on his time; and when William Buchanan published his notorious review of Rossetti's *Poems,* "The Fleshly School of Poetry," Rossetti became certain. Even an overdose of laudanum in 1872 failed to kill him (his much more frail wife, a tubercular as well as a victim of anorexia nervosa, had been more successful as a suicide years before); but in 1881 chloral and whiskey abuse finally overwhelmed his liver and kidneys. He was then only fifty-four. But had the real artist and poet been dead long before? Can the biographer make that judgment? And where does he draw the line?

A later writer (and one-time artist) to suffer from the Rossetti syndrone was Evelyn Waugh, who did put his paranoia and his hallucinations about overheard conspiracies into *The Ordeal of Gilbert Pinfold* (1957), which is as much case study as fiction. Suffering from chronic insomnia, Waugh, according to his psychiatrist, Eric Strauss, ingested large quantities of phenobarbital and gin, and "overheard" and imagined events even after writing *Pinfold,* which proved to be only a temporary exorcism. Neither the insomnia nor the paranoia ever left Waugh completely, and the internal damage from alcohol and drug abuse contributed to his relatively early death at sixty-two. Ironically, Waugh's first major book—before he became famous as a novelist—had been a biography of Rossetti.[3]

Another kind of obsession haunted Virginia Woolf, whose mother died when Virginia was thirteen. She attempted suicide several times, and received no medical or psychiatric help that was useful. Julia Stephen was literally a presence in her daughter's waking life. "I could hear her voice, see her, imagine what she would do or say as I went about my day's doings," Virginia recalled, explaining, as if it were true of everyone, that her mother "was one of the invisible presences who after all play so important a part in every life." When she was forty-four, Mrs. Woolf recalled,

> One day walking round Tavistock Square I made up, as I some-times make up my books, *To the Lighthouse* [1927]; in a great, apparently involuntary, rush. One thing burst into another. Blow-ing bubbles out of a pipe gives the feeling of the rapid crowd of ideas and scenes which blew out of my mind, so that my lips seemed syllabling of their own accord as I walked. What blew the bubbles? Why then? I have no notion. But I wrote the book very quickly; and when it was written, I ceased to be obsessed by my mother. I no longer hear her voice; I do not see her. I suppose that I did for myself what psycho-analysts do for their patients. I ex-pressed some very long felt and deeply felt emotion. And in ex-pressing it I explained it and then laid it to rest. But what is the meaning of 'explained' it? Why, because I described her and my feeling for her in that book, should my vision of her and my feeling for her become so much dimmer and weaker? Perhaps one of these days I shall hit on the reason; and if so, I will give it, but at the moment I will go on, describing what I can remember for it may be true that what I remember of her now will weaken still further.[4]

Medicine, unfortunately, cannot offer a prescription, even to the creative person, how to undo one's mental ills that way. More likely one is offered, now, tranquilizers to fuzz the brain rather than anything to excite it into the creativity that might release the ghosts. And in Mrs. Woolf's case, there would be still other ghosts, and a successful suicide attempt in 1941. Yet the biographer must ask, how much of the creative achievement is owed to the illness and how much is owed to the conscious artist, if there is such a thing? Is the history of great creative achievements often the history of mental and physical illness? (Certainly we must accept the idea that some great works have emanated from organically and mentally sound artists unless we take the position that there is no such thing as a balanced mind or a balanced metabolism.)

The classic example of the marriage of illness to creativity has been the effect attributed, over centuries, at least until the discovery of strepto-mycin and later drugs, to tuberculosis. "The White Plague" not only decimated families, it raised the sensibility of the creative spirit and it finely tuned as well as heated the artistic imagination. Leaving the opera one wintry evening in the 1890s, Aubrey Beardsley, only a few years from his death, at twenty-six, from tuberculosis, would be chastised for not wearing his overcoat. "But I am always burning," he would say; and it is reasonable to assume that such ambulatory tuberculars as Beardsley or D. H. Lawrence ran a continual low-grade fever. Like some others ill with a disease that was certain to contribute to, if not cause, their deaths, Beardsley reacted to the numbering of his days with an intensity of creative purpose that excluded almost everything else.[5]

The same diagnosis might be made of a Beardsley contemporary, Marcel Proust, the son of a distinguished physician. Although he suffered from asthma from the age of nine, the ailment did not even interfere with his compulsory military service at eighteen; yet as a law student and in a library sinecure in his twenties he used his chronic illness to avoid doing what he had no desire to do. He spent his convalescence in writing when it was the occupation of a gentleman rather than a professional. When hay fever aggravated his asthma, and labored breathing made sleeping difficult, both were treated with drugs; and since he breathed better by day, he began a regimen of going to sleep when other Parisians were breakfasting, awakening in the late afternoon, and working through the night.

The million and a quarter words of *A La Recherche du temps perdu,* many times rewritten and many more times revised, and one of the great literary works of the twentieth century, cannot be understood in all its overheated, claustrophobic intensity without a knowledge of Proust's medical and psychological history. Indeed his *chef-d'oeuvre* could not have been written had he not indulged his bronchial asthma. To assure sleep he huddled under blankets in a torrid, cork-lined room, meant to insulate him from external noises, which also distrubed his writing when he was awake. His accommodation to his asthma may well have been psychoneurotic, but it enabled him to live in the half-wakeful state that stimulated the unconscious memories upon which he constructed his books, and gave him the leisure of the indulged eccentric to write them. Inevitably he surrendered to the drugs and the neuroses and was in no condition to recover from a siege of bronchopneumonia.[6] But literature owes to his hypersensitive bronchi his opportunity to plumb his hypersensitive psyche.

Another often-written-about figure might be mentioned without hypothesizing upon the possible causes of his illness. Like Proust, Charles Darwin (after the famous voyage of the *Beagle*) was a wealthy invalid recluse of great energy. Self-freed from normal obligations, he lived the life of the mind. But the problem for the biographer is not only why he did so but what was accomplished. Does a work of the mind created under conditions of illness, actual or induced, have a subtext that might be elucidated through medical analysis of both the work and its creator? We have yet to probe the possibility.

Other kinds of medical evidence suggest that the biographer has much to learn and that otherwise sound biographies are significantly flawed by inadequate knowledge of medicine. Have revolutions in aesthetics occurred because the view of reality insisted upon by a gifted artist was actually a distortion caused by a physical defect, but developed into an artistic philosophy? For example, the blurring of detail in the great landscapes and waterscapes of J. M. W. Turner may have been the result of astigmatism, a defect in the contour of the lens that prevents the focusing of clear, sharp images. Similarly, James McNeill Whistler, the myopic and monocled London Yankee for whom distant objects appeared blurred, preached in his famous "Ten O'Clock Lecture" that "when the evening mist clothes the riverside with poetry, as with a veil, and the poor buildings lose themselves in the dim sky, and the tall chimneys become campanili, and the warehouses are palaces in the night, and the whole city hangs in the heavens, and fairy-land is before us—then . . . Nature, who for once, has sung in tune, sings her exquisite song to the artist alone, her son and her master. . . ." What the painter was describing was the way he always saw things around him, and the near-sighted view became the prevailing one for a time. Monet's late paintings are analyzed for their revolutionary aesthetics by art historians, but their real lens should be a facsimile of his double cataract; for when he submitted to corrective surgery in 1923 he began enthusiastically retouching his paintings until his friends and relatives persuaded him to leave his great canvases unimproved. Is he thus diminished as an artist? And how should we look at the much-praised work that he painted during his twenty years of defective vision? We might speculate in general about how different art would be if great visual artists had worn corrective eyeglasses or had corrective surgery.[7]

Perhaps the same thing might be said of the auditory world. Proust shut it out with cork and nocturnal habits. Other creative artists suffered from various states of deafness. Despite a general assumption that a composer can "hear" every note in his mind's ear, would Beethoven have written the immensely difficult solo-voice sections of his Ninth Symphony the way he did had he been able to hear them? Jonathan Swift, among his other problems, was increasingly deaf in his later years, and suffered from concurrent nausea and giddiness. Biographers have ascribed the ailment to many causes, including neurosis, sexual excess and drink, and have given it many names. Yet it is important to understand what it was, because Swift, melancholy and eccentric at the best times, put his ailments into his verse, as in his lines prophesying his end:

> See how the Dean begins to break:
> Poor gentleman, he droops apace,
> You plainly find it in his face;
> That old vertigo in his head
> Will never leave him till he's dead;
> Besides, his memory decays,
> He recollects not what he says.

It must have been a poet whose hearing was an alternating jumble of silence and disordered sound who wrote the attack on the Irish House of Commons in College Green:

> Could I from the building's top
> Hear the ratt'ling thunder drop,
> While the devil upon the roof
> (If the devil be thunder-proof)
> Should with poker fiery-red

> Crack the stones, and melt the lead;
> Drive them down on ev'ry scull,
> While the den of thieves is full;
> Quite destroy that harpies' nest,
> How might then our isle be blest!

Was it, rather a disordered mind at work? Biographers have speculated about insanity, especially since Swift did not conceal his dread of the prospect, and was indeed senile in his final five years. T. G. Wilson in the *Irish Journal of Medical Science* (1939) dismissed speculations about epilepsy, migraine, insanity, otosclerosis, eyestrain, syphilitic labyrinthitis and other possibilities in favor of Meniere's syndrome, an inner ear disorder that may have affected the gloomy Dean's temperament. That, and subsequent complications, are as close to an answer as we are likely to get. Was his outlook warped by the unpleasant manifestations of his disease? Would he have condemned the world around him with the same savage indignation had he not been the victim of recurrent giddiness, aphasia, deafness and nausea? Was the real man the hale or the ailing Swift?

The questions the biographer must *know* to ask may involve medicine whether the subject is past or contemporary. In what way was Montaigne, for example—and his *Essays*—affected by his painful kidney stone affliction? "I feel everywhere," he wrote, "Men tormented with the same disease: and am honor'd by the Fellowship, forasmuch as Men of the best Quality are most frequently afflicted with it; 'tis a noble and dignified Disease. And were it not a good office to a man to put him in mind of his end? My kidneys claw me to purpose."[8] Thus the calculi, he thought, altered his outlook. But for how long, and to what degree? For he compared the relief he felt after voiding a kidney stone to the pleasure claimed by Socrates in scratching the itch made by his chains immediately after he was free of them. Thus how does pain affect the man—and his work—both during the experience and after his relief? Are these two different people? Similar questions can be asked by the biographer about the creative person aware of his medical sentence of death—although all of us are under that sentence to some degree.

There are times, too, when the creative act incorporates medical phenomena observed in others rather than experienced by the artist; and the artist may not be aware of his motivations until they are explained to him. Samuel Beckett, for example, took aside Jean Martin, who was to play Lucky in the premiere of *Waiting for Godot* in 1953, and demonstrated how the role was to be played, complete to the stammering and stuttering. Puzzled, the actor went to a physician friend and described the movements and speech patterns that the playwright wanted. Unhesitatingly the doctor told Martin that someone who spoke and moved as Lucky did would probably be a victim of Parkinson's disease. In the theater that evening Martin told Beckett, who answered, "Yes, of course." His mother had died of Parkinson's disease, he confided, but he moved quickly to change the subject. Perhaps he had not realized until then how much of his mother he had put into the disturbing yet clownish figure of the unlucky Lucky.[9]

Other biographical questions include the revision of our ideas of cause and effect, or praise and blame, as a result of new medical knowledge that impels us to reexamine past assumptions. Much-maligned "Bloody Mary" is a case in point, not only in historical writing but in the imaginative literature that has grown up around her myth. How different history might have been had she permitted her husband, Philip II of Spain, to rule jointly with her; but she refused to permit him to be crowned as King of England on his marriage, and Philip long after her death would return with his Armada to attempt, again unsuccessfully, to claim his inheritance from yet another barren queen. Biographers stress Mary's religious fanaticism, her authoritarianism, her frustrated desire for a child to continue her dynasty, while Philip remained nervously at court almost like a wealthy guest, paying his household's expenses out of Spanish revenues. Even as Mary's girth subsided and foreign emissaries began reporting secretly to their capitals that the Queen, now in her late thirties, had had another hysterical pregnancy, Mary was busy having secretaries prepare letters to the pope and European kings and dukes announcing a safe delivery, leaving blank only the date of birth and sex of the new heir, these to be filled in at the proper time. But again there would be no child, and there had been no pregnancy. Instead of a birth there would be a death.

Over the centuries biographer after biographer has gone into detail about Mary's amenorrhea and false pregnancies without postulating a diagnosis that accounts for the symptoms. Carolly Erickson's 1978 biographer cites a "twentieth century" diagnosis of ovarian dropsy, which turns out to be a 1931 speculation that only gave some of the symptoms a nineteenth-century label.[10] Would a diagnosis of a virilizing corpus luteum ovarian cyst, one that could have caused amenorrhea, deepness and masculinization of voice (attested to by contemporary accounts), false pregnancies (the "dropsy") and eventual death help us better understand Mary's behavior as a woman and as queen?[11] It seems one of history's great ironies that she, who executed far fewer Englishmen than her father Henry or her sister Elizabeth, and who was, besides, subject to amenorrhea, should be known as "Bloody Mary."

This sampling of lives suggests that biographers who lack a medical perspective may misunderstand the subject's character, motives and accomplishments, and that the impact of medical phenomena upon creativity, if considered at all, is often imperfectly understood. Further, it becomes clear that biographers, assuming that most if not all elements of a personality are under control, have assigned to conscious and individual accomplishment what might more accurately be credited to their subjects' bacilli or to organic abnormalities and defects, and that whole political and aesthetic philosophies may have been generated from the accidents of organic malfunction. But does this mean that biographers must refrain from doing more than setting down chronicles—that *what, where* and *when,* but not the *how* and *why*—until they can acquire an M.D.? Or that only those with medical educations should write biographies? Clearly both suggestions are absurd, although we have a burgeoning biographical literature by physicians analyzing the ills of men and women who have long crumbled into dust, hypothesizing from the distance of centuries or even millenia the afflictions of Noah or Job, or speculating about the nature of Byron's foot deformity or the cause of Milton's blindness.

Somerset Maugham, who had trained as a physician before he wrote his first novel, claimed, in writing about another physician-writer, Anton Chekhov, "I have reasons for believing that the training a medical student has to go through is to a writer's benefit. . . . When people are ill, when they are afraid, they discard the mask which they wear in health. The doctor sees them as they really are, selfish, hard, grasping, cowardly; but brave, too, generous, kindly and good. He is tolerant of their frailties, awed by their virtues."[12] He also has, Maugham implies, a dimension of understanding—and of charity—unavailable to other writers. But the physician is no literary or historical scholar. He can be, and often is, shaky on evaluating documentary evidence, and although he can write a satisfactory prescription in a hand more legible than legend suggests, he may be less than a prose stylist. Besides, the curious physician only finds his curiosity whetted after the fact of the written word, thus coming into the analytical process after the biographer has appeared to provide him with his clues.

What then can be done to clear away the debris of biographical misunderstanding of, or ignorance of, medicine? Perhaps writers about lives should do at least enough medical homework to become sensitive to the possible existence of data that might be interpreted by a physician if he had the facts, or apparent facts, pulled together and laid before him in an appropriate context. Physicians whose brains I have picked have been happy to help. But the problem is to be able to draw together a critical mass of information that is susceptible to medical analysis. There will be no perfect solution until biographers become physicians or physicians become biographers. Yet one must remember that Plato twenty-five centuries ago saw the need for philosophers to become kings or kings to become philosophers. We are no closer to that ideal either.

NOTES

    1. Ralph Martin, *Jennie,* 2 (New York: Doubleday, 1971), p. 15.
    2. Pearl Craigie's life and death were discussed in more detail in chapter 2 of my *The London Yankees* (New York: Harcourt Brace Jovanovich, 1979).

3. For more on both Rossetti and Waugh see my *Four Rossettis: A Victorian Biography* (New York: Weybright and Tally, 1977).

4. Virginia Woolf, *Moments of Being. Unpublished Autobiographical Writings,* ed., Jeanne Schulkind (New York: Harcourt Brace Jovanovich, 1976), pp. 80–81.

5. For more on Beardsley's life and death see my *Aubrey Beardsley: Imp of the Perverse* (University Park, Pa: The Pennsylvania State University Press, 1976).

6. Proust's ailments are described in loving detail by George Painter in his definitive *Marcel Proust* (Boston: Little, Brown, 1959).

7. A useful survey covering some but not all of the phenomena I have described is Patrick Trevor-Roper, *The World Through Blunted Sight* (New York: Bobbs-Merrill, 1970).

8. See Richard Selzer, "Stone," in *Mortal Lessons* (New York: Simon and Schuster, 1976), pp. 85–86.

9. Deirdre Bair, *Samuel Beckett* (New York and London: Harcourt Brace Jovanovich, 1978), p. 424.

10. Carolly Erickson, *Bloody Mary* (New York: Doubleday, 1978), pp. 414, 505. *The Curse,* by Janice Delaney, Mary Jane Lupton, and Emily Toth (New York: Bantam, 1977), basing its account on C. Frederic Fluhmann's *The Management of Menstrual Disorders* (Philadelphia: Saunders, 1956), discusses the amenorrhea without assigning cause or effect.

11. The suggestion is made by Rodelle Weintraub after consultation with practicing gynecologists.

12. W. S. Maugham, *Points of View* (New York: Doubleday, 1959), pp. 189–90.

The Poet as Patient:
Henri Michaux

Virginia A. La Charité

Henri Michaux (b. 1899) has been variously viewed as a poet, a painter, a philosopher, a pessimist, an optimist, a prose writer, a realist, a dreamer, a clinician, a critic. His work is so multivalent and diverse in both mode of expression and content that nearly any approach may be valid, any description acceptable, any interpretation credible. Hence, the immediate problem that confronts his reader is that of identity, for, at first glance, his creative universe is all-inclusive and nondefinable—a labyrinth in which a reader may wander at will, only to be checked by impasses. Yet, there are patterns that unify his artistry and account in part for what on the surface may be said to be paradoxical, contradictory, and unresolved.

In the first place, Michaux's work is based on personal encounters with pain and his own attempts to overcome, if not nullify, the fact that the human body is a vulnerable organism. In the second place, man has a terrain that is free from the disease that characterizes his existence in the physical world: the space within.[1] The problem, then, for the reader is to accept Michaux's war on the external intrusion of pain and enter his labyrinth of inner space. For Michaux, pain is the one sensation that affects man on all levels: physical, moral, intellectual, social, emotional, artistic. Pain links man to a sordid world in which there is a loss of all initiative to act and eventually the loss of control over one's existence. Pain renders its sufferer so weak and so deficient that he literally becomes depersonalized, tied only to a dehumanized state of submission, despair, and impotence. Victory over pain resides in the liberation of inner space, affirmation of the self, health in the fullest meaning of the term. Consequently, Michaux's work from 1923 to the present is structured at all turns on the problem of suffering: "*Suffering* is the word."

Michaux's emphasis on suffering and pain arises from his own experiences. Beginning with an asthmatic childhood that compelled his parents to send him to the country for his early schooling, he even attended medical school for one year (1919) in an intellectual and academic attempt to try to come to grips with bodily affliction and suffering. His first major work of poetry, *Who I Was* (1927), examines the feelings of alienation and solitude that afflict a sufferer and leads Michaux to speculate about an "inner hygiene" that might neutralize, if not conquer, the victimization caused by physical weakness.

During a trip to Ecuador (1927–28), the high altitude so adversely affected his stomach, his breathing, his heart that he describes himself as "born full of holes." The cardiac condition that afflicts Michaux the man in South America is effectively transposed into his work, *Ecuador* (1928) —a text that remains highly personal but in which he elects a diary form in prose, dialogue, and free verse poetry. Michaux's first "crisis of dimension" in personal and artistic terms stems from his sensation of impotency, as his body takes over and dictates his existence. Election of the subjective diary form and its multiple styles for *Ecuador* testifies to the fragmentation that occurs when Michaux as man and poet faces his vulnerability to attack from without; he actually has no identifiable mode of expression, having lost control over the space within.

The poet is, then, a sufferer who is subject to the ordeals of the flesh and its organs. In order to recuperate, he becomes a patient, forced to a prone position in bed, the dimension of flatness and solitude. In *My Properties* (1929), the poet-patient begins to turn for the first time to his inner space in order to counterbalance his horizontally immobile position by vertically thrusting his imagination against "A Rotten Life." Deprived of physical stamina, he finds that there is strength and relief in creations of his own. As the doctors examine his urine and decide that "A Prudent Man" is one who follows endless pieces of cautious advice (no smoking, special diet, rest), the poet-patient decides that just staying alive in the outer space is the main problem. Writing "In Bed," he equates immobility with boredom and vulnerability; illness is inactivity and the loss of equilibrium (the earlier crisis of dimension), while convalescence becomes the recovery of self-mastery. In "Shouting," Michaux finds that the pain caused by the inflammation of his big toe is so unbearable that he is led to scream; the release of these screams brings a moment of relief from the oppressiveness of the pain and at the same time results in a creative act: the poem of release that momentarily negates the anguish of actual suffering. His "Intervention" in the medical world alleviates the problem. The expulsion of sound—the scream—is an immediate reaction that does not pass through the brain for its formulation; rather, it is a direct response to a stimulus and, in its expansion from scream to yell, it overcomes the actuality of immobility and containment in the body. Temporarily, the sufferer becomes the master of his suffering through verbal expression. With the series of texts in *My Properties*, Michaux establishes the use of unformed sounds as a poetic means of remedy and discovers that the text of inner space can invade corporeal existence. The creative act has therapeutic value.

The subsequent creation of the fictive character Plume in *A Certain Plume* (1930) continues Michaux's view of inner space as the potential terrain for therapy. Plume is the foil to the sufferer, for Plume is neither vulnerable nor victimized by physical reality; he is immune to affliction and does not even react to stimuli. Plume does not experience pain. In "Plume Had a Sore Finger," for example, Plume undergoes the amputation of a finger, but it does not bother him because he still has nine left! Plume never aches, never hurts, never suffers. He is a scapegoat on whom Michaux releases his own suffering: "I play out my ailment through him."

Following the Plume texts, Michaux undertook a long trip to Southeast Asia and the Far East. In *A Barbarian in Asia* (1933), he is struck by Oriental attitudes to the human body, illness, suffering, and death. He finds in India that health is mainly a matter of self-treatment, and he notes in China that death is not viewed in a tragic perspective. The stoicism of the Orient provides the Western poet-patient with a counterbalance to Occidental emphasis on life. Publishing *Night on the Move* (1935) and *The Far Away Inside* (1938), Michaux draws on his trip to Asia by using inner space to defeat, not just alleviate, suffering. Health lies in the attitude of hostility to the pus that infects the exterior world. "The Athlete in Bed" denies his immobility; rapid breathing in "On Breathing" is inverted into an image of hardiness; infection in a swollen leg disappears as it is blatantly ignored by the imagination in "Emme and the Old Doctor."

Projection of inner space onto the outer space in *Between Center and Absence* (the first part of *The Far Away Inside*) by means of the "Big Screen" of the mind enables the patient to envisage what is beyond the physical. Seeing what is not there brings about release in "A Head Comes Out of the Wall," for this kind of vision creates in turn a form of immunity to actual stimuli and displaces the moment of suffering. Although Michaux is too much of a realist to deny the fact that ailments such as toothaches and earaches occur and cause acute discomfort, he succeeds, nonetheless, in not permitting them to disrupt his equilibrium. In his world, the ill person can effectively counter his pain and choose his moment of suffering, as opposed to Huysmans's protagonist, Des Esseintes (*Against the Grain*, 1884), who commits metaphysical suicide because he cannot overcome the intrusion of a toothache into his private, sensate world. For Michaux, life is activity, expressed in "My Blood"; it is free, inner circulation that can make the patient so active that he can detach himself from his toothache and treat it as a separate entity, one of his "properties." The body in the form of a toothache no longer rules the way the heart condition ruled in *Ecuador;* rather, the possessor of the toothache can now look at it dispassionately and determine his relationship to it. Such intervention into the physical world on the part of the space within does not negate the pain, but it does enable the patient to cease being the victim of his pain (as Des Esseintes was prey to his toothache) and to become instead its master. Making an object of pain into a poetic image of desired presence even characterizes Michaux's *Voyage to Great Garabagne* (1936), his first travelogue of a journey to an imaginary country; the people of Aples cure illness by placing a dog in the sickroom; the dog's salutary presence enables the sufferer to get outside of his illness, just as Michaux had earlier cast his own ailment on Plume.

Countering pain is a matter of taking the initiative and attacking the paralysis that illness and suffering foster. Michaux's collection of texts and drawings, *Paintings* (1939), proposes the "poem-action" that is based on poet-patient aggressive behavior to neutralize the "abscess of being" that he evokes in "Clown." The "poem-action" is marked by intensity and is, consequently, more creative than the "thought-image," which is passive in its reflection of the physical world of the outer space. Whereas a "thought-image" repeats form and shape ("abscess of being"), a "poem-action" is the immediate response to a stimulus and therefore immune to disease and decay. In the later edition, *Paintings and Drawings* (1946), Michaux further demonstrates the curative power of the "poem-action" by having the texts of poems printed in red type on tissue paper over each drawing. No matter how the reader-viewer approaches the volume, he sees first the tissue paper and red-inked words; as the drawing circulates under the words, the words are freed from the enclosure of their ideographic form and circulate actively, like blood, signifying health. The poet-patient's blood is the initial stimulus to the reader, who then reacts to the drawing beneath, the vision of what is not, the vision beyond the physical "body." The drawings approach sketches of reflexes, as the words themselves decrease in their relationship to the "reading" of the text. The physical stasis of words on the tissued page and of drawings on the second page is overcome by the presence of circulation: movement and fluidity. The Michaux expression emerges as one that expels the "abscess of being," the body of flesh and its inherent bulk, and eliminates what is vulnerable to attack by pain.

Michaux's "expulsion-purgation" of physical shape in his drawings (what he describes as the rejection of portraits in favor of "temperaments") is verbally undertaken in *Trials, Exorcisms* (1945). Just as linearity (the horizontal position of the patient) is "cured" in *Paintings and Drawings,* Michaux overcomes the phlegmatic mode of expression through aggressive direct writing, "an act of curing." Verbal exorcism becomes the "prisoner's poem" because it is the text of recovery. As the poet-patient dislocates words, fractures syllables, and ruptures grammar, the sufferer expels the weight of the external world, the abscess, and projects outward his "interior sentence," the expression of the health within. Sound and the incantation of nonwords emerge as adjuncts to the fluidity of the drawings. Monsters from without are countered by monsters from within, as words go on the attack to displace verbal suffering.

Hence, existence is heavy, ponderous, and subject to disease; even memories are wounds. Michaux's wife's illness (tuberculosis) and her long period of recovery, which is nullified by her agonizing death in 1948 from burns received in a fire, lead Michaux as man and poet to experience additional levels of suffering; he no longer suffers physically, metaphysically, and metaphorically, for he now experiences the pain of emotions.

Life in the Folds (1949) is bitterly marked by suffering induced by experiences in the outer space; hypodermic injections intrude in the midst of the cure, as the pain of reality creates a puppetlike existence. In order to defy and devalue this level of suffering, which is brought about by both corporeal and emotional "folds" (memories, wounds, scars), Michaux turns to a plastic art and written expression, which literally and figuratively get under the skin in *Facing the Locks* (1954). In this work, new dimensions are added to his exorcism of the world of form and formation, as he treats man as an abstraction and repudiates man "according to his flesh." Texts of attack are written in aggressive capital letters ("I AM ROWING," "EFFICACIOUS," "TO ACT, I AM COMING") so that their visual impact amputates their relationship from the usual printed form (external body). In *Movements,* a 1951 text included in *Facing the Locks,* Michaux unlocks the human body by capturing man as circulation —inner space gestures in motion. His drawings and text become virtual renderings of circulation, free even from the corporeal limits of *Paintings and Drawings* and their use of special but no less physically delineated arrangements (tissue paper that overlays the drawings). In overcoming the form of expression, Michaux intersperses in *Movements* drawings of man's gestures with a free verse text; the reader-viewer can no longer distinguish where one mode ends and another begins, for the plastic and written are so complementary that each is essential to the "reading-viewing" of the other. The actual dimension of paginal space, limitation, and immobility (the situation of a sufferer) is "cured," as the reader now circulates freely in the poet's vision. Michaux's dedication to the noncorporeal is maintained in *Four Hundred Men on the Cross* (1956), where he proposes "A CRYSTAL MAN," one who is free from the crucifixion of life and its inherent pain. The body is a prison, and suffering is nonredemptive.

Michaux's exploration of the physical world and its exorcism through a purgation of form in both plastic and written modes are followed by sixteen years (1955–71) of investigation into the psychological level of human existence through drug experimentation. Using hallucinogens to reach inner space in its subconscious mode, Michaux finds that drugs indeed permit the patient to forget the existence of the body and they do eliminate pain, but the drug experience can also engender plurality, fragmentation, disorder, and the loss of self-control. Moreover, drug usage leaves the experimenter in a state of physical exhaustion and dependency; it reinforces corporeal weakness, impairs functions, induces disability and disorientation, and creates discomfort as well as feelings of vulnerability. Drugs are not creative in overcoming suffering; they are only revelatory of the fact that suffering can be overcome. The poet-clinician in *Miserable Miracle* (1956), *The Turbulent Infinite* (1957), *Peace in Debris* (1959), *Learning through Despair* (1961), *Winds and Dust* (1962), and *Towards Fulfillment* (1967) finds he is still a patient, who even years after the experiences has a crisis of dimension, a disruption of his equilibrium, an invasion of his health.

Abandonment of drug experimentation as a means of establishing a terrain of inner space that is completely free from the hypodermic real is followed by studies of dreams and daydreams in *Sleeping Modes, Waking Modes* (1969), yet in these texts Michaux retains the artistic attitude of the detached clinical observer of his drug works. Fusing scientist with poet, his examination of the dream world concludes that dreams reflect the corporeal world of "thought-images," while daydreams capture the fluidity and circulation of the space within of the "poem-action." Daydreams render intact the vibration and rhythm of the formless shapes of *Movements,* for they go beyond the basic physical form of words.

The collected volume *Moments: Passages of Time* (1973) examines how man can be taken out of the prison of his abscess of being: the work of artists, experiences of intense contemplation as practiced in the Orient, moments of unrestricted mobility such as that afforded by daydreams. Michaux does not set up a new optic for man nor the adoption of a special attitude towards existence such as Surrealist salvation through the imagination. On the contrary, he combines subject with object (poet-patient, clinician-clairvoyant), just as he combines written and plastic art in an affirmation of health: life in its vibratory, fluid evocations. As the words of *Moments* circulate across the page, they destroy the dimensions of the intrusive body by evoking passages outside time and space. Freedom from the confines of limitation and suffering is poetically rendered through a liberation of the word from its contextual situation; the text ceases to be linear and flat (the prone position of the patient) and becomes eruptive and motile, having no beginning, no end, only a vortex of formlessness, life itself.

Yet, the artistic victory of *Moments* is nearly negated by *Facing What Is Disappearing* (1975), in which the poet experiences a broken arm and a subsequent bone infection. Facing the loss of his right hand and consequently of his ability to write and to paint, Michaux must either accept his handicap or retrain his left hand. The loss of equilibrium is a loss of body symmetry; being off-balance in a new crisis of dimension in which the body is again controlling his existence, the poet-patient adopts the clinical stance that marks his drug and dream analyses, as he sets out to overcome this latest insult from the body, which threatens the very practice of his artistry. Prior to his bone complication, Michaux's written and plastic modes are structured around therapeutic counterbalances in which the forces of expression oppose their form. Now he faces the world of nature and applies to it the same attack technique of the "poem-action" by countering the futility of suffering with the usefulness of pain. Inverting the nonnatural, Michaux brings about a new physical balance to his own corporeal existence—he becomes left-handed and discovers that this new dimension is even preferable to his former right-handed situation. Suffering alone offers the opportunity for self-mastery over the outer space, and, as such, it is useful on all levels of existence, especially the creative one.

Michaux's personal and artistic triumph over suffering and sordid physical reality is summarized in *Along the Path of Rhythm* (1974). While this work could be described as strictly one of plastic art, for it contains no words and consists solely of drawn figures very like those of the earlier and right-handed created gestures of *Movements*, it is undeniably a work of poetry that demonstrates as no other Michaux text his ultimate triumph over the hostile real world and suffering. Drawn exclusively with his left hand, Michaux's figures *Along the Path of Rhythm* emerge from the horizontal confines of form into a vertical unmeasurable resurgence and reaffirmation of life forces; rhythm is the manifestation of inner circulation, health. Words are finally counterbalanced by silence, as suffering becomes the word that is its own cure. The patient creates the poet through *Emergences-Resurgences* (1972) of the space within.[2]

Notes

1. *The Space Within* is the title of Michaux's collected volume of poetry, and it is available in English under the title *Selected Writings: The Space Within*, trans. Richard Ellmann (New York: New Directions, 1968). Other Michaux works currently available in English include *A Barbarian in Asia*, trans. Sylvia Beach (New York: New Directions, 1972); *Ecuador*, trans. Robin Magowan (Seattle: University of Washington, 1970); *H. Michaux*, trans. Theo Savory (Santa Barbara, Calif.: Unicorn Press, 1967); *Light Through Darkness*, trans. H. Chevalier (New York: Orion Press, 1963); *The Major Ordeals of the Mind and the Countless Minor Ones*, trans. Richard Howard (New York: Harcourt Brace Jovanovich, 1974); *Miserable Miracle: Mescaline with Eight Drawings*, trans. Louise Varèse (San Francisco: City Lights Books, 1963).

2. Critical studies in English on Michaux include Malcolm Bowie, *Henri Michaux: A Study of His Literary Works* (Oxford: Clarendon Press, 1973); Virginia A. La Charité, *Henri Michaux* (New York: Twayne, 1977); Frederic J. Shepler, *Creatures Within: Imaginary Beings in the Work of Henri Michaux* (Bloomington, Indiana: Physsardt, 1977).

Syphilis as Muse in
Thomas Mann's Doctor Faustus

Laurence M. Porter

"Perhaps the most personal and characteristic of Thomas Mann's reflections on art and life is his concept of the relation between disease and genius."[1] His favorite characters among his creations were two diseased musicians, Hanno in *Buddenbrooks* and Adrian Leverkühn in *Doctor Faustus*. Personal experience contributed to the development of this idea. Mann underwent surgery for lung cancer during the 1940s, while writing *Doctor Faustus*. He remarked in himself, as well as in mankind generally, "the curious divergence between biological and intellectual vitality. . . . I wrote the best chapters of [my novel] *The Beloved Returns* during a six-month bout with infectious sciatica."[2] Almost from the outset of his career, Mann had associated illness with artistic inspiration.

This notion was hardly new. Plato had likened poetic creativity to madness. In *Doctor Faustus,* Mann had to take only two steps in order to transform the ancient Greeks' notion that the artist or oracle was possessed by a God into the notion that artistic inspiration could result from possession by the Devil, and that demonic possession of the soul could be represented metaphorically by a body invaded by the alien microorganisms of an infectious disease. Several of the German romantics, like E. T. A. Hoffmann and Friedrich Schlegel, considered illness "a spiritual phenomenon, closely associated with intellectual and emotional awakening." In his *Aphorisms,* Novalis claimed that sickness was necessary to individuation.[3] But Nietzsche and Dostoevsky were Mann's major sources for this view.

Ever since *Thus Spake Zarathustra,* Nietzsche had repeatedly stressed the mind's dependence on the body. In *The Genealogy of Morals* he said that "every table of values, every 'thou shalt' known to history or ethnology, requires first of all a *physiological* illumination and interpretation."[4] Mann owned several editions of Nietzsche's works, and about twenty-five books of Nietzsche scholarship. He admitted that *Doctor Faustus* was a Nietzsche novel, meaning that he had deliberately created many parallels between the philosopher's life and Leverkühn's. Mann's Devil quotes from Nietzsche's *Ecce Homo;* and Mann borrows Nietzsche's experience in the Cologne bordello, the symptomatology of his disease, and even his dietetic menus from Nice.[5]

As for Dostoevsky, Mann observed that during the composition of *Doctor Faustus,* when he had to witness from exile the spectacle of his native land dishonored by Hitler and defeated in the 1939–45 war, "I was greatly drawn to Dostoevsky's grotesque, apocalyptic realm of suffering, in contrast with my usual preference for Tolstoy's Homeric, primal strength."[6] Dostoevsky's Prince Myshkin, the hero of *The Idiot,* often wondered whether his flashes of insight were nothing more than disease, a departure from the normal. "What if it is disease?" he decided at last. "What does it matter that it is an abnormal intensity, if the result, if the minute of sensation, remembered and analyzed afterwards in health, turns out to be the acme of harmony and beauty, and gives a feeling, unknown and undefined till then, of completeness, of proportion, of reconciliation, and of ecstatic devotion merging in the highest synthesis of life?"[7] Mann himself distinguished two types of artists: the healthy, who have natural grandeur, and the sick, who have spiritual grandeur. In the essay "Goethe and Tolstoy," written in 1922, he contrasts these two vigorously healthy writers with the ailing Schiller and Dostoevsky. Mann categorically refused to identify himself with either type.

Mann's essay "Dostoevsky—Within Limits" develops his line of speculation concerning "genius as disease, disease as genius, the type of the afflicted and possessed, where saint and criminal become one." Mann continues: "However much Dostoevsky's ailment threatened his mental powers, it is no less certain that his genius was closely bound up with and colored by it." To be sure, the "average dull-witted man" cannot find inspiration in illness, but in the case of geniuses "something comes out in illness that is more important and conducive to life and growth than any medically guaranteed health or sanity . . . certain conquests made by the soul and the mind are impossible without disease, madness, crime of the spirit; the great morbid ones are the crucified, sacrifices on the altar of humanity, to the end that it shall be uplifted, its understanding and feeling enlarged, its health lifted to a higher plane." Such people "make us cautious altogether about the concept sickness, which we have been all too ready to mark with a biologically minus sign."[8]

Mann's novel *Doctor Faustus,* published in 1947, dramatizes this idealistic view of illness. The twentieth-century German composer Adrian Leverkühn willfully contracts syphilis with the understanding that the infection will be limited to the central nervous system, thanks to the intervention of the Devil; that it will stimulate his brain in such a way as to lead him to a stylistic breakthrough which will redeem modern music from sterility; and that he will enjoy twenty-four years of intense creativity. Mann had sketched the outline of this story as far back as 1905.[9] At that time the myth that the brain lesions of neurosyphilis might inspire original thought was already current. It recurs periodically to the present day, in such flights of fancy as B. Springer's *Die genialen Syphilitiker*

(*The Inspired Syphilitics,* 1926), Janos Plesch's *Rembrandts within Rembrandts* (1953), or Richard Selzer's "Museum Piece" in his *Rituals of Surgery* (1974).

Mann tells us that he read many books about neurosyphilis while he was composing *Doctor Faustus.* [10] Five unnumbered and undated handwritten pages describing the symptoms of the disease, drawn up perhaps by Mann's friend Dr. Martin Gumpert, were found among his papers after his death. They list the characteristic complaints of Adrian Leverkühn in the novel: severe headaches, stiffness of the pupils, psychic irritability, unconscious slips of the tongue, difficulty in pronouncing complicated words (a phenomenon quite evident in Adrian's farewell speech), and general luetic paralysis, alternating with periods of improvement even without treatment.[11] From a medical viewpoint, the major distortions in the description of Adrian's disease are the absence of secondary symptoms and the neat temporal divisions between relapses. Adrian becomes infected in 1906, and suffers periods of severe ill health in 1918, 1926, and 1930 when he becomes an idiot. In other words, the twenty-four years of creativity granted by the Devil are divided into periods of twelve, eight, and four years.

The real interest of Mann's treatment of syphilis in his novel, however, is not limited to his attempt to portray its symptoms faithfully. His characters engage in debate concerning the nature and meaning of disease itself. Mann links disease to the romantic concept of the artist inherited from his literary forebears. And he integrates disease into a conceptual framework which he had been elaborating ever since the beginning of his career, a constellation of ideas which associates artistic creativity with repressed sexuality, a pernicious euphoria, death, the demonic, and a self-absorbed rejection of the ethical demands of society.

From the standpoint of a medical anthropologist, "disease" is "a theoretical term that is used to designate or label harmful deviations . . . from optimal human functioning and adaptation. . . . The realization that physicians are urged to treat health crises and illnesses having no identifiable organic or biological substrate and that biological disease states often go unrecognized is compelling evidence that disease and human behavior as traditionally defined today are neither logically nor causally linked."[12] Therefore disease can be seen either as a biological or as a behavioral disturbance, or both. In one of the discussions between the narrator Serenus Zeitblom and the composer Adrian Leverkühn in *Doctor Faustus,* the former claims that Adrian's syphilis is just a biological disorder, while the latter insists that it results from his choice and is intimately related to his moral destiny.

When Mann speaks in his own voice elsewhere he considers disease primarily a behavioral disturbance. In his writings, the concept of disease functions primarily to associate the esthetic experience and artistic creativity with guilt.[13] Thus in his essay on Wagner, Mann comments that the chemical properties of the love potion in the Tristram legend are less important in determining the fateful passion of the two protagonists than is their attitude. Thinking that they have drunk poison and have only a short time to live, they consider themselves freed from their vows to King Mark and entitled to reveal their mutual love in their last moments.

Goethe, in a famous quip on the arts, said romanticism is sickness and classicism is health. This view is borne out by the behavior of many romantic artists who adopted a "sick role": they indulged in eccentric conduct, withdrew from society, and allowed themselves to be cared for by others. Since they did not seek treatment for their condition, they were socially condemned for their deviancy, as the addict, kleptomaniac, or sexually disturbed person might be condemned today unless he looked for help.[14] To put it another way, one might say that romanticism attempted to separate literature from the task of maintaining social order; to free the esthetic domain from ethical demands. The opposition of the esthetic and the ethical occurs throughout Mann's work.

The status of the diseased artist as Mann sees him is profoundly ambivalent. "The demonic and irrational have a disquieting share in this radiant sphere [of genius]," the narrator of *Doctor Faustus* asserts at the outset. Two-thirds of the way through the novel, he expatiates on this opinion: "The depressive and the exalted states of the artist, illness and health, are by no means sharply divided from each other. . . . In illness, as it were under the lee of it, elements of health are at work, and elements of illness, working geniuslike, are carried over into health. . . . Genius is a form of vital power deeply experienced in illness, creating out of illness, through illness creative." Moreover, *Doctor Faustus* draws many implicit parallels between Leverkühn and Christ. The ailing artist is a Christ figure whose suffering benefits future artists by showing them the way to a renewal of art; at the same time he is a damned soul who has signed a pact with the Devil in order to secure the specious boon of "the sinful and morbid corruption of natural gifts."[15]

Mann's artistic originality is not the result of his restatement of this familiar position, but rather of his skillful association of the notions of sin and disease with the very nature of Leverkühn's original discovery in music. In Chapter 19 the composer knowingly risks contracting syphilis from a whore, during the only genitally sexual act of his life. He does indeed become diseased. A series of five musical notes whose names in German correspond to five successive elements of his name for the woman he possessed come to form a frequent motif in his compositions: B ("H" in German), E, A, E and E^b (E-flat, which is "Es" in German)— Hetaera Esmeralda. So, as the woman is the source of an infection which invades the composer's body, likewise her name is the source of a pattern which comes to pervade his music. When in Chapter 22 Leverkühn discovers the twelve-tone system (his version is a simplification and parody of the method of composition with twelve tones developed by Schönberg, for Leverkühn always presents the twelve tones in the same order, regardless of other considerations, and he allows anarchy to reign in other areas of his music), the tone rows become omnipresent, like a foreign organism in an infected body, and his final, major composition again features the five-note sequence as the dominant element among the tone rows.

Mann interpreted the syphilis in *Doctor Faustus* as "a means provided by the Devil to induce creativity in an artist inhibited by knowledge."[16] Leverkühn hallucinates the Devil in Chapter 25. (Actually Mann suggests that this figure has emanated from the composer's unconscious. Mann himself had undergone a Freudian analysis and was familiar with Freud's writings.) The Devil retrospectively explains that Leverkühn's syphilis derives from a demonic pact. So far as the fate of the composer himself is concerned, strictly speaking the Devil is dramatically unnecessary: the syphilitic infection itself, together with Leverkühn's belief that it can provide him with artistic inspiration, accounts adequately for his destiny. But the Devil's role is necessary to add mythic-religious overtones to three other levels of meaning in the novel, on which Leverkühn functions respectively as a Christ figure, as the legendary Faustus of the 1587 chapbook, and as the German people intoxicated with the poisonous cant of Hitlerism. The latter two of these levels, like the first, associate the esthetic experience with guilt.

The title story of Mann's first book, *Little Herr Friedemann*, takes up the Kierkegaardian association of music with sexuality and the demonic. He added narcosis and death to this constellation of motifs in his masterpiece, *The Magic Mountain*. *Doctor Faustus* brings to their full development this set of notions, which had been familiar to Mann for fifty years. Broadly speaking, music, self-sufficient and nonrepresentational as it is, stands for Mann's own intricate, self-engrossed, and "apolitical" art[17] as he surveyed it at the twilight of his career. In this perspective, disease in *Doctor Faustus* metaphorically assumes the burden of Mann's uneasy conscience vis-à-vis the bourgeois. Bourgeois normalcy has the virtue of affirming human solidarity, the dominant ethical principle which Mann's artists feel they must neglect in order to be creative. Mann never resolved his inner tension between ethics and esthetics. In his last great novel, *The Confessions of Felix Krull, Confidence Man,* the rascality of the protagonist— comparable to the syphilis of *Doctor Faustus*—reasserts the scandalousness of trying to be different from others.

NOTES

1. Joseph Gerard Brennan, *Thomas Mann's World* (New York: Russell and Russell, 1962 [orig. pub. 1942]), p. xi.

2. Thomas Mann, *The Story of a Novel: The Genesis of "Doctor Faustus"* (New York: Knopf, 1961), p. 5.

3. Brennan, *Thomas Mann's World,* pp. 39, 40.

4. R. J. Hollingdale, *Thomas Mann: A Critical Study* (London: Rupert Hart-Davis, 1971), p. 143.

5. Mann, *The Story of a Novel,* p. 32.

6. Ibid., p. 125.

7. Quoted by Brennan, *Thomas Mann's World,* p. 39.

8. Joseph Warner Angell, ed., *The Thomas Mann Reader* (New York: Knopf, 1950), pp. 435, 439, 443, 444.

9. Thomas Mann, "Notebook 7" (unpublished), cited by T. J. Reed, *Thomas Mann: The Uses of Tradition* (Oxford, England: The Clarendon Press, 1974), p. 361. Mann mistakenly dates this note 1901 in *The Story of a Novel.*

10. Mann, *The Story of a Novel,* pp. 62, 217. He also read many books on spinal meningitis, the disease that kills the fictional composer's beloved nephew.

11. Gunilla Bergsten, *Thomas Mann's "Doctor Faustus"* (Chicago, Ill.: University of Chicago Press, 1969 [orig. pub. 1963]), p. 57. Compare, e.g., Elmer E. Southard and Harry C. Solomon, *Neurosyphilis. Modern Systematic Diagnosis and Treatment* (New York: Arno Press, 1973), pp. 5, 17–18, 31, 116, 120, et passim.

12. Horacio Fabrega, *Disease and Social Behavior* (Cambridge, Mass.: MIT Press, 1974), pp. 124, 161.

13. Bernhard Blume, "Aspects of Contradiction: On Recent Criticisms of Thomas Mann," in Henry Hatfield, ed., *Thomas Mann: A Collection of Critical Essays* (Englewood Cliffs, N.J.: Prentice-Hall, 1964), p. 164.

14. Robert Dingwall, *Aspects of Illness* (New York: Saint Martin's Press, 1976), p. 31, citing Talcott Parson's *The Social System.*

15. Mann, *Doctor Faustus: The Life of the German Composer Adrian Leverkühn, as Told by a Friend* (New York: Knopf, 1963 [orig. pub. 1947]), pp. 4, 354–55, 4.

16. Patrick Carnegy, *Faust as Musician: A Study of Thomas Mann's Novel "Doctor Faustus"* (London: Chatto and Windus, 1973), p. 2, citing Mann's correspondence.

17. In 1918 Mann published an autobiographical book entitled *Betrachtungen eines Unpolitischen* (Reflections of an Apolitical Man).

From Heart to Spleen:
The Lyrics of Pathology in Nineteenth-Century French Poetry
Robert L. Mitchell

At the beginning of the nineteenth century in France, both the strict rules of acceptable poetic vocabulary codified two centuries before (which proscribed the use of vulgar, "unpoetic" terms) and the ideology of a Romantic conception of the poet encouraged verse that was ethereal and relatively limited in terms of imaginative power. The harsh realities of everyday existence were consistently cloaked by euphemism and coated over by rhetorical flourishes. By the end of the century, however, French poetry had undergone an extraordinary revolution in expressive freedom, broadening its horizons of permissable vocabulary. This evolution in the conception of poetic expression was characterized by an increasing self-consciousness of the poem's own language. Poetic vocabulary ceased simply to follow well-established constrictive rules of the "noble style" and began to tap an increasing number of outside resources to express the poet's vision or attitudes. Medical and scientific terms, theretofore proscribed for the poetic text, were among these.

At the beginning of the century, the use of medical terms in poetry was relatively uncommon, and the only consistently "mentionable" organ of the human body was the heart. Even this was not conceived as a bodily organ of blood and muscle, but rather—to reflect the sensitive, Romantic hero—as a symbol of joy and pain, the repository of desire, passion, and profound sentiment. Chateaubriand's lyric prose, for instance—his *René* in particular—is pervaded by the word *heart,* which is also vital to his definition of the Romantic "vagueness of passions": "One lives with a full heart, in an empty world; and having used nothing, one is abused by everything."[1] The heart of another celebrated Romantic, Alfred de Musset, would frequently beat on demand, as in "To My Friend Édouard B." (1832): "Ah! beat your heart, 'tis where genius is. / 'Tis there where pity, suffering, and love are."[2]

After the century's midpoint there came a new generation of extraordinarily imaginative poets—Baudelaire, Rimbaud, and Corbière (to name only a few)—who, as Victor Hugo put it, were among the first to "place a revolutionary bonnet on the old dictionary," to pulverize the traditional, accepted values in French poetry by, among many new techniques, exploring the possibilities of using traditionally unpoetic words, including vulgar or common terms, neologisms, and medical and scientific expressions. Like Du Bellay in the *Defense and Illustration of the French Language* three centuries before, these poets attempted to broaden the lexical base of poetic language, to include theretofore tabooed expressions. Generally, the vocabulary developed by these innovators was of a much more physical nature (the heart, we have seen, had been constantly spiritualized) than that of their predecessors; they frequently dared to choose expressions that were scatalogical, sexual, anatomical, and pathological. The word *spleen,* used in the title of this essay (as well as by many late nineteenth-century poets), exemplifies this trait. Its literary sense is a profound and disturbing malaise, far more visceral than the Romantic boredom or melancholy; its connotations of blackness and corporeal— as well as spiritual—oppression (it is, of course, the English word gallicized) justifies its use as an antonym to the "heart."

Before exploring some of the "lyrics of pathology" that cropped up in late nineteenth-century French poetry (and, more important, the various uses to which they were put), we might first take a brief look at two texts written in the early 1870s that specifically attempted to pervert the poetic status of the "heart" so dearly cherished by the Romantics. The first example is the opening line of Arthur Rimbaud's "Le Coeur volé" ("The Pilfered Heart"): "Mon triste coeur bave à la poupe" ("My sad heart dribbles at the poop").[3] On the literal level, the poem describes the physical and moral revulsion that the adolescent Rimbaud experiences in the orgiastic company of soldiers during the Paris Commune. On a symbolic level, this opening verse ironically derides Rimbaud's susceptible, "Romantic" heart: the first four syllables ("Mon triste coeur"), an eminently Romantic phrasing, are quickly and brutally undermined by the four that follow ("bave à la poupe"). In fact, the young Rimbaud's heart not only dribbles (sickened by the antics of the soldiers) but, in the second line, is just as repulsively "covered with tobacco." (It is spat on by the same soldiers.)

A second, even more significant illustration of the deromanticizing of the heart occurs in Tristan Corbière's poem of social and sexual isolation, "Paria" ("Pariah"): "Moi,—coeur eunuque, dératé / De ce qui mouille et ce qui vibre" ("I,—eunuch heart, despleened / Of what moistens and what trembles"). Here, the Romantic conception of the heart is doubly perverted. First, modified by "eunuch," it is emasculated and thus no longer valid as the seat of (virile) emotions such as desire and passion. Second, it is then "despleened" (or, figuratively, "deprived") of tears (and perhaps semen?) and heartbeat (orgasm?). This juxtaposition of heart and spleen is especially noteworthy (particularly for our study), as the very mention of the spleen serves to contaminate the usually affective connotations of the heart.

What makes the following examination of medical vocabulary in lyrical texts so meaningful is that we are not dealing with a group of mediocre poets: they are, on the contrary, important figures in the development of what we think of as "modern" poetry, in France and elsewhere.

Charles Baudelaire (1821–67) is generally considered to be the "father of modern poetry": his texts are not only far more self-conscious than those of his predecessors, but they also demonstrate a new, daring conception of poetic imagery at the center of which was the imagination (and not the heart). The heart was certainly not abolished from his poetry, since Baudelaire had not entirely liberated himself from the Romantic influence. In fact, the word appears no fewer than 142 times in his major collection, *Les Fleurs du mal (Flowers of Evil),* which first appeared in 1857. But there is no doubt that his poetry introduced into the French tradition a language that attempts, on the imaginative level, to come to grips with the corporeal, the ugly, the visceral, the macabre, the gnawingly oppressive qualities and vices of the human condition—in short, the "spleen" of man's existence. The way in which this language (part of which uses terms from anatomy and pathology) functions is, paradoxically, by transforming—by image or symbol—what is repugnant into something beautiful, as Baudelaire affirms in a fragment that suggests this "alchemy": "Tu m'as donné ta boue et j'en ai fait de l'or" ("You gave me your mud [vice, ugliness, etc.] and I fashioned gold out of it").

Apart from the familiar "heart," the following selective list of specifically medical expressions gives us an idea of the variety of disease perceptions and anatomical realism that Baudelaire infused into his poetry: atrabiliary, bowels, brain (fourteen times), cadaver (eleven times), canker, chlorosis, clavicles, convulsion, dropsical, fetus, hospital, infection, lungs, marrow, nerves, olibanum, paralytic, phthisical, saliva, spleen, triturate, ulcerated, vertebrae.

One of Baudelaire's favorite tactics is to express an abstract, intangible feeling of oppression by means of concrete (often medical) imagery: this was considered a shocking technique in his day. In the prefatory poem of *Flowers of Evil,* "Au lecteur" ("To the Reader"), for example, he expresses sinning and vice with images such as beggars nourishing vermin, the Devil rocking us on his "pillow of evil," and a debaucher biting an old whore's breast. In the sixth stanza, anatomical terminology (brains and lungs) effectively helps to transform the "Demons" of vice and the specter of Death—both abstractions—into eerie, concrete, hauntingly *real* entities. The former becomes a squirming army of worms; the latter, an invisible, plaintive river:

> Close, swarming, like a million worms,
> In our brains is a world of Demons on a spree,
> And Death in our lungs, when we breathe,
> Descends, an invisible river, with deaf groaning squirms.

Medical terms also help create the macabre element of Baudelaire's poetic universe: the stinking, infected, but (as always, the Baudelairian paradox) beautiful carcass of "Une Charogne" ("A Carcass"); the anatomical horrors of the Skeletons and the Flayed Ones who inhabit the quais of Paris in "Le Squelette laboureur" ("The Skeleton-Laborer"); and the "charming horror" of, and bizarre attraction to, the "dancing skeleton"—complete with clavicles, vertebrae, and teeth—that represents all of humanity in "Danse macabre" ("Macabre Dance"). But it is perhaps "Spleen *(Pluviôse, irrité . . .)*" ("Spleen [*Pluviôse, irritated . . .*]") that best illustrates the lyrical function of medical terminology. Here, Baudelaire presents the reader with a series of disconnected, concrete images that collectively represent the generally oppressive nature of "spleen," its powerful figurative and spiritual connotations. Contributing to this impression are descriptions of the malnourished and scabby body of the poet's cat, the influenzal wheezing of the clock, and the dirty deck of gossiping cards, the legacy of a mysterious, dropsical old woman. As is often the case in Baudelaire's poetry, medical terms are used to create a collective metaphor of the sickness of the human condition.

Arthur Rimbaud (1854–91), *the* Wunderkind of French—perhaps of all—poetry (he abandoned writing at the age of nineteen or thereabouts, leaving us with a legacy of some of the most bewildering and imaginative poems ever attempted), used medical terms to quite different ends than did Baudelaire. We shall take a look at some of his earlier, developmental poems, for it is there that the two functions of this specialized vocabulary are most apparent: (1) Irony: the adolescent Rimbaud wished to lash out at, and pervert, "adult" institutions, including love, beauty, religion, and the French bourgeois mentality in general by describing these entities in terms that were pathological, scatological, corporeal, and sexually aberrant. (2) Innovation: Rimbaud would soon develop an obsessive theory of "finding a [new] language" to replace the worn-out, conventional, impoverished manner of writing French poetry. His practice of novel linguistic usages, including neologism and scientific vocabulary, is pervasive (particularly in these very early poems). A selective list of medical terms which appear in his poetry includes anus, bile, bowels, brain (five times), cataplasm, cephalagia, chilblain, cloaca, cough, cupping-glass, enemas, epileptic, femur, fetus, gums, heart, hypogastrium, leprous, liver, migraine, occiput, ovaries, pectoral, phalanges, phthisical, rachitic, scapula, sinciput, skeleton, spasms, syphilitic, tonsils, triturate, ulcer, urine, vertigo, vomiting.

In several instances, Rimbaud mischievously perverts feminine beauty by anatomical description or distortion. "Vénus anadyomène" ("Venus Emerging from the Sea") presents a marvelously sardonic description of a "contemporary" Venus—here, a tattooed tart—emerging slowly and bestially from an ancient bathtub (rather than from the classical seashell!). Instead of Botticellian beauty, she has "touched-up deficits," broad scapulae, hyperactive sebaceous glands, a plethoric dorsal region, and "singularities that one ought to observe with a magnifying glass" (warts? lesions? . . .). And then the bottom line: this very un-Venus-like "Venus" presents us her broad horselike rump ("sa large croupe"): "Belle hideusement d'un ulcère à l'anus" ("Hideously beautiful with an ulcer on its anus").

It is, however, in "Les Assis" ("The Seated Ones") that Rimbaud most brilliantly allows medical terminology to function in a lyrical text. If the major theme of this poem is the sexual perversion of the "seated ones," the librarians who represent for the adolescent poet the hostile, adult world, Rimbaud's grotesque anatomical and pathological character-ization of them also dominates the poem. Medical imagery, densely con-centrated particularly in the first two stanzas, distorts the seated function-aries: they have black "wens," "knotted" fingers clenched tight to their femurs, sinciputs plated with vague "cantankers" (the French word is *hargnosités,* a neologism taken from the adjective *hargneux,* "ill-tempered"; like Baudelaire, Rimbaud has concretized in eminently physical terms an abstract personality trait, and my translation is a combination of "canker" and "cantankerous"), which resemble the "leprous efflorescences" of old walls. Further, they have grafted in "epileptic loves" their fantastic osse-ous frameworks to their chairs' black "skeletons," and their feet are intertwined in the chairs' "rachitic crossbars." As the poem develops, the librarians are maliciously depicted not with normal fantasies, but dream-ing of desks and chairs, of ink-flowers spitting comma-semen; finally, they fall asleep, and their "members" are aroused by the wicker of their chair seats. The description of the functionaires' grotesque, aberrant physical traits at the beginning of the poem appropriately leads to the poet's portrayal of their bizarre onanistic activity. The cumulative effect, as we have mentioned, is twofold: by means of medical vocabulary, Rimbaud has verbally demolished the librarians as well as established himself as an innovative and imaginative Wielder of the Word.

Yet a third, but no less imaginative use of medical vocabulary occurs in the poetry of the Breton Tristan Corbière (1845–75). Even more than Rimbaud's, Corbière's poetry is fundamentally ironic; and one of the many targets of this irony is "normal," heterosexual love. (As in Rim-baud's life, this element was almost certainly, as far as we know, absent in Corbière's.) Corbière's "loves" (his "mock love poems") are "jaun-diced." In fact, the title of his only collection of verse is *Les Amours jaunes (Jaundiced Loves).* In "A L'Etna" ("To Etna"), the volcanic mountain replaces any potential "real" lover: it is compared to a woman for its "soul/Of baked flint." The love between Etna (the surrogate female) and Corbière is, as always, contaminated, figuratively and literally, as jaun-dice, consumption, and cancer conspire to thwart any consummation:

> —You laugh yellow and cough: no doubt,
> Spitting an old sick love right out;
> The lava flows beneath the crust
> Of your chronic cancer of the breast.

—Let's hit the sack, Confrere!
My flank against your sick flank—there:
We're brothers, by Venus,
Volcano! . . .
          More . . . or less . . .

But it is "La Rapsode foraine et le pardon de Sainte-Anne" ("The Itinerant Rhapsodist and the Pardon of Sainte-Anne") that reflects a very different lyrical use of medical terminology. Here Corbière eloquently expresses his admiration and compassion for ugliness, malady, and deformity. It is a touching piece, which has its roots in Breton folklore; the Breton tradition, instead of deriding these qualities, reveres them and considers them saintly. The passage in which Corbière describes in clinical detail the nobility and faithful devotion of a group of Breton crusaders —a group composed of rachitics, epileptics, idiots, lepers, cripples and one-eyed souls, sufferers of ulcers, St. Vitus' dance, and cankers—is particularly poignant and succeeds in transforming a simple procession of diseased creatures into a touchingly lyrical moment. Two stanzas from this lengthy passage poignantly reflect Corbière's unique "lyrics of pathology":

Aren't they divine on their trays,
All haloed in vermilion,
These proprietors of open wounds as they pray,
Living rubies under the sun! . . .
. . . .
Votive piles of tainted meat,
Charnel houses for heaven's elect,
At home in His house, which God will protect!
—Was their making not his own feat . . .

Baudelaire, Rimbaud, and Corbière have thus provided some idea of the revolution that took place in nineteenth-century French poetry. Medical terms, as we have seen, play various essential and novel roles in this evolution, including the poetic transformation of a brutal reality; the epitomizing of the human condition; social and self-directed irony; a distortion of traditional values; and at times an apotheosis of pathological conditions. The real importance of this lexical and imaginative breakthrough is that besides creating works of great interest and value, these poets enabled those who followed to expand the boundaries of "acceptable" poetic vocabulary and, in particular, to exploit further the poetic possibilities of the (ostensibly alien) language of medicine. We can mention, in passing, the splenetic and lymphatic expressions of Jules Laforgue (1860–87), and especially his ironic "Complainte du foetus de poète" ("Complaint of the Poet-Fetus"), in which the poet, in the unlikely form of a fetus, describes his odyssey through Mom as he thrashes through the uterine "steppes of mucus" and placental decidua. Other examples include the motifs of neuropathological syndromes and physical atrophy that filled the verse of the "Decadent" poets in France during the 1880s. By then, the floodgates were open, and in the twentieth century the use of physical and mental anomaly had become an integral, "approved" part of poetic expression. The cleft between medicine and poetry had been, at least partially, sutured; the grafting had been performed successfully; and, stripped of its "alien" status, the former discipline had at last begun to be exploited (in the best sense) for its rich potential as thematic material by the latter.

NOTES

1. François René de Chateaubriand, *Atala, René, Les Aventures du dernier Abencérage* (Paris: Garnier, 1958), p. 170.

2. Alfred de Musset, *Poésies complètes* (Paris: Gallimard, Bibliothèque de la Pléiade, 1957), p. 128.

3. All translations are my own. I used the following editions: Charles Baudelaire, *Oeuvres complètes* (Paris: Gallimard, Bibliothèque de la Pléiade, 1975); Arthur Rimbaud, *Oeuvres* (Paris: Garnier, 1960); Charles Cros, Tristan Corbière, *Oeuvres complètes* (Paris: Gallimard, Bibliothèque de la Pléiade, 1970).

André Breton and Psychiatry
Anna Balakian

André Breton, the creator of Surrealism, came from a modest Breton family; born in 1896 in a provincial environment, he was sent to Paris in 1907 to one of the better secondary schools, the Lycée Chaptal, from which he graduated in 1912. He began his medical studies at the Sorbonne in 1913, one year before the declaration of World War I. After only two years of medical school he was assigned to a paramedical post in the Army at a hospital in Nantes where he tended the shell-shocked; and a little later, still during the war, he got even more practical experience at the psychiatric center of Saint-Dizier near Paris, where he became in 1917 the assistant of Dr. Raoul Leroy. He recalled these experiences in his memoirs, *Entretiens:* "I was able to try out experimentally on the patients the process of (psychoanalytical) investigation, keep records of interpretation of dreams, of dissociations of involuntary thought."[1] And he claimed that these were the first raw materials of surrealism.

In terms of theory, the three prominent workers in the field who attracted Breton's attention were the pioneer Jean-Martin Charcot, Pierre Janet, and Sigmund Freud. If the fundamental purpose of the surrealist doctrine was to widen the frontiers of reality, enlarging the power of the mind to grasp the phenomena of life, it was obvious that the most fertile research activity in the field was being done by psychiatrists. Breton dropped out of the study of medicine after the war; his mother was so distressed that she has been reported to have said, "I would have preferred to have heard that he had been killed in action." Brutal though this statement is, it can be understood in the context of social economics: for the lower bourgeois class medicine was the surest way to climb into economic security in the absence of family inheritances. Many of Breton's colleagues in the new literature were, like him, dropouts from medical studies. But this fact explains the spirit of teamwork among a number of the surrealists who had been to medical school and applied their methods of collaborative scientific experimentation to the scrutiny of the creative process related to writing as well as to living, which was at the core of the surrealist movement. The identification by psychiatrists of mental states outside of the standard rational ones, whether in the case of traumas produced on the battlefield, or in ordinary social behavior, gave these young people insights into the mind's potential for variation in the inter- pretation of reality. Mysticism in standard religions is based on aspira- tions for transcendence of the admitted limits of human reality. It seemed that the early stages of the work of psychiatry opened up knowledge of mental processes that could admit the transcendental without casting its target outside of earthly, sensory limits. The surrealists proposed for themselves a materiomysticism bound by the limits of human life and dedicated to the intensification of the sense of reality. Surrealism, pro- posed not as a denial of reality but as a search for a deeper knowledge of it, sought support in the methodologies of the psychiatrists.

In his first surrealist manifesto Breton asked: "Is it not true that the possibility for the mind to err is all to the good?" That was to be the crux of Breton's dispute with psychiatry.

In 1928, four years after the First Manifesto, in their magazine *La Révolution Surréaliste* (vol. 9, p. 20) Breton and his colleague, Louis Ara- gon, who had also been a medical student, celebrated the Fiftieth Anni- versary of Hysteria, calling the work of Charcot the greatest poetic discov- ery of the nineteenth century. Charcot's work had attracted attention among the lay public since his findings had been accompanied by an iconography, edited by his colleague Bourneville and an expert photog- rapher, P. Regnard. This Iconography of the Salpêtrière had been worked out between 1875 and 1880, and publication had begun in 1878. Charcot had been the first link between medicine and surrealism. Charcot seemed to have confirmed in his observation of clinical cases that it was possible for the human mind to conciliate objective reality with the dream without outside stimuli such as drugs or hypnosis. Charcot had noticed that the attitudes, positions, visionary stances of those called "hysterics" in the Salpêtrière hospital for the mentally deranged, right in the heart of Paris, were not dissimilar to those of saints and martyrs that one could observe in icons and statues of the Middle Ages. The similarity between mystical exaltation and the behavior of contemporary clinical cases had made Charcot believe that this kind of open-eyed visionary stance was more common than previously thought, not simply limited to female hysterics, but evident in men as well and existent outside of strictly medical cases. From these studies of Charcot and from the strange, hal- lucinated expression of the photographed cases, Breton and Aragon came to the conclusion that it was a state that could be simulated by the sane and used as a means of poetic expression to carry the writer and the reader to a level of communication more intense and more vibrant than that achieved by that infamously popular form of literature called narra- tive prose. Drawing their own conclusions from Charcot's scientific ob- servations, they declared, "Hysteria is not a pathological phenomenon and can, in all respects, be considered a means of expression."[2]

The study of hysteria led Breton to the investigation of other forms of so-called insanity that could be applied to enlarge the field of poetic investigation; the intention was to begin to redefine poetry by endowing it with an epistemological aim as well as an aesthetic one. This attempted relationship of poetry to scientific research was the motivating force that led to the declaration that to survive in the scientific age poetry must be considered a vital need to mental health and viewed as part of the modus vivendi rather than merely as a form of artistic communication. It must be regarded as a channel of release from the ever-increasing and over-powering determinism of the modern world. The provocation of an active state of benign derangement would then produce fortuitous visions that could be identified as surrealist poetry.

Although Breton had been impressed by the earlier observations of Charcot, the works of Janet and Freud were closer to his time. Pierre Janet was a professor of experimental and comparative psychology at the Collège de France and the intermediary between Charcot and the pure scientists on the one hand, and Freud and the pragmatists of medicine on the other. Janet's works had been on the required reading list of medical students of Breton's vintage. He had also been the teacher of Jung. Although there are resemblances between Jung's search for the collective unconscious through alchemical processes and the surrealists' ventures into the same sites of psychic discovery, it would be erroneous to conclude that Jung had an influence on the surrealists; rather they derive from common sources, the major one of which is Pierre Janet, who used in his lectures alchemical terminology and process not because he believed in spiritualism but for the devices that helped the rational mind to probe the recesses of what we call imagination, intuition, ecstasy, and so on. In reading the monumental work of Pierre Janet we encounter the very vocabulary that André Breton put in vogue in surrealism, and whereby he deconstructed and transformed such banal notions as reality, nature, anguish, *amour fou,* automatism, and even and perhaps foremost the notion of human liberty.

A few months after the death of André Breton in 1966, when I went in search of clues to the formation of the man and the poet in preparation for my critical biography, *André Breton: Magus of Surrealism,* I met Philippe Soupault, Breton's earliest literary collaborator, who had also been a medical student. It was he who, in relating the circumstances under which the first surrealist text, *Les Champs magnétiques,*[3] was written, pointed out the importance of Dr. Pierre Janet in the surrealist venture into automatic writing. The term came from a thick volume by Pierre Janet called *L'Automatisme psychologique,* first edition 1889, ninth edition 1921, indicating the popularity and availability of the work to students of psychology.

It is interesting to note from the perspective of surrealism that Janet made a clear distinction between *automatic* and *mechanical* writing. Two centuries earlier La Mettrie, the materialist philosopher, had disclosed the so-called mechanical structure of animal response to sensory stimuli, manifesting an automatic chain pattern of cause and effect. Janet's notion of automatism was quite different. He had realized that in his definition of psychological automatism he had to distinguish clearly between animal automatism, free of moral considerations, and the human form of automatism that attempts to free writing from moral constraints to varying degrees by interrupting the rational structure of the habitual stream of thought. These seemingly artificial distractions and deviations from the logical sequence of thinking were intended to provide revelations into the substrata of human cognizance and were not intended mechanically to obliterate what is normally assumed to be mental lucidity. This process is a far cry from forms of writing that intentionally present man as an absurd and irrational being, identifying him as an idiot or fool or as what the world diagnoses as "insane." If I may quote from my own analysis of Janet's thought as I have stated it in my book on Breton:

> Janet thought that . . . his notion of automatism could end a battle long waged between determinists and idealists, and could conciliate the two points of view by considering them not in antithesis but in correlation. If man on the whole can control his reactions to his environment, there is an area, a most primordial one, the most elementary and most difficult to unveil, in which volition plays no part, and of which he is not aware unless it interferes with his conscious thought. This intrusion occurs in the mentally ill, but it is of no use to the subject because he has lost at the same time his sense of awareness of the intervention. However, it could reveal to the observer clues to the patient's fears and desires. If the normal person cannot lift the self-censuring mechanism of reason that bars access to automatic thought, he can in a moment of inattentive writing squeeze out the data stored in the deep recesses of the mind. The simplest example that occurs to Janet is the automatic recall of the spelling of a word when rational memory has had a lapse. If the spelling cannot be rationally conjured up, a moment of inattentive writing may bring it out of the area of the automatic functioning of the mind.[4]

Pierre Janet adds: "Let the pen wander automatically, on the page even as the medium interrogates his mind." (9th ed., p. 468)

Indeed, for the surrealists, experimenting with automatic writing as a device to reflect their innermost sensory and moral rebellion also simulated the verbal automatism of the medium as had been demonstrated in Janet's laboratory experiments. An Open Letter by Breton to the "Voyantes"[5] in 1925 is in praise and recognition of the insight they bring to those bent on conquering the obscure recesses of human cognizance. Janet had experimented with crystal bowls in the middle of psychology lectures; he had traced the history of divination from Egypt to Greek antiquity and on to the Middle Ages. As a supporting document he referred to F. W. Myers's *The Subliminal Consciousness, Sensory Automatism and Induced Hallucination* (1892). Janet identified the unexpected and involuntary character of images in the crystal bowl with the notion of the *marvelous,* giving it a scientific rather than a supernatural base. Crystal and mirror images were indeed to become obsessively recurrent in surrealist poetry and art. The surrealists were to call "marvelous" not the image itself produced under mediumesque situations but the mental power to catalyze images like those induced by the crystal bowl into a chain reaction; like automatic writing, gazing into crystal or mirror was to be a device to unchain the freedom of the mind to create its own universe, giving it a sacred quality. In his autobiographical narrative, *Nadja,* concerning a woman considered deranged by society, Breton under her momentary influence asks her and himself at the same time: "Is it true that the *beyond,* the total beyond, is in this life?"

It is interesting to note that Pierre Janet's experiments in written and verbal automatism had not been conducted exclusively on clinical patients. He had involved his students as subjects after having first warned them that there were dangers to mental health, particularly to certain individuals more impressionable and more easily freed from the constraints of will than others. He said, "I have advised you to try the experiment yourselves; I shall add softly: don't abuse, for I am convinced that its perfect success is not favorable to good mental health."[6] The danger was that the conductor of the experiment could turn into a hypnotizer vis-à-vis certain persons who had propensities for the role of medium. This was indeed to prove the case with surrealists such as René Crevel and Robert Desnos who participated rather too assiduously in the surrealist experiments into heightened consciousness.

In his discussion of hysterics and lay mystics verging on states classified as aberrations, Janet talked of "amour fou" and "convulsive" visions in a voluminous study called *De L'Angoisse à l'extase.*[7] Breton refers to this work in his collected essays called *La Clé des champs.*[8] He was to make key words out of *amour fou* and *convulsive beauty,* turning these expressions from their medical sense into poetic ones. *Influence* is an often misunderstood word. It is equated with imitation. Certainly, Breton was not imitative of Janet or for that matter of any other psychologist. In appropriating certain procedures and words, he gave them new targets and new dimensions. They served as catalysts and stimuli to the creative process.

Breton felt that at the point in time when he emerged as a thinking youth, concerned with the physical and social quality of the human condition, the forces of sciences had to be brought into collaboration with creative literary or artistic talents that would not be satisfied to give simply aesthetic pleasure and amusement. The arts had to play a major role, in his estimation, in improving the quality of life, or they had no business to exist at all. Literature had become totally stagnant, and a nihilistic and intentional breakdown of it as manifested in some of the avant-garde movements was not sufficient. As in the case of the sciences, so in the case of the arts, the ultimate objective had to be the opening of the gates of the mind to a more vivid, intensified apprehension of existence. To recuperate from the gods the power man himself had granted to them was the motto Breton proposed in one of his earliest, and "automatically" written texts, *Poisson soluble,*[9] which he joined to his first Manifesto.

"Amour fou," that troubled passion that a mentally deranged person may be directing to some veiled god and the "convulsive" visions that an irrational rapture produces in such a person, become for the poet something else. "Amour fou," which is the title of one of Breton's most beautiful narratives of self-discovery and which unfortunately remains untranslated in English—I tremble that it may be translated as "crazy love" when indeed it means "madly in love"—rejuvenates for Breton the whole range of sexual love in this particular book, but elsewhere in his work it goes further to encompass the constricted, life-giving forces of the human mechanism, its power of embrace, relating not only to the sexual partner but to the immanent elements of the entire spectrum of exterior reality. When he speaks of rendering the flesh sacred he thinks in terms of mystical ecstasies: "I have never ceased to unite the flesh of the woman I love with the snow-topped summits in the rising sun."

As for the use of *convulsive,* he ends his narrative, *Nadja,* with it, by saying that "beauty must be convulsive or it must not be at all." This rather assertive, doctrinaire statement comes as the conclusion to the experience he has had with the character, a waiflike woman, whom he met in the streets of Paris, accidentally, fortuitously, and whom society eventually committed to an insane asylum. Beauty, a word slowly disappearing from the artist's lexicon during the years of Breton's literary development, had to be retrieved, according to the surrealists. Aragon wrote a very interesting picaresque novel on the subject in 1920 called *Anicet;* it also unhappily remains untranslated for the English reading public. Beauty, first immutable, perfect in symmetry, serene in posture, classical, dispassionate, had become incompatible with the modern world. At the end of the nineteenth century, it had taken on an agonized, artificial, intentionally static character. At the beginning of the twentieth century, there were two choices: to destroy the notion of beauty totally, or to change its connotation. Some artists were intent on destruction; the surrealists under the direction of Breton wanted to endow it with a new dynamism, which Breton qualified as *convulsive,* incorporating the signification of involuntary movement (as the convulsions of the deranged), unexpected, and, by its power to astonish both its creator and receiver, acting like earthquakes and leading to *action.* It was part of the notion of a dynamic materialism as opposed to the static determinism of the prior age of positivistic scientific attitudes. A thing or phenomenon would be deemed beautiful if it led to greater insight of being, to keener perceptions of our universe. Above all it would provoke not the passive pleasure of reception but *move* the receiver to breathless wonder and fortuitous encounter. After his analysis of his brief episode with Nadja, Breton came to this sense of convulsive beauty much in keeping with the conclusions that Dr. Janet had reached after his numerous case studies recorded in *Automatisme psychologique.* Janet had said, "All this teaches us that we are richer than we think, we have more ideas and sensations than we thought. Our mind is full of beautiful thoughts of which we have no knowledge, which should console us for all the mediocre thoughts that we recognize so easily."[10]

Reading in the annals of Dr. Janet's medical case histories in *De l'Angoisse à l'extase,* I discovered a twenty-eight-year-old, anemic girl, called Nadia: he records her as being orphaned, yet as talking of her mother as if she were alive; she is wide-eyed and particularly wise to her own condition. The Nadja of Breton's book is not a reminiscence of earlier readings; she is a living contemporary, as evidenced by the fact that many of Breton's friends met her and even dated her. Yet I find a telling connection with Janet's case history. When Breton encounters her and asks her name she answers that she calls herself "Nadja." We know that it is not her real name because Breton tells us that it is the name she had chosen for herself; the reason she gives for the choice is that it contained the beginning and only the beginning of the Russian word for hope. Immediately, then, Breton destroys the very authenticity of the situation that he had belabored by surrounding it as he had with the circumstantial elements of his own daily life. What ensues in the course of the narrative is an experiment testing the hypothesis he had earlier expressed that one can love a deranged woman better than any other kind. He followed the test through and found that his hypothesis was false. In associating Breton's Nadja with the casebook Nadia, my purpose was not to prove that Breton had stolen the character from the annals of medicine. On the contrary, if indeed the seed of the name and the general situation create a link with the clinical case, the resulting Nadja of Breton demonstrates the very wide difference between the medical attitude and the literary one. It is my judgment that although an authentic wisp of a woman did come across Breton's path and he did flirt with her, probe her mind, watch the degrees of dislocation of reality evident in her behavior, he created more than her name. He also gave her some of his speech, the contrived irrationality of some of her metaphors, the poetic language in which she clothes some of her unusual perceptions. For this alchemical language with concordances of emblematic water and fire, and concrete representations of the invisible but felt presences surrounding Nadja, is not believably the discourse of an uneducated woman; rather it seems to emanate from the poet as he catches the contagion of the irrational in his proximity to Nadja. But as Nadja crosses the thin barrier that separates insanity from sanity, the poet cannot follow her. In fact, he loses track of her, only to find out some time later that she has been locked up. And there we have the basic parting of the ways between doctor and poet. The poet protests the incarceration. He challenges psychiatry's definition of "autism" as a pathological egocentrism, and claims that under that label *derangement* would cover "all that in man resists pure and simple adaptation to the exterior conditions of life, since they would aim secretely to exhaust all cases of refusal, nonsubmission, and desertion." In short, poetry, art, love, revolutionary passion could all be considered forms of derangement. In an excess of consternation, Breton even suggested that if he were interned for insanity, in a moment of lucidity he could well see himself assassinating the first attendant, preferably a doctor, who came across his path. This comment of Breton's attracted the attention of a medicopsychological session in which a dialogue between a certain Dr. De Clérambault and the very doctor from whom Breton had learned so much, Pierre Janet, heatedly disputed his impertinence. The dialogue was to be reprinted as a preamble to Breton's Second Manifesto in 1930, two years after the publication of *Nadja*.

The dispute, however, had no true relevance to Breton's ontological attitude. For him, vindictive attack on psychiatry and asylums was to be understood in a larger context; the asylum was the metaphor of the larger prison englobing all mankind. The incarceration of Nadja was symptomatic of the forces in general that bind the human imagination. The plight of Nadja as she vanished behind prison bars came to symbolize the plight of humanity as a whole; if Breton's point of departure was a medical case, he had proceeded to the spiritual, and there was at that point only one more step to the political as he extended the individual problem to the universal problems of human liberty: "Human emancipation conceived definitively in its most revolutionary form . . . remains the only cause worth serving," he concluded.

Breton did not liberate Nadja from prison; nor did his participation in varied libertarian causes give him political solutions. But on the personal plane Nadja proved to be a moment in Breton's psychic history; through Nadja he understood himself better, his own motivations were divested of some social hypocrisies, he discovered his own need for a freer expression of love than he had previously experienced. Above all, in her innocent way, Nadja had revealed to the poet the continuum between the exterior world and the subjective. Without this encounter he would not have learned to love passionately nor perhaps to write such poems as "L'Union libre" (Free Union), where the continuum acquires a brilliant literary reality.

Nadja was written under the aegis of Pierre Janet; the next volume of narrative prose, *Les Vases communicants* [11] (another work as yet unavailable to Anglo-American readers), was dedicated to Freud. The title identifies existence as a composite of two urns, the dream and the state of wakefulness, constantly charging each other with power. Breton's knowledge of Freud dated back to the war years, although in view of Breton's faulty knowledge of German it is unlikely that he went to primary texts. Indeed, Freud was to be translated into French much later than into English. [12] Nonetheless Freud had granted the young poet–medical student an interview in Vienna in 1921 in answer to a letter from Breton that he called "the most touching that I have ever received." He had been rather reticent in his responses to the young writer's questions. However, Breton and his colleagues gave Freud much credit in their two periodicals, *La Révolution Surréaliste,* and *Le Surréalisme au Service de la Révolution* (1924–33). In his First Manifesto, Breton extolled Freud for his discoveries in dream interpretation, for his method of investigation, and the new rights he thereby granted to the human imagination. He found in Freud's work the scientific support he needed for his own belief in the marriage of the two states, in appearance so contradictory, of dream and reality, into a fusion of absolute reality that he called surreality.

The most thorough analysis of Breton's point of departure in Freud and his subsequent deviation from Freudian psychology appeared in *Les Vases communicants*. Upon receiving Breton's book Freud had confessed in a letter to Breton that he was not at all clear as to what surrealism was. "Perhaps," he said, diplomatically, "I am not made to understand it, for I am so far removed from art."[13] The fact of the matter was that if Breton learned of the close relationship between the two states of dream and consciousness, the purpose of his recognition of these connecting states was not interpretation of dreams as a source of explanation of psychosis and as a clue to obsessions. The artist's aim in the understanding of dreams was the colonization of the subconscious. The dream helped the psychiatrist to interpret the disintegration of personality; it was to reveal to the artist the basis of a unification of personality by his adjustment to two planes of reality deemed not antithetical any longer but complementary. Moreover, Freud's methods had pointed to a level of cognizance where the distinction between the sensory and the intellectual faculties is erased and where these two faculties work together toward a monistic sense of reality. Too long, thought Breton, man had limited his ambitions to interpretative functions; it was time to use the knowledge of subconscious forces for the transformation of reality.

It seemed strange that although Freud's methods would imply a monistic philosophy Freud continued to insist on a distinction between psychic reality and material reality. Breton on the other hand, from *Nadja* to *Les Vases communicants* and *L'Amour fou*, was trying to convince his readers that psychic reality is the better part of material reality, the inherent reservoir of the magic of the artist, even as a rich involvement in the material reality can resituate for everyman the notion of the "sacred" within the range of human experience. The study of dreams had for Freud a corrective purpose in the analysis of neurosis and derangement; his influence on the surrealist poets was to use dream analysis as a source of restoration of primal states, for the capture of glimpses of the golden age, of a purity of sensation beyond tears, of the sparking of desire. For what Breton had learned from his experience of psychiatry was that the dream need not be considered merely as a channel of escape from reality but rather as an expansion and transfiguration of the real world. The result of the surrealist application of psychiatry in ways unimagined by the medical scientists is manifest in the writings and paintings of those who worked under Breton's impetus. It may be too early to pass definitive judgment on these works in terms of their artistic value, but one thing is clear: the notion of madness loses its pathological meaning when one is dealing with the artist, and the artistic function can be viewed as the paradox sensed by that precocious French predecessor of the surrealists, Arthur Rimbaud, who had defined the poetic process as "the reasoned disturbance of all his senses." This approach became more than a verbal statement by the unwitting collaboration of the psychiatrists with the surrealists.

NOTES

1. *Entretiens* means Conversations and consists for the most part of a series of interviews given by André Breton on national radio between March and June 1952. The book (Paris: Gallimard, 1952) has not yet been translated into English.

2. The subject has been explored at greater length in my book, *Literary Origins of Surrealism,* 2nd ed. (New York: New York University Press, 1966).

3. *Les Champs magnétiques* means Magnetic Fields. Written in the summer of 1919, the work was recognized by its authors, André Breton and Philippe Soupault as the first surrealist text, although its publication in 1920 at Au Sans Pareil editions predates the official beginning of the Surrealist School by four years. Motivated by the psychiatric studies of Dr. Janet, it is the first example of collaborative automatic writing. "We listened to ourselves think," says one of the most important statements in the automatically transcribed text. The title was inspired by the graphic representations of a physical magnetic field posted in an exposition in the Bois de Boulogne that the two poet-medics had observed.

4. *André Breton: Magus of Surrealism* (New York: Oxford University Press, 1971).

5. The "Voyantes" are the visionary ladies who are known sometimes as mind readers, as fortune tellers, mediums, and psychological advisers. Breton was on the side of all those whose psychic powers are derided by society; he championed the "voyantes" because he thought of them not as mystifiers but as sources of automatic thinking, as probers of the subconscious. One of the most famous was Mme Sacco, whose portrait is featured in Breton's autobiographical narrative, *Nadja,* and whose wisdom of foresight he trusted. An important disagreement Breton had with Freud was on the subject of prophecy and prescience as an index of psychic power. Freud rejected the validity of the prophetic dream; Breton took prophecies seriously; one instance of verification in retrospect is a statement he made in the "Lettre aux Voyantes" written after a visit to one of these persecuted ladies: "There are people who contend that the war has taught them something; I am ahead of them for I know what the year 1939 has in store for me." The essay, written in 1929, can be found in a volume, called *Manifestoes of Surrealism,* a Jacques Pauvert collection of manifestoes and other essays of Breton, translated by Richard Seaver and Helen R. Lane (Ann Arbor: University of Michigan Press, 1969).

6. Pierre Janet, *L'Automatisme psychologique,* 9th ed. (Paris: Felix Alcan, 1921), p. 421.

7. *De L'Angoisse à l'extase* means From Anguish to Ecstasy. The volume consulted was the eighth edition (Paris: Felix Alcan, 1926). It originally appeared in the laboratory works in psychology of the Salpêtrière, series 9–10, the famous Mental Hospital in Paris.

8. *La Clé des champs* is the title of a collection of Breton's essays, not yet translated into English. The term (literally: "Key to the Fields") is linked to alchemical language and means freedom to go where one pleases, and by extension, to go in search of the secrets of the universe.

9. *Poisson soluble* is an automatic text by Breton appendaged to his first Manifesto, which appeared in 1924. *Poisson,* fish, is explained by the fact that he was born on February 19 under the sign of Pisces. (Some commentators on Breton give the date of birth as the eighteenth; but the form he filled out for *Contemporary Authors* gives the nineteenth in his own handwriting.) *Soluble* is presumed to indicate that all men are solvent in the vast pool

of their thought; the main subject of the text is self-identification. I can attest to the fact that the manuscript I saw of the work gives no evidence of any struggle in composition; the language seems in fact to have flowed uninterruptedly. The translation can be found in the University of Michigan volume of *The Manifestoes* cited in note 5.

10. Janet, *L'Automatisme psychologique,* p. 421 (the translation is mine).

11. *Les Vases communicants,* meaning Connecting Vessels, uses the analogy of the laboratory siphons to suggest the uninterrupted flow of dream and reality into each other. It is a quasi-scientific study of the power of the dream in quotidian experience. It contains many references to scientific and scholarly studies of the dream and continues the autoanalysis of Breton's own life and desires, picking up where *Nadja* ended.

12. For an elaboration of the study of Freudian influences on surrealism and particularly on Breton, see the chapter "Breton and the Surrealist Mind" in my book *Surrealism: The Road to the Absolute,* 2nd ed. (New York: Dutton, 1970), pp. 123–40.

13. Breton-Freud Correspondence at the end of *Les Vases communicants* (Paris: Gallimard, 1955), p. 204. The letters were originally included in the fifth issue of *Le Surrealisme au Service de la Révolution,* published in 1930–31.

Disease As Language:
The Case of the Writer and the Madman
Gian-Paolo Biasin

> Life is a little like disease, with its crises and periods of quiescence,
> its daily improvements and setbacks.
>
> Italo Svevo

It is interesting to note that while in medicine the science of symptoms is called *semeiotics,* in literary criticism a similar word, *semiotics* (also employed in medicine as a synonym of *semeiotics*), is used to define the science of signs.

A sign, as broadly defined by Umberto Eco, is "anything that can be taken as significantly substituting for something else"; systems of signs enable men to communicate. Words are the signs *par excellence* of the things to which they refer in a totally arbitrary, but nonetheless systematic and necessary way. At times the symptoms of a disease may become the signs of a language.

My purpose is to explore how literature deals with disease—more precisely, with mental disease—not only at the realistic and metaphoric levels, but also and above all at the level of communication.[1] At this level, symptoms become indeed the signs of a language that the writer tries to decode and interpret, in order to understand the Other, the sick person, and through the sick person disease itself, the irrational, what by definition seems incommunicable.

Among the novels recently published in Italy, one stands out precisely for its powerful, poignant, and revealing treatment of disease as language: *Fratelli* (Brothers), by Carmelo Samonà, born at Palermo in 1926.[2] In Italian literature, mental diseases have traditionally been the object of inquiry by many writers, most notably Luigi Pirandello (especially in *Henry IV*); with the "economic boom" of the fifties and the consequent social tensions and changes of life patterns in large segments of the population, mental diseases have multiplied, and have become the subject of many novels, diaries, stories. The importance of Samonà's book is that it is the first one written by a writer who is neither a patient nor a doctor, the first one in which disease is presented and analyzed *explicitly* as language, and the first one in which the contemporary trend to reform mental institutions radically (carried on in Italy by Dr. Franco Basaglia) is reflected in the fictional situation of the characters, who do not live inside an asylum.

Fratelli is the story of two brothers, one sane and the other insane, who live together in a semideserted, huge apartment high above an unnamed city. The apartment, half-empty, provides them with ample space for their daily life and gives the kind of isolation comparable with ideal laboratory conditions for the observation of the basic manifestations of madness; this observation becomes more difficult when the two venture outside, into the more complex space of the city, with its intertwining streets and public gardens.

The sane brother, who is the narrator of the story, takes care of the insane one, helps him eat, dress, and clean himself; in so doing, he doggedly tries to understand the fragmentary and absurd language of the other, to decipher his behavior, decode his gestures. He searches for a meaning that would be clear-cut, univocal, reducible to reason and to normalcy. He tries to establish contact with the other, a contact that is first of all physical (touching, embracing) but more subtly spiritual (a meaningful glance, the exchange of some sort of dialogue). But in order to communicate, he is forced to adopt some of the behavior of the insane brother: everything becomes play, theater, imagination—where the freedom of action is virtually unlimited, unlimited precisely by the boundaries of reason and logic. Hence the pretended "Great Voyages" the two brothers undertake together, hence their role playing, as well as their gratuitous exchanges of food and clothes; hence, too, the gradual sensation, conveyed by the narrator, that *he* is not sure any longer of his own Self, of his own meaning. The two are, after all, "brothers."

Since the narrator specifically refers to himself as a writer (in that he accumulates notes describing the illness of the other), his writing is posited against disease in a long, subtle meditation involving not only the meaning, but also the values of Western civilization—such as the notions of personal identity and society, the cause-effect principle, the laws of profit or of the maximum result obtained with the minimal effort. Nothing particularly eventful happens in the plot. But throughout, the narrator continues his desperate effort to establish a dialogue, to decipher the language of madness, to find out the meaning, a meaning, for the other's sickness as well as for his own health.

Beautifully written in a style that combines the pathos and compassion of a personal diary with the clarity and intelligence of a *conte philosophique*, *Fratelli* can be read at face value, as a very realistic (one suspects even autobiographical) story. It can also be read at a metaphoric level: the brother's sickness is not really, or not only, madness, but everything that does not belong to the realm of reason and that influences our lives outside of our control. Finally it can be read at the level of communication, as an inquiry into the nature of human language(s) and into the way in which people relate to one another through speech, silence, gestures, and especially the written word, literature. Without the obscure force of sickness, the writer would not be able to write, or to understand himself, or others, or his writing.

The problems of communication involved in the text inevitably lead to a process of interpretation, a process that starts with symptoms (the medical "semeiotics") and ends with signs (the literary "semiotics"). The correlation between medicine and literature could not be asserted more powerfully than in these two synonyms, which share the same classical, Greek etymology.

Let us examine the text of *Fratelli* in some detail. Samonà carefully emphasizes the nature of his narrator's quest: "I shall not give it a name," he says, referring to his brother's sickness, because for him sickness is "a sort of invisible object even more than a hostile force":

> I have never given up the idea of fighting this calamity with every possible means. I follow it closely, as if it had a shape, I spy on it, I carefully note down its symptoms and put them into relationships among themselves. I am so doggedly hunting, pursuing, finding it, that at times it might even seem that I am courting it.
> . . . I have learned that one must pretend to accept disease as something which integrates and belongs to us, like an insane extension of our bodies: hence a sacred ceremony, capillary and incessant; a homely code rooted in our gestures. (pp. 8–9)

In this passage, the obsessive presence of sickness is reflected in the medical terms used (from "disease," which is compared to "an insane extension of our bodies," to the biological and temporal adjectives "capillary and incessant"); this obsessive presence is turned into the acceptance of disease as an integral part of life, a recognition of its mysterious and humble character (in that it involves both a "sacred ceremony" and a "homely code").

No matter how hard the narrator tries to imitate the sickness of his brother in order to identify with him, he knows that he is not obliged to *live* this sickness, that he can control it from the outside. Yet, he says:

> While I try to snatch my brother from the condition in which he happens to be, I feel that he is performing on me an action somehow equal and opposite to mine: hunted by me, in his turn he follows me incessantly. . . . Our story consists wholly of these violations of territory which are repeated until the names and the faces of the respective invaders become confused. (p. 10)

Time and space are the frame within which the confrontation between the two brothers takes place. It is a confrontation (a fight, a courtship, a ritual) between two different languages, two ways of conveying messages, two sets of meaning. A whole universe of communication is explored in which words are a minimal part, and gestures, silences, glances, exchanges of various things are the predominant and most valuable elements. This universe is divided into two spaces: on the one hand the language of normalcy, rationality, order, cause-effect relationship, predictability, limitation, embodied in and written by the sane narrator; on the other hand the language of abnormality, irrationality, chaos, chance, unpredictability, limitlessness, embodied in and uttered (or acted out) by the insane brother. The fascination of *Fratelli* is that the latter language has to be and is in fact described and conveyed through the former. The examples are numerous, but a few will suffice:

> We speak: but the form of our messages begins to become different: while mine are fast, neat, coherent with the line of my will and thought, his are almost always hindered or reluctant to follow faithfully the orders that his desire to communicate . . . must have transmitted to his vocal chords and lips. . . . One would say they are lucid fragments of a discourse which has lost its cohesiveness because of a distant, terrifying explosion: during the centrifugal movement the links were shattered, the meanings upset and overturned, but shining bits of that ancient linguistic treasure still emerge on his lips. . . . I cannot explain how in him difficulty and gracefulness can be combined with such nonchalance. In my brother the use of words is similar to the movement of his body: an ensemble of panting and light rhythms. (pp. 21–22)

In the following description—the rendering through written words of the sick brother sitting under a pine tree—disease symptoms become the signs of a language itself:

> I have understood that he has an intense relationship with the old bark, the roots, the bits of moss covering the ground beneath him. The language he uses to explore them must be complicated. A sign of it is the very slow movement of his fingertips on the knots of the roots, different from the one he makes on the moss, more similar to a caress, and different as well from the way he adheres to the trunk with his nape and back. You could say he is waiting for some signal. I have no choice but to enter the great wood by myself or to sit next to him and watch his behavior, without understanding it. (p. 86)

In another instance it is no longer a question of deciphering words, gestures, or bodily movements, but a matter of decoding things charged with meaning; the narrator finds certain small gifts ("presences") from his brother, such as bread crumbs or even small flakes of dried excrement:

> These collected presences make up a network of combinations which later on I try to decipher in solitude, as if they were an

articulated discourse which cannot reach me except through that series of small, innumerable stages. I have the feeling that another language is coming forth, richer in innuendoes than the one sufficient to communicate elementary needs, such as "I am cold, I want to dress" or "I am hungry, I want to eat"; a language turned upside down or astray, moving in the opposite direction from the desires and the impulses I vainly believe I have foreseen, every time. (p. 36)

The importance of the linguistic dimension in the relationship between the two brothers cannot be underestimated. Because of it the sane narrator can invent games in order to involve the insane brother in some sort of communication; because of it, theatrical scenes can be enacted, the two brothers can play and exchange roles—and in so doing keep in touch. The notion of play, inherent in language, becomes crystallized in the "dramatic action" of theater. In fact the sick brother can immerse himself rapidly and completely in a theatrical action, a role:

This pulls him immediately out of his language. Not only is he capable of becoming interested in any given well-wrought plot, but he penetrates it happily, and his language profits from this disguise to the point that lexicon and intonation are changed, and his body is compelled to have an economy of gestures which seemed unreachable before. (p. 14)

But the sick brother cannot accept books, including opera *libretti*, Italian classics, and children's stories (such as Collodi's *Pinocchio*), because

the written texts, soon mastered and feared by him, weighed on him with an ambiguous authority which always hid a shadow of disillusionment. In his opinion, stories were no longer invented by me so that he could disassemble them; they were rigid plots, bottled up within the signs, . . . distant from the sonorous flow of words, of gestures. Writing was the tomb of all the stories. (p. 19)

Indeed, writing marks the insuperable difference between the narrator and his sick brother:

The advantage of writing in comparison with oral discourses is that here my brother is not present and, as a consequence, cannot introduce variants. It is up to me alone to document or invent, test hypotheses or limit myself to sure data. When the sheet is motionless and white on my desk, I can do everything. . . . And I have some advantage over time. . . . While writing, I can go back for days or weeks, or destroy an entire epoch with a single stroke of my pen; or on the contrary I can keep what I have already written and preserve it from the menace of future disavowals. (pp. 93–94)

These words are extremely important because they characterize the complex and arbitrary nature of literature, revealed to the narrator by his constant contact and experience with disease. The contrast is here not only between writing (on disease) and the spoken discourse (of disease), but also between artificial order and natural chaos, between health and madness, between literature and life.

As the novel comes closer to its conclusion, the narrator diminishes his careful, anxious annotations and begins to fear "the end of writing" (p. 103); so, too, does his brother close himself up in an ever expanding "inscrutable domain of silence" (p. 104). But not all is lost. At the very moment when he confesses the failure of writing to account for disease, the narrator uses this very same writing to account for his unfinished quest, for his unending pursuit:

> It is a fact that only while I take care of him in a material way do I find in him some echo of the old moods and am still able to snatch tenuous fragments of phrases resembling a prelude to a discourse with me. Since I help him, as always, to dress, we find ourselves one in front of the other and touch our arms and shoulders lightly. . . . In his combinative art (a word and a glance, a word and his tongue's smacking against his palate, a gesture contrary to the word accompanying it, or the cross of two opposite words), I read some clue of a meaning travelling toward me. There are moments when I seem to be nearing a gleam of truth, to grasp a transparence similar to a whole meaning. I concentrate, then, and stop every movement. I am on the verge of piercing a curtain at whose base, with my fingernails, I am digging a passage. (p. 108)

This is the end of *Fratelli,* an end open to various possibilities, an end that does not preclude the discovery of a truth, the achievement of an understanding; the expressions "on the verge of" and "a passage" underline the temporal and spatial dimensions of a process (a progress) that is still going on as the reader closes the book: the "curtain" veiling knowledge is not pierced yet. Confronted with disease, literature has explored its own nature while also exploring the object of its investigation; and like medicine, literature continues its quest to understand the unresolved mystery of our life and our death, of which the irrational is such an integral part.

Fratelli is a splendid example of how the confrontation with disease affects a heightened state of consciousness for the writer—and hence for the reader. Firstly, he has become aware of the enormous importance of the body—the biological factor—as part of the totality of man (one remembers those "fingernails" in the very last sentence of the novel); it might seem paradoxical that it is a *mental* disease that brings about the awareness of *the body,* but the paradox disappears when one thinks of Michel Foucault's definition of madness as "a global structure."

Secondly and perhaps more importantly, in meditating upon his own writing, Carmelo Samonà has understood the "gleam of truth" that shines in the title of his book from the very beginning and that becomes finally transparent: the languages of reason and unreason, notwithstanding their differences, derive from the same matrix, are fundamentally the same.

The Writer and the Madman are, indeed, Brothers.

NOTES

1. I have treated this subject at some length in my *Literary Diseases: Theme and Metaphor in the Italian Novel* (Austin and London: University of Texas Press, 1975).

2. Carmelo Samonà, *Fratelli* (Turin: Einaudi, 1978). All references are to this edition; page references are given in parentheses. All translations are my own.

Words and Wounds
Geoffrey H. Hartman

Hush! Caution! Echoland!

James Joyce *(Finnegans Wake)*

Preliminary Reflections

Once upon a time there was a poet who wanted to be a doctor. But when he wrote his greatest poem he was already under the shadow of the tuberculosis that killed his mother and brother, and would allow him but a few years to live. John Keats, writing "The Fall of Hyperion" in 1819, imagines a dream in which he confronts a High Priestess who is at one and the same time the ghost of his dead mother and the conscience of all the great poets before him who had wished for a role equal in importance to that of healing the sick. Moneta (the High Priestess) does not mince her words. She asks contemptuously:

> What benefit canst thou do, or all thy tribe
> To the great world? Thou art a dreaming thing;
> A fever of thyself . . .

Stung by the accusation, Keats tries to answer with a classic defense of poetry:

> surely not all
> Those melodies sung into the world's ear
> Are useless: sure a poet is a sage;
> A humanist, Physician to all men.

But Moneta then challenges him to distinguish between *dreamer* and *poet* (unfair, if one recalls that Keats subtitles his poem "A Dream"):

> 'Art thou not of the dreamer tribe?
> The poet and the dreamer are distinct,
> Diverse, sheer opposite, antipodes.
> The one pours out a balm upon the world,
> The other vexes it.'

The debate raises an essential question for those interested in the relation of medicine and literature. Is there a healing power or "balm" in poetic words, or are they not useless and even pernicious, weakening our sense of reality, poisoning the mind with images of a world more wonderful—in terror or beauty—than the one we know? "Only the dreamer venoms all his days," is how Keats's Voice of Conscience, the High Priestess, puts it.

I would like to understand what is meant by the healing power of words. To do so, I will circumvent the religious and also the magical view, except as they provide testimony that the issue is a real one. I must also decline to say anything about the clinical or curative aspects of "logo-therapy": my aim will be to show how deeply the issue of wounds and words is reflected in imaginative literature. The poets themselves are those who represent most clearly the power of words, their balm or venom. Yet except for the obscure notion of "catharsis" (proposed by Aristotle to explain why dramatic portrayals of tragic events may give pleasure rather than pain) we do not have a useful concept with which to understand the tremendous impact words may have on psychic life.

Where do we begin? We know something about the power of words. As Othello charms Desdemona with the "witchcraft" of speech, so Iago maddens Othello using the very same means. And William Blake, in the midst of his visionary poem *Milton,* allows us to glimpse a part of its pathetic and human base:

> armed with power, to say
> The most irritating things in the midst of tears and love
> These are the stings of the Serpent!

That words can wound is a clearer fact than their capacity to heal, and Blake punctures his sublime rhetoric to make that point. Yet his poem remains the best evidence that words may redress the wound they inflict.

This brings us back to literature. What kind of a physic is it? Shakespeare depicts madness in a faithful yet bearable manner. He does not analyze or define Ophelia's disturbance: he represents it. But in the way some illnesses are self-limiting, so with his representation of madness. The disease and the cure come together in the poet's web of words. Shakespeare has Ophelia speak a "balmy" language, one that exhibits her wound by denying it, or by dressing it with the plaster of euphemistic words. How desperately her "language of flowers" speaks of a realm of *simples,* that is, of herbs with a magical or medicinal effect strong enough to heal the perturbed soul:

> There's rosemary, that's for remembrance. Pray, love, remember.
> And there's pansies, that's for thoughts. . . . There's fennel for you,
> and columbines. There's rue for you, and here's some for me. We
> may call it herb of grace o' Sundays . . .
>
> *(Hamlet,* 4.7.)

If only words were simples, like those flowers, or Ophelia's childlike tone! But they are maddingly complex and equivocal. Literature, I surmise, moves us beyond the fallacious hope that words can heal without also wounding. They are at most homeopathic, curing like by like, in the manner suggested by Edmund Spenser's "myrrh sweet bleeding in the bitter wound" (*The Fairie Queene* 1.1.9).[1]

Hypothesis

Let me suppose, then, that words are always armed and capable of wounding: either because, expecting so much of them, looking to them as potentially definitive or clarifying, we are hurt by their equivocal nature; or because the ear, as a *psychic* organ, is at least as vulnerable as the eye. What is unclear about the first hypothesis is why we should expect so much of words. This overestimation, which may turn of course into its opposite, into contempt of talk, can suggest that words themselves caused the hurt we still feel, as we look to them for restitution or comfort. (Where there is a word-cure, there must be a word-wound.) I prefer, initially, the other way of stating our hypothesis, that within the economy of the psyche the ear is peculiarly vulnerable or passes through phases of vulnerability. The "cell of Hearing, dark and blind," Wordsworth writes in *On the Power of Sound,* is an "Intricate labyrinth, more dread for thought / To enter than oracular cave."

Every literary interpreter and some psychoanalysts enter that cell when they follow the allusive character of words, their intentional or unintentional, condensed or extended resonance. "Strict passage," Wordsworth continues, describing the auditory labyrinth, "through which sighs are brought, / And whispers for the heart, their slave. . . ." There exists a lust of the ears as strong and auspicious as the lust of the eyes about which so much has been written since Saint Augustine. The two are, doubtless, interactive: the Story of the Eye (see Georges Bataille's pornosophic novella of that title) always turns out to be, also, the Story of the Ear. But whereas "the ineluctable modality of the visible" (Joyce) has been explored, especially by analysts interested in primal scene imagery, the ineluctable ear, its ghostly, cavernous, echoic depths, has rarely been sounded with precision.

Wordsworth's phrase, "strict passage," points to the "constricted" or narrowing and therefore overdetermined character of the sounds that make it through, but also to a moral dilemma. The ear must deal with sounds that not only cannot be refused entry but penetrate and evoke something too powerful for any defense: Wordsworth depicts it as akin to sexual lust or the intoxication of a blood sport, "shrieks that revel in abuse / Of shivering flesh." The power of poetry, song or music to undo this wounding, "warbled air, / Whose piercing sweetness can unloose / The chains of frenzy, or entice a smile / Into the ambush of despair," suggests a sweet piercing that counters or sublimates a bitter one.[2]

"Chains of frenzy" tells us how close we are to the theme of madness; "the ambush of despair" how close to depression. Moreover, to "draw a smile / Into the ambush of despair" is ambiguous, and "unloose / The chains of frenzy" has a double negative effect that may undermine rather than reinforce the idea of a liberating cure. These phrases, like the ear itself, are constricted; and even should we attribute them to the highly condensed diction of the Pindaric ode Wordsworth is imitating, this merely rehearses the entire problem, and does not bring us a step forward. For though limitation can be therapeutic, it can also be compulsive, or expressive of a word-wound that still binds the hearer. At this point, obviously, clinical material on the relation of word and wound should be adduced; not being a clinician I shall fall back on literary examples.

Names and Wounds

Psychology and anthropology agree on the importance of the motif of the *wounded name.* To achieve a good name, or to maintain it, has been a motivating force in both heroic and bourgeois contexts. Fiction corresponds to life at least in one respect, that slander and rumor—hearsay more than sightsay—determine the drama of errors that besets reputation. A peculiar and powerful theory of what it means to redress a wounded name is developed by Jean-Paul Sartre, the French philosopher and critic. He speculates that his contemporary, Jean Genet, a convict turned writer, fashioned his identity out of a "dizzying word" addressed to him when he was a young boy.

The word was a vocative, an insult, a common malediction like "You thief!" flung at him by a foster parent. It is said to have made Genet aware of his radically disinherited state. Genet was an illegitimate child; his mother too was a thief, or of the insulted and despised; that word, therefore, became a call, a vocation, which helped to establish not only a negative identity for Genet but redeemed that of his mother through him. Genet grows up a thief, a homosexual, a powerful writer with his own magnificat and gospel: John (Jean) becomes Saint John. The connections are very complex, and it takes Sartre a voluminous and immensely dialectical book to account for what happened.[3]

I am interested more in the elements that go into the theory than in the exact truth-value of the theory itself. What in Sartre's view wakes the child to the problem of identity is not a sight, an ocular fixation as in the famous case of Augustine's friend Alypius, but an *aural experience.*[4] Moreover, the verbal structure of what Genet hears is a vocative, and ritually it approaches an act of nomination or even annunciation. Identity is bestowed on Genet by a ghostly scene of naming, a curse that is taken to be an act of grace.

Genet is word-wounded by the insult or curse, but he makes it into an identity badge by a psychic reflex, and then by a life-long fixation. And rendering him vulnerable in the first place is the very absence of an authentic *name,* and therefore the necessity of endless fillers or substitutes. "You thief!" while only one such filler, happens to suggest that Genet must *steal* a name if he is to own one. For *Genet* is a name that points to the absence of a proper name: it is the mother's surname, and suggests moreover a figurative origin because it is a "flower of speech." Genet takes *genêt* ("broom flower," Leopardi's "ginestra") and turns it via his ritualistic and flower-name laden novels into a literal figure: into something truly his own.

"Flowers of speech" is a designation for the figures or metaphors that characterize literary discourse and distinguish it from apparently straighter or more scientific kinds of writing. Genet links figurative language, or flowers of speech, with the "language of flowers," or the principle of euphemistic and courtly diction. He depicts what are criminal events in the eyes of bourgeois society by means of a sublime and flowery style.

No one is deceived, of course: the reader sees through to the sordid wound, and understands this inverse magnificat. Genet steals back his name, and insists on it as a source of healing and salvation. Yet this stealing back of a name is not as naive or exceptional as it seems. For those who have a name may also seek a more authentic and defining one. This *other* name is usually kept secret precisely because it is sacred to the individual, or numinous *(nomen numen),* as if the concentrated soul of the person lodged in it. A perilous or taboo relation may arise between the given name and the truly "proper" name, and then a psychic search unfolds for this hidden word under all words, this spectral name.[5] It is a quest that often leads to the adoption of pseudonymns and nicknames, and even to anonymity.

Thus naming and the problem of identity cannot be dissociated. Thus literature and the problem of identity cannot be dissociated. Literature is at once onomatopeic (name-making) and onomatoclastic (name-breaking). The true name of a writer is not given by his signature but is spelled out by his entire work. Or, as Thoreau remarks, in an instructive and amusing paragraph contrasting the given and the secret name, "There is nothing in a name. The name Menschikoff, for instance, has nothing in it to my ears more human than a whisker, and it may belong to a rat. As the names of the Poles and the Russians are to us, so are ours to them. It is as if they had been named by the child's rigmarole, *Iery wiery ichery van, tittle-tol-tam.* . . . At present our only true names are nicknames. . . . We have a wild savage in us, and a savage name is perchance somewhere recorded as ours. . . . I seem to hear pronounced [the] original wild name in some jaw-breaking or else melodious tongue" *(Walking,* 1862).

"Look with thine ears" *(King Lear).*

The motif of the wounded name, which at first seemed rather special, leads into the crucial problem of self-identity and its relation to art and writing. But let us also consider the issue from the reader's point of view.

It may prove difficult to say anything definitive about the capacity of words to wound; or about the obverse effect, their medicinal, defensive qualities. The whole theory of defenses, originated by Freud, is involved in metaphor, and becomes ever more elaborate. Moreover, we have to recognize that hearing—a receptive and, as overhearing, involuntary act —is already within the sphere of hurt. We are in bondage to our ears as to our eyes. We are all like Shakespeare's Emilia (*Othello*, 5.7.) when it comes to the aggressing power of words. "Thou hast not half that power to do me harm / As I have to be hurt." That statement is itself a converted threat, and suggests how much depends on hearing what is said in what is being said.

Yet this is where the study of literature enters. Reading is, or can be, an active kind of hearing. We really do "look with ears" when we read a book of some complexity. A book has the capacity to put us on the defensive, or make us envious, or inflict some other "narcissistic injury." When literary critics remark of literature, "there's magic in the web," they characterize not only what distinguishes the literary from the merely verbal, but what distinguishes critical from passive kinds of reading. Critical reading (which almost always leads to writing) allows us to estimate words as words, to use rather than abuse their affective powers, to determine as well as be determined by them. These things are obvious, and it seems preachy to be repeating them; but we too often conceive of critical reading as a scrutiny of content or form rather than more generally of the status of words in the psyche and the environing culture.

What active reading discloses is a structure of *words within words,* a structure so deeply mediated, ghostly and echoic that we find it hard to locate the *res* in the *verba.* The *res,* or subject matter, seems to be already words. Even images, as Freud noticed in his analysis of dreams, turn out to have the form of a *rebus,* or words (parts of words) that appear in the disguise of things. These reified verbal entities must then be translated back into the original sounds, like a charade. But words themselves, of course, may reify, by being taken too literally or absolutely. Psychoanalysis, with its emphasis on the overdetermined or ambivalent symbol, and semiotics with its disclosure of the radical obliquity of signification, undertake to correct that abuse.

Writing and reading of the active sort are certainly homeopathic vis-à-vis the "wound" left by literalism *and* the "wound" that the literalism of the word seeks to cure: equivocation. The search for the absolute word, or minimally for the *mot juste,* is like that search for the good name. There is bound to be a noncorrespondence of demand and response: an inadequacy or lack of mutuality that relates to our drive to make words into things. However precise words may seem to be, there is always understatement or overstatement, and each "verbal action" involves itself in redressing that imbalance.

"Nothing" as the *mot juste*

Take Cordelia's famous "Nothing," which sets going one of the bloodiest of Shakespeare's plays. It is only ponderable when we think about the status of words. Cordelia exercises, of course, her power of nonreceiver, of not responding to a "Speak" that would enjoin the very words to be heard. But within this paralegal situation her "nothing" raises a more basic issue. Lear wants to exchange power for love; more precisely, words of power for words of love. Cordelia's reply contains not only a judgment that the quality of love cannot be constrained but that there may be something disjunctive in language itself that makes such an exchange— or reversal, if Lear who wants to "crawl unburdened toward death" desires a licensed regression to childhood—as unlikely as reconciling love and power in the real world. Lear's fiat remains naked of response, therefore; and since the original fiat in Genesis was answered not only by obedience ("Let there be. . . . And there was") but also by recognition and blessing ("And God saw it was good" "And God blessed. . . ."), Cordelia's "nothing" has, in its very flatness, the ring of a curse.

Lear gives all, Cordelia nothing. The disproportion is too great. In Lear's view, order itself is threatened, and his great rage is just. But order, here, is the order of words, the mutual bonding they establish. Lear is asking no more than his daughter's blessing; which is, moreover, his one guarantee in a situation where he is about to divest himself. And instead of word-issue Cordelia utters something that sounds as sterile to him ("Nothing will come of nothing") as a malediction. It is painful to recall how much of the ensuing drama is curse, rant, slander and impotent fiat:

> Hear, Nature, hear: dear goddess, hear:
> Suspend thy purpose if thou didst intend
> To make this creature fruitful.
> Into her womb convey sterility,
> Dry up in her the organs of increase,
> And from her derogate body never spring
> A babe to honor her.
> (1.4.265 ff.)

> You nimble lightnings, dart you blinding flames
> Into her scornful eyes! Infect her beauty,
> You fensucked fogs drawn by the pow'rful sun
> To fall and blister.
> (2.4.160 ff.)

> Blow, winds, and crack your cheeks! rage! blow!
> (3.2.56)

Cordelia's "Nothing" proves to be sadly prophetic. It exhibits the power of words in seeming to deny them. As such it may be representative of all word-wounds, given or suffered, as they approach the status of *curse* or the incapacity to *bless*. Perhaps our speculations are becoming a shade more definitive.

". . . the bruised heart was pierced through the ear" *(Othello)*.

Curse and blessing are among the oldest types of formalized speech. Like oaths and commandments, to which they are akin, they seek to bind the action of those to whom they are addressed. Yet unlike oaths or commandments they are resorted to when legal instruments are not appropriate or have failed. Legal codes may contain curses as a reinforcement or obversely seek to limit a curse—but it is clear that curse and blessing have a psychological aspect, as well as a legal or ritual role.

Supposing now that the psyche demands to be cursed or blessed—that it cannot be satisfied, that it cannot even exist as a nameable and conscious entity—as ego or self—except when defined by direct speech of that kind, then we have a situation where the absence of a blessing wounds, where the presence of a curse also wounds, but at least defines.

Perhaps direct speech itself, or the need for it, is the problem here: the desire for a *fiat* or absolute speech-act. Moreover, because the demand to be cursed or blessed stems from the same source, and life is as ambivalent in this regard as words are equivocal, the psyche may have to live in perpetual tension with its desire to be worded. It may turn against as well as toward words. The equivocations put into the mouth of Shakespeare's clowns or fools are, thus, a babble that breaks language down because it cannot draw a "just" or "definitive" statement out of the crying need to curse or bless or to do both at once.

"Do you *hear* how Fury sounds her blessings forth?" (Aeschylus, *Eumenides*)

We have seen that *Lear* opens with something like a curse, a decreating as well as a deflating word. Ordinary language, influenced perhaps by literary stereotypes, teaches us to think of "a father's curse" and "a mother's blessing." It is as if the action of *Lear* strove toward "a mother's blessing" but could only attain "a father's curse."

Shakespeare, in fact, is so puissant because he is explicit, because everything becomes utterable as direct speech. There is an Aeschylean and cathartic quality in him absent from most other poets. The defining wound is always before us, in every brazen word. And the dramatic action is as direct as the words. When Edgar, disguised as Tom o'Bedlam, meets Gloucester, his blind and beggared father, he utters a foolish cry that manages to word a terrible wound. "Bless thy sweet eyes, they bleed" *(King Lear,* 4.1.54).

This outrageous pun, one of several about eyes, suggests on the basis of a link between "blessing" and "bleed" (the etymological meaning of blessing is to mark with blood in order to hallow) that *since* the eyes bleed, *therefore* are they blessed. Shakespeare's inner eye moves repeatedly toward imagining the worst in the form of a divestment, a making naked, a making vulnerable, of which one ultimate symbol is this castration of the eyes. But when Shakespeare calls on that darkness, in his play's general *fiat nox,* the curse the action labors under can still generate a bearable blessing.

Blessing and curse, euphemism and malediction, praise and slander, undermine statement. However neutral or objective words seem to be, there is always a tilt of this kind, produced by the very effort to speak. There are those who must curse in order to speak, and those who must bless in order to speak: some interlard their words with obscenities, some kill them with kindness expressions. These are the extreme cases that suggest how close we are to muteness: to not speaking at all unless we untangle these contrary modes. Their tension is, for the purpose of literature at least, more basic than any other; and it needs no witch doctor or psychiatrist to tell us that despite our will to bring forth unambiguous issue, words that point one way rather than the other, we remain in an atmosphere as equivocal as that of the witches' chorus greeting a Macbeth who ponders the future: "Fair is foul and foul is fair / Hover in the fog and filthy air."

Let me also mention Aeschylus's *The Eumenides:* how, by a retrospective myth, it founds a city-state on a transfiguration of the cursing principle. The judicial process instituted by Athena is merely a breathing space or asylum in the play, like the navel stone or her idol. The real issue is the breathless rush of the Furies, unremitting, unrelenting.

> We are the everlasting children of the Night,
> Deep in the halls of Earth they call us Curses.

The final chorus, therefore, has to convert the Curses into an energy that is equal and contrary. It must honor the Furies in terms they understand, which affirms them in their onrush, their dark and eternal function:

> You great good Furies, bless the land with kindly hearts,
> you awesome Spirits, come—exult in the blazing torch,
> exultant in our fires, journey on.
> Cry, cry in triumph, carry on the dancing on and on![6]

Flowers of Speech

How thoroughly the human condition is a verbal condition! The medicinal function of literature is to word a wound words have made. But if we have learnt something about the limit of poet as medicine man, we have also learnt something about the limit of all verbal expression. Objectivity in language is always a form of "You great good Furies": a neutralizing or musicalizing of badmouthing. The very production of speech may depend on a disentangling of blessing and curse, on the outwitting of that eternal complex. Everything we say has to bind the Furies in the fetters of benevolence. Flowers of speech, as Baudelaire made explicit (laying the ground for Genet) are also flowers of evil. These equivocal flowers or figures characterize the literary use of language.

I conclude with two examples of how a great writer outwits the intolerable tension of curse and blessing, and founds a language of his own that enables, and sometimes disables, ours.[7]

In *Finnegans Wake* James Joyce's hero (or Jeems Joker's, as he signed himself) is HCE. This acronym, though given various interpretations, may be a truncated palindrome of ECHO, reinforcing HCE's name of "Earwicker." The ear does become ineluctable in this book, which is the extended ballad of *Perce-Oreille.*[8] Joyce methodically exposes the vulnerable ear by showing the unvirginal or contaminated state of language. In his "mamafesta," no phrase remains simple. Words betray their compound or compoundable nature: they are not from eternity but rather created and adulterated, of equivocal generation, beautiful in corruption. "In the name of Annah the Allmaziful, the Everliving, the Bringer of Plurabilities, haloed be her eve, her singtime sung, her rill be run, unhemmed as it is uneven!"

Yet here the wounded name is joyfully plural. Language has suffered a fortunate fall ("O fortunous casualitas"). Blasphemy is reconciled with good humor; and lust sings in obscene echoes that perpetually hollow and hallow this prose, as in the following "joycing" of the language of flowers:

> Bulbul, bulbulone! I will shally. Thou shalt willy. You would not should as youd rememser. I hypnot. "Tis golden sickle's hour. Holy moon priestess, we'd love our grappes of mistellose! Moths the matter? Pschtt! Tabarins comes. To fell our fairest. O gui, O gui! Salam, salms, salum! Carolus! O indeed and we are! And hoddy crow was ere. I soared from the peach and Missmolly showed her pear too, onto three and away. Whet the bee as to deflowret greendy grassies yellow-horse. Kematitis, cele our erdours! Did you aye, did you eye, did you eversee suchaway, suchawhy, eeriewhigg airywhugger?

An ancient belief held that there was in nature a "general balm" (see John Donne's *A Nocturnal upon St. Lucie's Day,* 1.6) with the virtue of sealing all wounds. A related group of superstitions considered excretions like sweat or blood or even excrement as therapeutic. Joyce releases into language a "Thinking of the Body" which would be unthinkable but for a "language of flowers." Literature sweats balm, and heals the wound that words help to produce.

I end with an episode from *King Lear.* In act 4, scene 6, Lear enters "fantastically dressed with wild flowers." The scene is marked by ear-piercing puns as well as moments of terrible pathos. At one point Lear's rambling language, itself tricked with wild figures, culminates in the dialogue:

> *Lear:* . . . Give the word.
> *Edgar:* Sweet marjoram.
> *Lear:* Pass.

What is being reenacted by Lear in his traumatized and defenseless condition is a type-scene of defense: getting past sentinel or guard. Also being reenacted is the first scene of the tragedy, his command to Cordelia, the "Speak" which led to "Nothing." But Edgar plays along, and the password he gives is taken from a language of flowers close to the mother tongue. "Sweet marjoram." Literature, as figurative language, extends that password.

NOTES

1. While "sweet" and "bitter" stand in an allopathic relation, the idea of a curative "bleeding" into or from within the "wound" carries the homeopathic idea. I mention later the ancient notion of therapeutic excretions: myrrh, balsam, and so on exude their unguents, sometimes through cuts in the bark. They are "wounded" in order to release a sweet or healing "blood," that is, resin. It was natural to associate this phenomenon with the efficacy of Christ's blood. Cf. Lynn Thorndyke, *A History of Magic and Experimental Science* (New York, 1923), I, p. xvi.

2. Wordsworth's lines are themselves already allusive: they echo the ending of Milton's *L'Allegro*, the Cheerful Man, which counters the poem of *Il Penseroso*, the Melancholy Man.

3. See J.-P. Sartre, *Saint Genet: Actor and Martyr*, trans. B. Frechtman (New York: Braziller, 1963).

4. Alypius succumbs to a spectacle in the Circus: "As soon as he saw that blood, he drunk down savageness with it; he did not turn away but fixed his eye and drunk in frenzy unawares, delighted with the guilty combat, intoxicated with the bloody sport" (*Confessions*, book 6, chap. 13).

5. I develop the idea of a spectral name more fully in "Psychoanalysis: The French Connection," *Psychoanalysis and the Question of the Text*, ed. G.H. Hartman (Baltimore: Johns Hopkins, 1978). In applying the idea to Genet I owe a debt to Jacques Derrida, especially to *Glas* (Paris: Galilée, 1974).

6. I quote from the Robert Fagles translation of *The Orestia* (New York: Penguin Books, 1977).

7. The cycle of words-and-wounds continues, because great writers so often reduce us to muteness, or else to echo them directly or deviously. The creative way in which this "curse" of the precursor's greatness weighs on later poets is the subject of Harold Bloom's work on the anxiety of influence.

8. I quote from or allude to the eighth printing (1958) of the Viking Press edition of *Finnegans Wake:* pp. 44, 175, 104, 360.

Whitman's Romance of the Body: A Note on "This Compost"

Alan Trachtenberg

> His favorite occupation seemed to be strolling or sauntering about
> outdoors by himself, looking at the grass, the trees, the flowers,
> the vistas of light, the varying aspects of the sky and listening to
> the birds, the crickets, the tree-frogs, the wind in the trees, and all
> the hundreds of natural sounds. It was evident that these things
> gave him a feeling of pleasure far beyond what they give to ordi-
> nary people.
>
> Richard Maurice Bucke, M.D.
> *Cosmic Consciousness* (1901)

Whitman made himself out to be at home among the birds and flowers,
loving to touch his flesh to earth and sea, to lean and loaf at his ease.
Dr. Bucke's picture finds support in the poetry and other writings in
which Whitman presents himself as an innocent communicant with nature. So he seems to us, at peace in his own flesh and in the sensuous
delights of flesh. "I will go to the bank by the wood, and become undis-
guised and naked / I am mad for it to be in contact with me." He
seems, and surely in a certain sense is, our great poet of health, of what
William James named "healthy-mindedness." But Dr. Bucke, and James
taking the doctor too faithfully, fail to specify that certain sense in
which the poet of health confirms himself most reliably when confront-
ing disease, decay, and death. This is not to say that Whitman shared in
that powerfully generative idea among modern writers like Gide and
Mann, "that," in Edmund Wilson's words, "genius and disease, like
strength and mutilation, may be inextricably bound up together."[1]
Whitman acknowledges no crippling mutilation, no permanent wound
of body or spirit (though he lived the last two decades of his life virtually crippled by a stroke), and in this sense cannot be included among
Romantic and modern agonists. And yet:

> Agonies are one of my changes of garments,
> I do not ask the wounded person how he feels, I

> myself become the wounded person,
> My hurts turn livid as I lean on a cane and observe.[2]
>
>   ("Song of Myself," 74–75)

This image, about which I will have more to say, tantalizes us with a concern for the place of wounds and livid hurts in the poet's regime of health.

According to James, Whitman "owes his importance in literature to the systematic expulsion from his writings of all contractile elements. The only sentiments he allowed himself to express were of the expansive order."[3] Many readers would concur, yet the description is astonishingly inaccurate. Dr. Bucke's picture of a Wordsworthian Whitman, which James cites, drives all complications before it. The "flexions and contractions" that James observes to be absent in Whitman's poems are precisely the rhythms of his strongest poems, poems in which the ebb and flow of confidence, of embrace and retreat, derives from a facing of wounds, agonies, and afflictions. How far James misses the mark can be gathered from his own explanation of the reasons perfectly intelligent people might cultivate "healthy-mindedness": "We divert attention from disease and death as much as we can; and the slaughter-houses and indecencies without end on which our life is founded are huddled out of sight and never mentioned, so that the world we recognize officially in literature and in society is a poetic fiction far handsomer and cleaner and better than the world that really is."[4] Whitman himself might have uttered the sentence in his own defense.

Unmentionable facts of physical and psychic distress appear with striking regularity in Whitman's poems.

> The suicide sprawls on the bloody floor of the bedroom;
> It is so—I witnessed the corpse—there the pistol had fallen.
>
>   (32)

In "Song of Myself" alone we hear "What groans of over-fed or half-starved who fall sunstruck, or in fits," (32) and see

> The malformed limbs are tied to the anatomist's table,
> What is removed drops horribly in a pail.
>
>   (40)

And in "The Sleepers,"

> The wretched features of the ennuyés, the white features
> of corpses, the livid faces of drunkards, the sickgrey
> faces of onanists,
> The gashed bodies on battle-fields, the insane in their
> strong-doored rooms, the sacred idiots. . . .
>
>   (426)

We hear of fevers, syphilis, rheumatism, consumption, erysipelas, of insanity, idiocy, blindness, deafness. The categories of the medical in Whitman astound in their abundance and specificity. The vividness of his descriptions, as well as the obsessive recurrence of sickly detail, owes something to his family; one brother died of tuberculosis, another of syphilitic insanity, yet another suffered from imbecility and epilepsy, and a favorite sister was afflicted with paranoia and drunkenness. The sight of physical pain and suffering seemed to draw him. During the Civil War he haunted hospitals in Washington and at the front, tending to the wounded. Odor of blood and cries of pain fill his journals during these years, and in "The Wound-Dresser" he writes:

> From the stump of the arm, the amputated hand,
> I undo the clotted lint, remove the slough, wash off the
> matter and blood,
> Back on his pillow the soldier bends with curv'd neck and
> side-falling head,
> His eyes are closed, his face is pale, he dares not look on
> the bloody stump,
> And has not yet look'd on it.

It cannot be said that Whitman himself failed to look, or flinched in the face of death's more gruesome aspects.

Still, James is not entirely mistaken in appraising Whitman as belonging finally to "healthy-mindedness." In his personal life cleanliness and well-being—no wonder, in light of the distempered scenes he witnessed —were fetishes. "I have this day, this hour," he wrote in 1862, "resolved to inaugurate for myself a pure, perfect, sweet, clean-bodied robust body, by ignoring all drinks but water and pure milk, and all fat meats, late suppers—a great body, a purged, cleansed, spiritualized, invigorated body."[5] Looking back over his career in 1881 he wrote of his ambition "to formulate a poem whose every thought or fact should directly or indirectly be or connive at an implicit belief in the wisdom, health, mystery, beauty of every process, every concrete object, every human or other existence, not only consider'd from the point of view of all, but of each. . . . My book ought to emanate buoyancy and gladness."[6] In part this is the resounding voice of the late Whitman, the "good grey poet," the prophetic bard, but even in the darker, tragic poems of 1856–60, even where the mood is somber, the stance toward more embattled and tense, and even where death occupied his deepest thoughts, "wisdom, health, mystery, beauty" (if not "buoyancy and gladness") pervade his resolutions. Was Whitman simply determined to affirm, even against the grain of experience? Or do disease and health serve each other in his poems in ways the popular picture of Whitman among the trees and flowers obscures?

James remarks that Whitman's optimism seemed "defiant," as if the poet willed himself into an expansiveness that obliterated thoughts of disease, decay, and evil. Who can deny this is often the case? But in his major poems Whitman reaches his affirmative resolutions (and often they are qualified) through a more exacting modulation of idea and feeling than rhetorical assertion allows. Rather than a simple negative to be overcome, disease is tied up with one of the predominant elements in Whitman's poetry: the trope of the body as a presence, or put somewhat differently, the trope of the speaker's being present to the reader as a physical body.

> This is no book,
> Who touches this, touches a man,
> (Is it night? Are we here alone?)
> It is I you hold, and who holds you,
> I spring from the pages into your arms—decease calls me forth.
>
> ("So Long!", 455)

Whitman wishes the poem to materialize itself in a reader as a voice, or to arise out of inert words on a page not as writing but as "living and buried speech": a voiced speech implying the presence (though invisible) of a body. What gives his verse its own unmistakable character is precisely this wish to coerce, to tease, to hector, and to seduce the reader into a denial of the experience of reading: a wish to negate the very act by which the reader encounters the poem in the first place. Of course that wish stops short of absolute negation, and thus we can speak of Whitman's making a trope of the figure of the body. The trope demands that the reader wrestle with the meaning of "decease calls me forth": the poet's decease from writing (in the usual sense of the word), and the reader's from reading. Decease, which also implicates a *dying* into presence, requires that the reader re-create for himself the ground of poetry, the ground of encounter between himself and the poet's voice. Passwords to the entire *Leaves of Grass*—a terrain of hidden corridors and cunning passages—are "the words of my book nothing, the drift of it everything," and "what I assume you shall assume."

Contemporary readers were quick to detect, and reject, the unusual physical character of Whitman's verse and were undeceived about its calculated offensive against not only Victorian propriety but more outrageously against the very notion of a "higher" realm of spirit.

> I do not press my finger across my mouth,
> I keep as delicate around the bowels as around the head and heart,
> Copulation is no more rank to me than death is.
>
> ("Song of Myself," 55)

"Simply disgustingly coarse," wrote Charles Eliot Norton, who did admire the "vivid writing" and "great stretches of imagination" in the poetry. And not without affectionate indulgence mixed with incomprehension Emerson spoke of "our wild Whitman, with real inspiration but choked by Titanic abdomen."[7] "Choked" is curious, for it was exactly his acceptance of abdomen, his romance of the body, that unchoked, released, and projected Whitman's song. My poem, Whitman wrote, is "avowedly" physical. And as for the offending abdominal lines, such as these from the "Children of Adam" poems that embarrassed Emerson,

> The young man that wakes, deep at night, the hot hand seeking to
> repress what would master him—the strange half-welcome
> pangs, visions, sweats,
> The pulse pounding through palms and trembling encircling fingers—
> the young man all colored, red, ashamed angry,

> (306)

the "espousing principle" of such lines, he wrote, "so give breath of life to my whole scheme that the bulk of the pieces might as well have been left unwritten were those lines omitted."[8] His entire enterprise rested upon the insertion of body into poem in a manner without precedent, certainly in polite literature, and if anywhere, only in the popular pornography that circulated underground in his day. Whitman willingly risked the charge of prurience not for the moral sake of undermining Victorian attitudes but for the much more strenuous and dangerous aesthetic sake of achieving a new ground for poetry.

The new ground lay in the body, and just as the poem was newly conceived as body, thus urging upon the reader a wariness of its implications (see "Whoever You Are Holding Me Now In Hand") so body was now conceived as poem, not only as source but as substance of poem. In a daring, even reckless act of extending the aesthetic into life and life into the aesthetic, Whitman attempted a radical conjunction of materiality and poetic form. He arrived here, at the initiating utterance of *Leaves of Grass* —"I celebrate myself"—in part by working through to a conclusion certain ideas he found in Emerson, though the reworked propositions returned to Emerson with a revulsive shock. The issue between them after the "Children of Adam" scandal of 1856 was not merely the violation of codes governing speech about the erotic, but the very nature of body. Emerson had theorized a unity of body and spirit, a wholeness of being in nature. But "body" remained abstract, not so much an autonomous physical realm as the locus of natural experience, the medium of sensation and perception. Transcendence moved through and beyond body, coming to rest in thought and spirit. Transcendence finally escaped the ground from which it launched itself. Thus in a passage that will not only point up differences between Whitman and his great teacher but will also help identify the place of disease in the poet's scheme of things, Emerson writes, "As fast as you conform your life to the pure idea in your mind, that will unfold its great proportions. A correspondent revolution in things will attend the influx of spirit. So fast will disagreeable appearances, swine, spiders, snakes, pests, mad-houses, prisons, enemies, vanish; they are temporary and shall be no more seen. The sordor and filths of nature, the sun shall dry up and the wind exhale."[9]

"They are temporary and shall be seen no more." Is Emerson merely indulging in James's "systematic healthy-mindedness," which "deliberately excludes evil from its field of vision?" Not necessarily, for the notion rests upon an at least thinkable proposition that the self bears responsibility for its own sense of the world, that what it takes as agreeable or disagreeable devolves from its own outlook. Emerson weights the act of seeing with the full burden of accountability for what is seen. True seeing will recognize defects as partial truths; what is disagreeable (by virtue of its partiality) will disappear into (or reappear as) the agreeable whole. "The ruin or blank that we see when we look at nature, is in our own eye. The axis of vision is not coincident with the axis of things, and so they appear not transparent but opaque."[10] In the axis of things what the sun dries up and the wind exhales has only a provisional, a momentary, and thus an incomplete reality. To the visionary eye "sordor and filths" cannot be granted full existence.

Whitman's eye also possesses powers of bestowing being, but with a crucial difference. In the end Emerson's eye disembodies: "I am nothing; I see all." Whitman restores eye to body and body to eye. His eye is present to the world as body; he not only sees but feels sight as bodily sensation, and the disagreeable achieves a heightened reality by virtue of his kinetic and affective seeing.

> Agonies are one of my changes of garments,
> I do not ask the wounded person how he feels, I myself
> become the wounded person,
> My hurts turn livid as I lean on a cane and observe.
> (74–75)

The third line points to Whitman's version of Emerson's restorative eye. He at once observes the hurt and feels it. He balances himself between an unbearably disagreeable sensation and a comfortably detached posture, between the immediacy of hurt and a view of it mediated (and distanced) by the notion of its being *one* of his "changes of garments." The fulcrum of the emotive balance is the physical balancing act on the cane, the act of leaning and observing that recurs throughout the poetry:

> I lean and loaf at my ease, observing a spear of summer grass.
> ("Song of Myself")

"Change of garment" confesses the capacity to turn at will from this hurt to that one, or to another pleasure. The body, bearer of each garment, is the ground, then, of a promiscuous identification with being as such. Yet the condition for experiencing any sensation is the provisionality of all. Thus the body is medium as much of evasion ("leavings") as of immediate sensation; by making himself present to all sensations the poet defensively makes himself immune to the permanent effects of any particular one.

We might wish to take immunization as a version of the "systematic expulsion" of "healthy-mindedness," as nothing but a difference in degree from Emerson's disappearance of the disagreeable. But the method is really a form of homeopathy. A disease-bearing body is introduced in order to generate anti-bodies that will embrace, contain, and incorporate the diseased entity. The medicinal process frequently begins with a disruption of the balanced composure of the state of health: leaning and loafing "at my ease."

Something startles me where I thought I was safest.

This remarkable opening line of an important early poem, "This Compost," instigates a process of revulsion from and return to the body analogous to medical immunization. Here Whitman takes Emerson's sordor and filths full in the face, and while he too has the sun dry up and the wind exhale, the difference lies in what is left over, in the leavings.

With the suddenness registered in the opening line, the poet "withdraws" from the ground of his ease, the earth he elsewhere addresses: "Earth! My likeness!"

> I will not go now on the pastures to walk,
> I will not strip the clothes from my body to meet my lover the sea,
> I will not touch my flesh to the earth as to other flesh to renew me.
>
> ("Earth! My Likeness!" 208)

Revulsion arises from the eruptive thought that the very ground, the ground of ease and safety, is also the ground of sickness, corruption, filth:

> O Earth!
> O how can the ground of you not sicken?
> How can you be alive, you growths of spring?
> How can you furnish health, you blood of herbs, roots, orchards, grain?
> Are they not continually putting distempered corpses in you?
> Is not every continent worked over and over with sour dead?
>
> Where have you disposed of those carcasses of the drunkards and gluttons of so many generations?
> Where have you drawn off all the foul liquid and meat?
> I do not see any of it upon you to-day—or perhaps I am deceived,
> I will run a furrow with my plow—I will press my spade through the sod, and turn it up underneath,
> I am sure I will expose some of the foul meat.
>
> (209)

The poem thus opens with a challenge to both an idea (earth as source of health) and a physical posture (ease, composure, safety). The challenge takes physical form (the sudden start) and evokes physical response (withdrawal, plow and spade). Can one return from such revulsion? Can earth again serve as sanative "likeness," as health?

But the challenge startles at an even deeper level than that of the poet's ease and safety. It starts him from his own physicalness itself, from his safety in the notion of body as the ground of being. For if the ground of earth sickens, then is his own body safe? And if his body is sickness, or if it cannot contain and somehow transfigure its inherent (because physical) vulnerability to sickness, can it sustain its claim to an authority equal to that of soul in the constitution of the self? And further, can he sustain his invitation to readers to partake of his body, to "lean and loaf" with him, in fact to identify (in the most dazzling extension of the body trope) poet and poetry itself with earth, dirt, grass? The startling, discomposing question reflects broodingly upon the comic-pastoral coda of "Song of Myself":

> I depart as air—I shake my white locks at the run-away sun,
> I effuse my flesh in eddies, and drift it in lacy jags.
>
> I bequeath myself to the dirt, to grow from the grass I love,
> If you want me again, look for me under your boot-soles.
>
> You will hardly know who I am, or what I mean,
> But I shall be good health to you nevertheless,
> And filter and fibre your blood.
>
> (104)

Now the underside of the trope comes rudely home, the rot, the stench, the offensive foulness of death. "How can you furnish health . . . ?"

Of course the rude start is but another change, another garment the poet assumes as he swivels on his cane. In this case the garment does not sit with equanimity; it is itself a dis-ease, an imbalance, a shifting of the center. Now at the periphery, vision is baffled. "I do not see any of it upon you to-day—or perhaps I am deceived." This physical equivalent to the thought of disease and foulness, this disequilibrium, is the homeopathic charge, the start of immunization. It is the negative necessary to the recovery and confirmation of ease. The process proceeds not by defiant incantation, but like true immunization by the addition (or inoculation) of a new element into the body of the poem: the renaming of earth as *compost*.

> Behold!
> This is the compost of billions of premature corpses,
> Perhaps every mite has once formed part of a sick person—.

Renaming proceeds from the eyesight, as the poet beholds the visible as the ground of the invisible, preparing for the following lines, where the visible is reseen in a new relation to the invisible and to itself: "Yet behold! The grass covers the prairies." Compost mediates visibility and invisibility. The immediate sense is as of compost heap: "a mixture of various ingredients for fertilizing or enriching land, a prepared manure or mould" (OED). To behold earth itself as compost (rather than a small section or heap of it) is to behold it in the condition of rottedness and manure, of waste and leavings. But the shift is not only tonal or textural, from sweet green growth to fetid brown decay. Renaming elicits from earth its buried inner and secret truth, its meaning as a process of (in the earliest sense of compost) "composition, combination, compound." As compost, earth composes by decomposing. From decomposition arises the composure the poet next beholds:

> —Yet behold!
> The grass covers the prairies,
> The bean bursts noiselessly through the mould in the garden,
> The delicate spear of the onion pierces upward,
> The apple-buds cluster together on the apple-branches,
> The resurrection of the wheat appears with pale visage out of its graves,
> The tinge awakes over the willow-trees and the mulberry tree,
> The he-birds carol mornings and evenings, while the she-birds sit on their nests,
> The young of poultry break through the hatched eggs,
> The new-born of animals appear—the calf is dropt from the cow, the colt from the mare,
> Out of its little hill faithfully rise the potato's dark green leaves,
> Out of its hill rises the yellow maize-stalk;
> The summer growth is innocent and disdainful above all those strata of sour dead.
>
> (209–10)

From the potent "yet" flow images that convey the countervailing and composing thought: in spite of disease (and perhaps because of it) life continues. The sexual figures of bursting, piercing, dropping, rising are confirmed by "the resurrection of the wheat . . . out of its graves" as a triumph over death.

The innocent, triumphant disdain prefigures the poet's own recovery, but only partially. The recovery will seem a kind of growth or resurrection, but disdain and innocence will give way to a wonder premised on a new knowledge. So far what has been beheld is vision, not yet a praxis of return. Return proper, the poet's own resurrection of spirit, begins in the stanza that follows, a return to a life of the body in nature: tasting, touching, once more reclining at ease.

What chemistry!
That the winds are really not infectious,
That this is no cheat, this transparent green-wash of the sea,
which is so amorous after me,
That it is safe to allow it to lick my naked body all over
with its tongues,
That it will not endanger me with the fevers that have
deposited themselves in it,
That all is clean, forever and forever,
That the cool drink from the well tastes so good,
That blackberries are so flavorous and juicy,
That the fruits of the apple-orchard, and of the orange-orchard—
that melons, grapes, peaches, plums, will none of them
poison me,
That when I recline on the grass I do not catch any disease,
Though probably every spear of grass rises out of what was
once a catching disease.

(210)

The return to ease and safety is now mediated by the powerful opening note—"What chemistry!"—which translates the dominating image of compost and forbids any forgetting of the initial startlement and the thought of a befouled earth. Chemistry translates the secret life of earth as compost: composition (and composure) out of decomposition. Like manure, then, decomposition appears now as a necessary moment in earth's makings. And thus the thought in the last two lines arrives as the groundwork of the poem: that grass itself cannot be conceived except as the out-growth and negation of disease in the endless symbiosis of life and death.

To be on the ground is to be of the body. And to be of the body is to be vulnerable to the start from forgetfulness that sordor and filths comprise the bodiliness of body. That start into alarm is the necessary start toward the imaginative equivalent of resurrection: the awareness, neither innocent nor disdainful but sublime, of the true terror (not the false alarms) of existence in the body:

Now I am terrified at the Earth! it is that calm and patient,
It grows such sweet things out of such corruptions,
It turns harmless and stainless on its axis, with such endless
successions of diseased corpses,
It distils such exquisite winds out of such infused fetor,
It renews, with such unwitting looks, its prodigal, annual, sumptuous
crops,
It gives such divine materials to men, and accepts such
leavings from them at last.

(210–11)

In the closing line the poem confesses one of its own secrets, that in "leaves of grass" lies buried the pun that unlocks the mystery, and the sublimity, of natural being: the oneness of leaf and leaving, of resurrection and grave, of life and death. But the mystery within the mystery, and the source of the terror that is "calm and patient," is that the oneness is not simply of body and soul. It occurs within the ground of the body— the body of flesh and desire that registers startlement as dis-ease, that withdraws and returns, plows and spades, bursts and pierces and rises, and which through the chemistry that assures the poet of tangible immortality achieves (in another sacred pun) composure (and composition) in compost.

NOTES

1. *The Wound and the Bow* (London: Methuen, 1941), p. 259.

2. The text throughout (except for the selection from "The Wound-Dresser" below, which is obtainable in any standard edition) is from the third (1860) edition of *Leaves of Grass.* Page numbers are to the "Facsimile Edition" of the 1860 text, ed. Roy Harvey Pearce (Ithaca, N.Y.: Cornell University Press, 1961).

3. *The Varieties of Religious Experience* (New York: New American Library, 1958), p. 81.

4. Ibid., p. 85.

5. Quoted in *Walt Whitman and the Civil War,* ed. Charles I. Glicksberg (Philadelphia: A.S. Barnes and Co., 1933), n. 15.

6. "A Backward Glance O'er Travel'd Roads" in *Leaves of Grass,* ed. Harold Blodgett and Sculley Bradley (New York: New York University Press, 1965), p. 572.

7. Quoted in Edmund Wilson, ed., *The Shock of Recognition* (New York: Farrar, Straus and Cudahy, 1955), pp. 249, 266.

8. "A Backward Glance," pp. 272–73.

9. Stephen E. Whicher, ed., *Selections from Ralph Waldo Emerson* (Boston: Houghton Mifflin and Co., 1957), p. 56.

10. Ibid., p. 55.

About the Authors

ENID RHODES PESCHEL, editor of *Medicine and Literature,* was Assistant Professor of French at Yale University until 1973. Her books include Arthur Rimbaud, *A Season in Hell* and *The Illuminations,* translation and introduction (Oxford University Press, 1973), *Flux and Reflux: Ambivalence in the Poems of Arthur Rimbaud* (Droz, 1977), and two volumes of essays that she edited: *Intoxication and Literature* (vol. 50 of *Yale French Studies,* 1974), and *French Symbolist Poetry* (Special Issue of *The Sou'wester,* Southern Illinois University, vol. 6, no. 1, Winter 1978). Her newest book is *Four French Symbolist Poets: Baudelaire, Rimbaud, Verlaine, Mallarmé,* translation and introduction (Ohio University Press, in press). Some of her writing about medicine and literature has been published in *The Pharos.*

EDMUND D. PELLEGRINO, M.D., President of the Catholic University of America, was President of the Yale–New Haven Medical Center until 1978. He is the author of *Humanism and the Physician* (University of Tennessee Press, 1979), and of numerous articles on medicine, and on medicine in its relation to the humanities. A founder and past President of the Institute for Health and Human Values in Medicine, he is also the founder and editor-in-chief of the *Journal of Medicine and Philosophy.*

ANNA BALAKIAN, Professor of French and Comparative Literature and Chairman of Comparative Literature at New York University, is the author of *Literary Origins of Surrealism, Surrealism: The Road to the Absolute, The Symbolist Movement: A Critical Appraisal,* and *André Breton: Magus of Surrealism.* She has just finished editing a collaborative volume on Symbolism as part of the *Comparative History of Literature in European Languages.*

GIAN-PAOLO BIASIN, Professor of Italian and Comparative Literature at the University of Texas at Austin, is the author of *The Smile of the Gods: A Thematic Study of Cesare Pavese's Works* (1968) and *Literary Diseases: Theme and Metaphor in the Italian Novel* (1975). He is associate editor of *Forum Italicum.*

MARIE BORROFF, William Lampson Professor of English at Yale University, is a poet and scholar. Among her books on Middle English poetry and twentieth-century poetry are *Sir Gawain and the Green Knight: A Stylistic and Metrical Study* (Yale University Press, 1962), *Sir Gawain and the Green Knight: A New Verse Translation* (Norton, 1967), and *Language and the Poet: Verbal Artistry in Frost, Stevens, and Moore* (University of Chicago Press, 1979). Her own poems have appeared in *The Yale Review* and *The New Republic.*

GERMAINE BRÉE, Kenan Professor of the Humanities at Wake Forest University, was for thirteen years Professor of French and Vilas Professor at the Institute for Research in the Humanities at the University of Wisconsin (Madison). In 1975, she was president of the M.L.A. Her many books include *André Gide* (1956, 1970), *An Age of Fiction* (1957), *Camus* (1959, 1961), *The World of Marcel Proust* (1966), *Camus and Sartre: Crisis and Commitment* (1972), and *Women Writers in France* (1973). Some of her anthologies and textbooks include *Twentieth-Century French Literature* (1962), *Defeat and Beyond* (an anthology of French wartime writing, 1970), and *Camus: A Collection of Critical Essays* (1962).

DIANA FESTA-McCORMICK, Associate Professor French at Brooklyn College, is the author of *Les Nouvelles de Balzac* (Nizet), for which she received the Prix Guizot from the French Academy in 1973. Her other books are *The City as Catalyst* (Fairleigh Dickinson University Press, 1979) and *Balzac* (Twayne, 1979).

MARJORIE GARBER, Associate Professor of English at Yale University, is the author of *Dream in Shakespeare: From Metaphor to Metamorphosis* (Yale University Press, 1974).

EUGENE F. GRAY, Associate Professor of French at Michigan State University, has published articles on Flaubert in *Nineteenth-Century French Studies.*

STEPHEN GRECCO, playwright and Associate Professor of English at Pennsylvania State University, has received playwrighting grants from the Rockefeller Foundation's Office for Advanced Drama Research and from the National Endowment for the Arts. His stage plays include *The Bowlers* and *The Orientals;* his radio plays, *The Vacation, I Miss Them All,* and *Coffee and Dessert.*

MARY JEAN GREEN, Assistant Professor of French at Dartmouth College, is the author of *Louis Guilloux: An Artisan of Letters* (French Literature Publications, in press).

GEOFFREY H. HARTMAN, Professor of English and Comparative Literature at Yale University, is the author of several books. His latest is *The Fate of Reading* (Yale University Press, 1975). A new book, *Criticism in the Wilderness,* will appear in 1980. He is the editor of *Psychoanalysis and the Question of the Text* (Johns Hopkins University Press, 1978) and a contributor to *Psychiatry in the Humanities 3,* ed., Joseph Smith (Yale University Press, 1979).

BETTINA L. KNAPP, Professor of Romance Languages and Comparative Literature at the Graduate Center of C.U.N.Y. and at Hunter College, is the author of several books, including *Louis Jouvet: Man of the Theater, Jean Genet: An Analytical Study, Jean Racine: Mythos and Renewal, Antonin Artaud: Man of Vision, Maurice Maeterlinck: An Analytical Study, Off-Stage Voices, French Writers Speak Out, The Prometheus Syndrome, Dream and Image, Céline: Man of Hate, Anaïs Nin.*

RAYMOND C. LA CHARITÉ, Professor of French at the University of Kentucky, is coeditor of *French Forum* and French Forum Monographs. He is the author of *The Concept of Judgment in Montaigne;* the editor and translator of *Bonaventure des Périer's Novel Pastimes and Merry Tales,* and the editor of: *From Marot to Montaigne: Essays on French Renaissance Literature; O un amy! Essays on Montaigne in Honor of Donald M. Frame; Recreation, Reflection, and Re-creation: Perspectives on Rabelais's "Pantagruel";* and Vol. 2 of *A Critical Bibliography of French Literature* (Cabeen). He is currently working on an annotated bibliography of *Rabelais Criticism.*

VIRGINIA A. LA CHARITÉ is Professor of French at the University of Kentucky, where she has also served as Chariman of Comparative Literature. She is the author of books on René Char (1968), Bonaventure des Périers (1972), and Henri Michaux (1977). She is also cofounder and coeditor of *French Forum.*

RICHARD H. LAWSON, Chairman of the Department of Germanic Languages at the University of North Carolina at Chapel Hill, is the author of numerous articles on Schnitzler and other Austrian and German authors, as well as on comparative literature. His recent books include *Edith Wharton and German Literature* (Bonn: Bouvier, 1974) and *Edith Wharton* (Ungar, 1977).

ROBERT L. MITCHELL, Assistant Professor of French at Ohio State University, is the author of books on Charles Cros and Tristan Corbière and the editor of *Pre-text/Text/Context* (Ohio State University Press, in press). He will be the next Managing Editor of the *French Review.*

HAROLD GENE MOSS, Assistant Director for Institutional Grants at the National Endowment for the Humanities, was Associate Professor of English and Associate Professor of Community Health and Family Medicine at the University of Florida. He has published articles on eighteenth-century British literature.

HENRI PEYRE was for many years Sterling Professor of French and Chairman of the French Department at Yale University. Since he retired from Yale, he has been Chairman of the French Department at the Graduate Center of the City University of New York. He is the author of numerous books, a member of the American Philosophical Society, the American Academy of Arts and Sciences, and has been the recipient of some fifteen honorary doctorates.

LAURENCE M. PORTER, Professor of French and Comparative Literature at Michigan State University, is the author of *The Renaissance of the Lyric in French Romanticism* and *The Literary Dream in French Romanticism*. He is on the editorial board of *Degré Second.*

JOHN F. SENA, Associate Professor of English at Ohio State University, has published *A Bibliography of Melancholy* and several articles on satire, melancholy, and medicine in eighteenth-century British literature.

ANDREW E. SLABY, M.D., Ph.D., M.P. H., is Psychiatrist-in-Chief at the Rhode Island Hospital and Professor of Psychiatry at Brown University. He has authored and coauthored numerous books and articles, including *The Crisis Team: A Handbook for the Mental Health Professional* (Harper and Row, 1973), *The Healing Alliance* (W. W. Norton, 1975), *Integrated Psychiatric Treatment* (Harper and Row, 1975). Along with Laurence R. Tancredi (see below), he has written *Collusion for Conformity* (Jason Aronson, 1975), *Legal Issues in Psychiatric Care* (Harper and Row, 1975), *Handbook of Psychiatric Emergencies* (Medical Examination Publishing Company, 1975), *Ethical Policy in Mental Health Care* (Neale Watson Academic Publications, 1977), *Textbook of Psychiatry* (Harper and Row, in press), and *Emergency Psychiatric Services: Methods and Management* (Neale Watson Academic Publications, in press).

LAURENCE R. TANCREDI, M.D., J.D., is Associate Professor of Psychiatry at New York University School of Medicine and Visiting Associate Professor of Law at New York University School of Law. He has authored and coauthored numerous books and articles, including *Ethics of Health Care* (Institute of Medicine, National Academy of Sciences, 1974) and the last six books listed above under the name of Andrew E. Slaby.

ALAN TRACHTENBERG, Professor of American Studies and English at Yale University, has written and edited several books on American literature, including *Brooklyn Bridge: Fact and Symbol* (Oxford University Press, 1975; rev. ed., University of Chicago Press, 1979), *Democratic Vistas, 1865–1880,* ed. (George Braziller, 1970), *The City: American Experience,* ed. (Oxford University Press, 1972), *Critics of Culture: Literature and Society in the Early Twentieth Century,* ed. (John Wiley & Sons, 1976), and *America in Literature,* ed. (John Wiley & Sons, 1977).

STANLEY WEINTRAUB, Research Professor and Director of the Institute for the Arts and Humanistic Studies at Pennsylvania State University, is the author of twenty-nine books, nine of which are about George Bernard Shaw. He also edits *The Shaw Review.* His writing is largely in the area of biography, for which he received a National Book Award nomination (for *Beardsley*) in 1968. Some of his other biographies are *Private Shaw and Public Shaw, The Last Great Cause, Whistler, Four Rossettis* and—most recently—*The London Yankees.*